Accumulation and Stability
Under Capitalism

Accumulation and Stability Under Capitalism

PRABHAT PATNAIK

CLARENDON PRESS · OXFORD
1997

Oxford University Press, Great Clarendon Street, Oxford OX2 6DP

Oxford New York
Athens Auckland Bangkok Bogota Bombay
Buenos Aires Calcutta Cape Town Dar es Salaam
Delhi Florence Hong Kong Istanbul Karachi
Kuala Lumpur Madras Madrid Melbourne
Mexico City Nairobi Paris Singapore
Taipei Tokyo Toronto
and associated companies in
Berlin Ibadan

Oxford is a trade mark of Oxford University Press

Published in the United States
by Oxford University Press Inc., New York

British Library Cataloguing in Publication Data
Data available

Library of Congress Cataloging in Publication Data
Patnaik, Prabhat.
Accumulation and stability under capitalism / Prabhat Patnaik.
Includes bibliographical references (p.).
1. Saving and investment. 2. Capitalism 3. Economic
stabilization. 4. Developing countries—Economic policy.
5. Economic policy. I. Title
HC79.S3P37 1996 339.4'3—dc20 96-18540

ISBN 0-19-828805-0

1 3 5 7 9 10 8 6 4 2

Typeset by BookMan Services, Ilfracombe
Printed in Great Britain
on acid-free paper by
Bookcraft (Bath) Ltd.,
Midsomer Norton, Avon

PREFACE

This book was conceived when I was a visiting faculty member at the University of California, Riverside, during 1989–90, and most of the first draft was written during a subsequent stay at the School of Oriental and African Studies, London. Over this period I had the benefit of discussions with a number of friends at both these places. Among them I am specially indebted to Keith Griffin, Aziz Khan, Bob Pollin, Victor Lipitt, Howard Sherman, Terry Byres, and Ben Fine, the last of whom was kind enough to read the draft of the first six chapters.

My colleagues at the Centre for Economic Studies and Planning, JNU, have been extremely generous with me in sparing time for discussions whenever I have sought their help. I am specially grateful to the late Krishna Bharadwaj, Anjan Mukherji, Sheila Bhalla, Sunanda Sen, Deepak Nayyar and Abhijit Sen. C. P. Chandrashekhar and Jayati Ghosh went through the entire first draft of the manuscript and made valuable suggestions for revision, though they are in no way responsible for the errors that doubtless remain. I should also like to thank Mrityunjay Mahanty, Sangeeta Pratap and Biswajit Dhar for helping me prepare the final manuscript. I am deeply grateful to J. Subbarao, Professor of Physics at my university, for sparing time to carry out a simulation exercise on the model contained in the appendix to Chapter 7.

My intellectual debt to Amiya Bagchi and Utsa Patnaik should be obvious from the text of the manuscript. The latter was always willing to offer suggestions and ponder over my problems. S. K. Rao played the same role during my stay in London.

My greatest debt however is to Laurence Harris who has been, during this entire period, a source of intellectual help and encouragement. But for his steady support this book would never have been written.

I should like to add a word here about the use of mathematics in the book. Despite the profusion of symbols and equations occurring in it, confined for the most part though to the Appendices, the book does not involve mathematical reasoning in any essential way. I have used mathematics literally as a language, as a sort of parallel text into which readers, to whom my prose appears unclear or imprecise, are free to dip. The basic ideas of the book are simple and straightforward, almost embarrassingly so, and while they require some knowledge of economics, what they require is not very arcane.

P.P.
July 1995

CONTENTS

1

Introduction

Capitalism has in practice proved to be far more durable than most of its critics and many of its admirers had anticipated. Marx certainly would have been surprised at the fact of its surviving in the advanced countries even a century after his death. When he wrote at the fall of the Paris Commune that 'after whit-Sunday there can neither be peace nor truce possible between the working men of France and the appropriators of their produce', and that 'the French working class is only the advanced guard of the modern proletariat', his presumption clearly was that a revolutionary overthrow of capitalism in the advanced countries had come on the historical agenda (Marx 1970, 306). He may have had some misgivings on this score towards the end of his life, when he turned his attention increasingly towards Russia.[1] But Engels's remark in 1886 that in England the decennial cycle 'seems indeed to have run its course, but only to land us in the slough of despond of a permanent and chronic depression in which the unemployed, losing patience, will take their own fate in their own hands', suggests that belief in the historical imminence of revolution in the advanced countries was never entirely given up (Engels 1967, 6). The Marxist tradition in this century carried over this vision, at any rate until the failure of the German Revolution around the 1920s. In some of his last writings Lenin cast his eyes towards China and India as potential theatres of revolution after Russia (Lenin 1975*a*), but while modifying the classical Marxist vision, he and his followers too regarded the overthrow of capitalism in its main bastions as only a more protracted process than hitherto believed, during which the system would be getting progressively weakened in

---

[1] On Marx's increasing interest in Russia and its impact on his thinking see Hobsbawm 1964, especially p. 49 *et seq*.

a historical sense. The concept of a 'general crisis' of capitalism was supposed to capture this.[2]

But the Marxists were by no means alone in their dire prognostications for capitalism. Joseph Schumpeter's admiration for the capitalist system can scarcely be concealed. Chakravarty (1982) uses the very title 'bourgeois Marx' (which Schumpeter reserved for Bohm-Bawerk) to refer to Schumpeter himself. Yet Schumpeter too saw an inevitable eclipse of capitalism through a progressive loss of social support. The introduction of Roosevelt's New Deal according to him was symptomatic of such loss of social support (Schumpeter 1961). Even Keynes, whose object was to introduce reforms into traditional capitalism in order to ensure the durability of the system, had a vision of future capitalism, involving for instance the euthanasia of the rentier and the socialisation of investment, which is at palpable variance with what capitalism, modified by incorporating doses of the Keynesian medicine, has actually come to look like (Keynes 1949, ch. 24).

Indeed one can go further. The writings of most of the giants among economists have been permeated by a sense of the transitoriness of capitalism; the recurring references to a falling tendency of the rate of profit (as Marx (1968, 541) said of Ricardo) are indicative of this. And yet what we find is the system apparently going from strength to strength; even the socialist challenge which was so powerful at one stage seems to be on the decline. In short, capitalism as a system appears to possess reserves of strength far greater than its friends and foes alike had imagined.

How does one account for the resilience and durability of the system? The conventional answer to this question runs along two different lines. The first states that capitalism is an intrinsically smoothly functioning system. The celebrated 'invisible hand' ensures that markets clear, that there is full employment of all resources, and that resources are allocated efficiently. To be sure, the argument is not as crude as this. Frictions of various kinds ensure that the economy is never exactly in an ideal state of equilibrium, but it is sufficiently close to such an ideal state to imply that claims that the system malfunctions put forward by the critics, whether Marxists or Keynesians, are simply invalid. If perchance there is some malfunctioning, that is a result not of the innate working of the capitalist

---

[2] The concept of the 'general crisis of capitalism' figured in the programme of the Communist International, drawn up for the first time in 1925 (see Degras 1971).

system, but of the fact that the markets are not allowed to work smoothly. There are in other words no contradictions of capitalism as such, no crises, no disruptions arising from its innate functioning, and above all no involuntary unemployment and no price instability. A system which provides free choice to individual agents, and, by the very fact of doing so, functions smoothly, is bound to be durable. Its functioning no doubt can be improved, but only by reducing the frictions and improving the freedom of individuals. Any other kind of interference in its functioning, and any supersession of this system by collectivist decision-making, not only amounts to an abridgement of individual freedom, which is reprehensible in itself, but also results in serious dislocations.[3] The durability of capitalism arises therefore from the fact of its being in conformity with human nature which is individualistic, and for that very reason being endowed with institutions, e.g. markets, which make its overall functioning smooth.

The second answer contests this. It argues that a capitalist economy left to its own devices does not in general bring about full utilisation of resources in any particular period. What is more, its functioning over time is marked not only by fluctuations of output but by a rate of growth of output which is not necessarily identical with the 'natural rate of growth', i.e. the rate of growth of the workforce in 'efficiency units'. In other words, the 'invisible hand' can ensure neither the elimination of involuntary unemployment in any single period, nor a secular limit to the rate of unemployment. If a system whose spontaneous working is so seriously flawed has nonetheless managed to display such remarkable durability, the explanation lies in the fact of State intervention which has succeeded in overcoming some of these flaws. It is not the untrammelled assertion of individualism that constitutes the secret of the strength of capitalism, but the fact that such assertion has been tempered by State intervention to rid it of its unwelcome consequences. Capitalism is durable precisely because it manages to provide scope for individual freedom of action in the economic terrain even while ensuring that the system as a whole functions smoothly through the institutionalisation of appropriate structures of intervention. This of course is the

---

[3] This view articulated by writers such as F. A. von Hayek (1946) had fallen into disrepute following the Keynesian Revolution, but is now enjoying a remarkable resurgence in the economic literature, especially in the USA, where the denial of the existence of involuntary unemployment as a systemic phenomenon has again become widespread.

Keynesian answer though many Marxists perhaps would go along with it.

The purpose of the present book is to contest both these answers, and to provide an altogether different view of the functioning of the capitalist system, and hence an altogether different explanation for its durability. The first part of the book is devoted to a demonstration of the inadequacy of the above two explanations, while the second part presents my own explanation. Later parts provide some historical material in support of the argument of this book, and discuss some of its implications, especially for the development of the Third World economies. A brief sketch of the argument, however, is presented in the rest of this chapter.

1. CONGLOMERATE AGENTS

The demonstration of full employment equilibrium through the operation of the market mechanism had been put forward by Walras (and has been rigorously carried out in recent years by Arrow and Debreu (1954) revealing clearly the assumptions necessary for it). The argument that the market does not ensure the full utilisation of all resources amounts therefore to the assertion that the actual state of rest of a capitalist economy in any period is different from what is captured by a Walrasian general equilibrium. This argument has been advanced at two levels. The first is logical: once the effect of expectations about the future upon current decisions, and the changes in expectations resulting from changes in current variables are recognised, then, even if an actual capitalist economy conformed exactly to the Walrasian stylisation, in the sense of all agents being individualistic, 'rational', and price-takers, there is nothing to ensure that starting from some initial state of underemployment the economy would converge to a Walrasian equilibrium.[4] It follows then that the state of rest of the economy in any period must be due to

4 For example if the economy is in a 'liquidity trap' and the elasticity of wage and price expectation is unity, then with a standard Keynesian consumption function, we can not only never get to a Walrasian equilibrium, but there can be no equilibrium with a finite value of money with flexible prices. The real balance effect can be brought in here as a possible equilibrating mechanism, but its impact upon aggregate demand is open to question in a world where money is of the 'inside' variety. (See also Grandmont 1982 for a different critique of the real balance effect.)

some other factor (such as the relative stickiness of money wages according to Keynes), rather than its being in a Walrasian equilibrium.

The second level of the argument in fact buttresses this, namely, that the actuality of a capitalist economy does not correspond to the Walrasian stylisation. Much has been written on this: there are externalities, increasing returns, imperfect information and so forth, all of which in varying degrees vitiate the practical relevance of a Walrasian general equilibrium (see Hahn 1984). But apart from these, a basic reason why the Walrasian stylisation does not capture the reality of a capitalist economy lies in the fact that the latter is characterised in several spheres by the existence of price-makers. If there are price-makers, the market functions quite differently from the way that Walras had visualised, and there is no necessary attainment of a full employment equilibrium.[5]

The existence of price-makers presupposes collusive behaviour. It also presupposes typically a degree of power which the collusion must bring to bear against 'outsiders' and against those who break ranks. If a trade union has negotiated a money wage, for this wage to be meaningful it must possess some power to prevent the employment of non-members and deviant members who may offer labour at a lower wage. If the capitalists collude to fix prices, for this collusion to be effective they must have some means of restraining deviants from undercutting the price fixed by collusion. To be sure, this power is never absolute; but no matter what it depends on, once we recognise its reality, we have to see the market situation as being characterised, in a number of instances, by the prevalence of conglomerate, as opposed to individual, agents.

The concept of conglomerate agents is fundamentally different from the concept of coalitions which latter-day neoclassical economics has come to recognise and analyse. The latter concept takes individuals as the starting point; individuals come together for a more or less prolonged period of time in order to better their economic position. A coalition is merely a modus operandi for the assertion of individualism. A conglomerate on the other hand is based on a renunciation, whether voluntary or involuntary, of individualism. Whether an individual worker's renunciation of individualism is

---

[5] What Malinvaud (1977) says about fix-price systems obviously holds when we have price-makers fixing these 'fixed-prices'. For a discussion of non-Walrasian equilibria see Mukherji 1990.

because the trade union is powerful enough to run a 'closed shop', whether it is because he believes 'in the long run' he will be helpless against the capitalists without the support of the union, or whether it is because joining the union is a part of 'working class culture', the fact of this renunciation means that he is not continuously comparing the benefits of being inside the union with those which he could get by being outside.[6] In short, the conglomerate agent becomes an irreducible unit of decision-making whose actions and achievements need no longer be comprehended in terms of the rationality of the constituent individual agents.

Keynes's logical demonstration that even wage and price flexibility need not ensure full employment, and hence his implicit belief that the state of rest of a capitalist economy in any period must be due to some factor other than its being in a Walrasian equilibrium, was complemented by his recognition that conglomerate price-making by the unions in the labour-market is a fact of life. With money wages thus fixed, and investment decisions arrived at by individual agents, the economy could well get stuck with involuntary unemployment. Kalecki (1971) took price-making in both labour and product markets and arrived at the same conclusion. The basic point of departure for both was the recognition that in the capitalist market-system, conglomerate decision-making rules in certain spheres and individual decision-making rules in others.

2. PRICE AND OUTPUT INSTABILITY

The real significance of conglomerate agents and price-making lies however not merely in the fact that it gives rise to involuntary unemployment in a single period, but in the instability it introduces into the dynamics of prices and output. If the unions bargain for and

[6] The most perceptive discussion of this point is to be found in Marx 1976, Vol. 6, 210–11: 'Large-scale industry concentrates in one place a crowd of people unknown to one another. Competition divides their interests. But the maintenance of wages, this common interest which they have against their boss, unites them in a common thought of resistance-combination. . . . If the first aim of resistance was merely the maintenance of wages, combinations, at first isolated, constitute themselves into groups as the capitalists in their turn unite for the purpose of repression, and in the face of always united capital, the maintenance of the association becomes more necessary to them than that of wages. This is so true that English economists are amazed to see the workers sacrifice a good part of their wages in favour of associations, which, in the eyes of these economists, are established solely in favour of wages.'

obtain particular levels of money wages for particular categories of workers in any period, and if the capitalists in the different sectors pursue mark-up pricing, then we can, without much violence to reality, conceptualise the picture in aggregate terms as 'workers' confronting 'capitalists'. If the workers always insist upon and succeed in obtaining a certain share of output at prices which they expect to rule, and if the capitalists, through mark-up pricing, enforce a share for themselves which leaves the workers less than what they had thought, then, as the workers learn from experience and adjust their price expectations to incorporate actual past inflation, the economy would move into accelerating inflation. In view of this obvious proposition, the concept of a 'non-accelerating inflation rate of unemployment' (NAIRU) has been put forward in recent literature which argues as follows. The share which the workers succeed in enforcing through their money wage bargain at the expected prices is inversely related to the unemployment rate in the economy. Hence, at some unemployment rate, this share and the capitalists' share dictated through mark-up pricing must add up exactly to unity, and at this unemployment rate expected and actual inflation rates must coincide preventing any acceleration of inflation. (This particular version of NAIRU theory which is based upon a model of bargaining is due to Rowthorn 1977.) A capitalist economy in other words can succeed in obtaining price stability, in the sense of non-accelerating inflation, provided it maintains a certain unemployment rate.

The NAIRU, it should be noted, entails (unlike the 'natural rate of unemployment' of the monetarists) significant involuntary unemployment. But the question arises: can the spontaneous working of a capitalist economy ensure the maintenance of NAIRU? The answer usually given is that if money supply grows at an exogenous rate, since the income velocity of circulation of money changes slowly and for independent reasons (having to do with 'habits and customs'), the inflation rate cannot possibly accelerate or decelerate secularly; the economy is bound therefore to stabilise itself around the NAIRU, and experience 'natural rate of growth', defined as the rate of growth of the work-force in 'efficiency units'. Quite apart from the fact that this does not amount to a proof of stability, this answer suffers from two obvious shortcomings.

First, money supply growth can scarcely be considered as an exogenously given datum. There is considerable empirical evidence (even for the pre-'credit card' era) in support of the hypothesis of endogenous money, i.e. for the proposition that the supply of money adjusts in a capitalist economy to the demand for it (see for instance Pollin 1990). Besides, even conceptually, to treat money supply as being exogenous is tantamount to the belief that the relative distribution of surplus between the rentiers and the entrepreneurs is a matter outside the purview of price-making, which is palpably unrealistic. If workers influence the money wage rate, surely rentiers are not so demure as not to influence the interest rate; and surely the entrepreneurs in fixing their profit margin also take account of their interest cost. A regime of fixed interest rates (altered no doubt from time to time) amounts to endogeneity of money supply. The chief weapon through which the stability of the NAIRU can at all be achieved in such a regime is variations in expenditure, in particular investment expenditure.

This brings us to the second point, namely there is no reason why investment should so behave as to stabilise the economy at the NAIRU. For such stability, investment should fall when unemployment is lower than the NAIRU and rise when unemployment is very high, which is patently unrealistic. True, accelerating inflation which is a result of low unemployment should have some discouraging effect upon investment (though so would decelerating inflation when unemployment is high), but there is nothing to suggest that this effect would always ensure convergence to the NAIRU before all sorts of things go wrong with the economy on account of accelerating inflation. Once again therefore we are forced to the conclusion that there is no inherent mechanism in a capitalist economy characterised by pervasive price-making which can spontaneously achieve both price and output stability (in the sense of steady growth in each).

And yet, on the whole, capitalism has performed for long stretches of time quite smoothly, punctuated no doubt by cyclical ups and downs but not marked by any violent oscillations which its spontaneous working would have led us to expect; and this surely has been one of the main factors behind its durability and continuing appeal. State intervention cannot explain this relatively stable performance. If the State is brought in as a *deus ex machina*, then formally one may be able to demonstrate that its intervention can stabilise prices and output in a capitalist economy. But the NAIRU at which it can achieve this would be different from and higher than the NAIRU without State intervention. And even if it is assumed to exist and have stability, it would certainly entail high levels of unemployment. But the State is not a mere *deus ex machina*; its activities respond to social pressures which tend to undermine its stabilising role. Moreover since it is an observed fact that State expenditure has accounted for a secularly growing proportion of the output of the advanced capitalist countries, if the State simultaneously had the entire onus of stabilising prices and output as well, the NAIRU should also have secularly increased, so that we should have observed higher and higher levels of unemployment as the 'normal' state of affairs under capitalism. (This is because with larger taxation by the State the intensity of conflict over distributive shares would have increased, necessitating a higher actual unemployment rate as a means of achieving price stability. See Chapter 5 below.) But this has obviously not been the case. Clearly therefore the observed smoothness in the functioning of capitalism must be owing to some other factor.

3. STABILITY THROUGH UNEQUAL INTERDEPENDENCE

This book argues that capitalism in the advanced countries manages to stabilise itself and perform smoothly because one section of the labour force which it employs indirectly, via the use of the commodities produced by this section, has the distinguishing characteristic that its *ex ante* wage claims relative to productivity (even in terms of expected prices) are compressible. This section consists mainly of the primary commodity producers of the outlying regions and the compressibility of its wage claims arises because of the vast labour reserves which surround it. If this section was located within the metropolitan centres themselves and produced the same commodities, the same result regarding output-cum-price stability should logically hold. But this would jeopardise social stability within the metropolis, apart from the fact that some of these commodities simply could not be produced within the metropolis itself. Under the existing arrangement, however, social stability is maintained in the metropolis, unemployment can on the whole be kept within 'tolerable' levels, real wages can rise more or less in tandem with productivity increases, and capitalism comes out in flying colours as a remarkably successful system, while the misery in the outlying regions is attributed to their specific national traits or 'outlandish' institutions or the social turmoil that this misery itself inevitably breeds.

Looking at the matter formally, once we introduce primary commodities as a separate category, the level of the NAIRU in the manufacturing sector depends upon the terms of trade between the manufacturing and the primary sectors. Or, alternatively, for any given level of the terms of trade, there is a certain associated level of the NAIRU in the manufacturing sector. By maintaining an appropriate level of the terms of trade, therefore, the manufacturing sector cannot only achieve output-cum-price stability, but, what is more, do so at levels of unemployment which are quite low.

Three questions immediately arise about this argument. First, how does the capitalist sector actually manage to get the 'appropriate' level of the terms of trade? Strange though this may appear, it does so by its spontaneous working. In other words, the proposition that the spontaneous working of a capitalist economy can bring about price-cum-output stability and that too at high levels of employment, is correct, but for reasons and in a manner quite different from what its defenders have traditionally visualised. There have always been massive labour reserves available for capitalism (which is why the concept of a 'natural rate of growth' is so unrealistic), but immigration for purposes of employment by metropolitan capital has always been controlled. On the whole it would not be incorrect to say that the unemployment rate in the metropolis, instead of being the outcome of two independent factors, namely the demand for and the supply of labour, has itself been a determinant of the rate of growth of the labour force immediately available to metropolitan capital in that it has provided the signal for tighter or looser immigration (or for emigration). If the inducement to invest is high, which it would be by the very availability of potential markets in outlying regions (even if these markets are not actually much encroached upon), the economy can operate near full capacity and achieve a growth rate depending on the investment ratio and the capital productivity. Whatever labour is required for this growth rate would be forthcoming, as long as a certain unemployment rate which gives the correct signal is maintained. At this unemployment rate any incompatibility between the capitalists' share and the workers' wage claims, and hence any possibility of secular price instability is removed because the primary sector simply gets the residue, namely whatever is left over after meeting these claims. This however has no adverse effects upon the supplies forthcoming from the primary sector because it is the workers in the latter sector who are in the position of residue-receivers (the capitalists get whatever rate of profit is necessary for making supplies come forth). In other words, it is the compressibility of the *ex ante* wage claims of the workers of this sector relative to productivity which makes the system as a whole operate spontaneously in a smooth manner. And likewise if the metropolitan State takes a secularly growing share of the output produced within the metropolis, this only means lower real wages in relation to productivity for the primary sector workers but no disruption in the overall smoothness in the system's operation. (Though lower real wages relative to productivity in the primary sector may be camouflaged by the fact of productivity growth in this sector itself taking the form of product innovations, such as new raw materials.)

The second question which can be raised is the following. If the above is correct, then surely the ratio of the value of primary commodities imported from the outlying regions to the gross value of manufacturing output produced in the metropolis would decline secularly over time, until the former has become so small that it ceases to have any importance as a stabilising mechanism. This is true. Primary commodities' terms of trade are only one of the possible stabilising mechanisms, though historically they have been the most significant. As their importance in this respect declines, other stabilising mechanisms, which are qualitatively similar to them, may take over, and indeed perhaps are taking over. One example of such an alternative mechanism is the induction of immigrant labour within the metropolis itself under conditions of a dual wage structure (though the wage that such labour receives may still be much higher than what it gets back home). Investment of capital in the outlying regions themselves provides another example, though to prognosticate on the basis of this possibility a 'diffusion' of successful capitalism from the metropolis to the outlying regions would be simple minded and grossly erroneous: quite apart from the obviously practical hurdles to any large-scale capital outmigration from the metropolis, any such outmigration would undermine the very social stability within the metropolis which has been so marked a feature of capitalism.

The third question can be stated as follows. Does the foregoing merely amount to a restatement of the old 'dependency theory' in a new garb? In particular, does it follow from what we have said that all that the outlying regions have to do is to institute 'import substituting industrialisation' and then they will be rid of their peculiar position? The answer unfortunately is no. We have so far talked as if the periphery produces only primary commodities. But it does produce manufactured goods, except that in the eyes of the purchasers, especially the affluent ones, within the periphery itself, these goods are not comparable to those produced in the metropolis, even when they cater to the same needs. They represent more 'primitive' commodities, or more primitive versions of the commodities being produced in the metropolis. Now, even if the periphery embarks on the production of what today are the 'frontier goods', by the time that it has mastered this production, product innovation in the metropolis shifts the concept of 'frontier goods'. In other words, we have a sort of product cycle, whereby new processes and products are being diffused (whether spontaneously or through deliberate 'import substitution') with a lag to the periphery, but this lag means that the periphery's products, in the eyes of some of its own residents, let alone those of the metropolis, are perpetually outdated. The relative prices in this situation are not very consequential for reversing the absolute preference, both within the metropolis as well as by a section of the periphery's population, for the goods of the metropolis. The periphery's growth rate, then, gets tethered willy-nilly to the growth of its exports, and its capacity to undertake conscious development effort on a scale that would release it from the status of being a stabiliser for the metropolis remains forever impaired. In short, the dominant status of the metropolis in this inter-relationship is maintained not necessarily because of political control (though that has been historically important and is never altogether absent even now), but because the periphery is incapable of being an innovator. It is incapable not necessarily because it lacks innovativeness *per se* but because tastes, including within it, and the definition of what constitutes an innovation are defined by the metropolis. The mere institution of import-substituting industrialisation cannot alter this predicament.

The view of imperialism developed here, in the sense of an institutionalisation of a global system of unequal interdependence being essential for the successful operation of capitalism in the metropolis, is reminiscent of Rosa Luxemburg, though its content is altogether different. Its concern is not with the possibility of capitalisation of surplus value within the capitalist system, but with that of output-cum-price stability. Likewise, underconsumptionism, in the sense of shifting income distribution secularly accentuating the contradiction between the capacity to produce and the capacity to consume and thereby creating problems for the system via deficiency of aggregate demand, not only plays no role whatsoever in our argument, but is even doubted as a phenomenon of significance. Secular shifts in income distribution against primary producing workers (in 'efficiency units') are seen here as a consequence of autonomous developments such as the growing expenditures of the capitalist State. The causation is not the other way round as underconsumptionism would suggest. What we have in other words is a view of imperialism *sui generis*. But this view only underscores its immense strength and resilience. The development of the Third World by breaking out of this system is by no means a hopeless task, but is far more difficult than was earlier believed. Yet if optimism of the will is essential for praxis, then so of course is pessimism of the intellect.

I

Accumulation and Stability

2

Accumulation and Economic Growth

In a world of price-making, output in any period depends upon expectations about the future, unlike in conventional equilibrium economics. In the latter, abstracting for simplicity from the problem of heterogeneity of output, expectations may affect the level of money wages and prices for a given nominal supply of money, and the division of output between consumption and investment, but not the level of equilibrium output itself, which is determined entirely by what is producible through the combination of available non-free resources under the existing technology. If all transactions take place at the market-clearing prices, this is the level of output that would actually prevail. If however money wages (or both money wages and prices) are fixed through conglomerate decision-making, output can be less than this level, entailing involuntary unemployment, or can at best be equal to this level, entailing profit-inflation (in which case prices are no longer fixed). While the term 'unemployment equilibrium' is sometimes used to describe the former situation, this is a misnomer: the concept of an equilibrium, in the sense of a configuration of economic variables at which different agents, given their endowments, are maximising their objective functions, loses all relevance.[1] At best, the term equilibrium can be used in this case as denoting merely a state of rest.

[1] Hahn (1984, 320) and others attempt to reconcile individual decision-making and institutional price-flexibility with the existence of involuntary unemployment by arguing that the latter represents an equilibrium state where the unemployed workers have no desire to seek jobs at lower-than-prevailing real wages because they care

The dynamics of a system characterised by price-making cannot obviously be captured by the usual concept of a moving equilibrium, where the economy is in full employment equilibrium in every single period and the successive equilibria are either on or converge towards a steady-state path. The movement of output through successive single-period states of rest would itself depend upon how expectations about the future are formed. The notion, prevalent in contemporary mainstream macroeconomics, that the expectation-formation process can be refined by learning from past mistakes until expectations become 'rational', in other words that they more or less correctly anticipate the future, is meaningless in this context, since a system characterised by price-making is not anchored upon any basic equilibrating tendency. If anything, such learning can have the perverse effect of moving output further away from full employment. (This can easily be seen with reference to the Harrodian notion of instability discussed below.) A discussion of how successive single period states of rest would behave over time under simple, unchanging expectation-formation rules was initiated in the post-Keynesian literature by Harrod (1939,1948), though Luxemburg (1914, reprinted in 1963), starting from Marx's schemes of expanded reproduction, had grappled with the problem earlier.

Harrod's conclusions are well-known. First, if we postulate, as a first approximation, a certain savings and investment behaviour for the economy as a whole, the latter derived from a simple expectation-formation rule, then on the basis of this postulated behaviour and the prevailing technology (captured by the capital–output ratio), there exists a unique growth path, which, if the economy happens to be on it, will be sustained into the future. Second, if the actual growth rate of the economy differs from this unique rate (the 'warranted rate'), far from there being a tendency towards convergence, the economy would further diverge away from the warranted rate. Third, this warranted rate, except by sheer accident, would be different from the 'natural rate of growth' of the economy, which is the rate of growth of the work-force in 'efficiency units'. In

---

about their relative position. This of course raises the question: why is the real wage what it is? Besides, if Hahn were right, there would never be the phenomenon of 'blacklegs'. Surely it is more sensible to jettison the notion of equilibrium based on the rationality of individual agents and to work in terms of such obvious and mundane concepts as conglomerate agents and price-making as Keynes himself in fact did (at any rate for trade unions).

other words, the only rate of steady growth which the economy could possibly experience, given its technology and investment and savings behaviour, is a rate that may spell growing unemployment or run into supply bottlenecks in the form of labour shortage. There are thus two distinct reasons why the successive single-period states of rest would not exhibit steady growth. The actual growth rate to start with may be different from the warranted growth rate, and the warranted growth rate may differ from the natural growth rate. The sequence of states of rest would in general be such that the economy is tossed from one disequilibrium position to another, exhibiting neither full employment, nor even a stable rate of unemployment, across successive periods. The invisible hand is singularly powerless to ensure any semblance of stability.

Harrod's argument brought forth the famous counter-attack by Solow (1956) and Swan (1956), who visualised the growth process under capitalism as a moving equilibrium through time which converges towards a steady state at the natural rate of growth, and re-emphasised consequently the essential inherent tendency of the capitalist system towards stability. Each period according to this conception inherits a certain stock of equipment and a certain labour-force. The existence of a multiplicity of techniques (captured by postulating an aggregate production function) makes possible the full employment of both 'factors' through the establishment of appropriate 'factor prices'; savings out of the full employment output are invested; the addition to current capital stock represented by current investment and the natural increase in the work-force, determine the next period's initial 'factor endowment'; and so the process goes on and approaches asymptotically the steady-state configuration.

The Solow–Swan picture, it is often claimed, introduced a multiplicity of techniques in the place of Harrod's postulate of a rigid capital–output ratio, and hence removed the artificially restrictive character of Harrod's model which had yielded spurious results on instability. In other words, it was only the rigidity of Harrod's assumptions, rather than anything essential in the working of a capitalist economy, that had given rise to Harrod's conclusions about instability. This claim however is not a valid one. Of the two causes of instability mentioned by Harrod, Solow-Swan completely assumed away one, namely the fact that the actual rate of growth need not equal the warranted rate of growth; this they did by postulating that full employment savings exactly equalled what was invested in every period (see A. Sen 1970*b*). Since there is no mechanism for achieving this equality in an actual capitalist system characterised by price-making, and since with the existence of unemployed resources little can be said on the profile of choice of techniques over time, the Solow–Swan demonstration of stability merely amounted to proving a case by asserting it.

There was however a second line of criticism of Harrod, namely that he had not fully worked through the implications of his own model. In a Harrodian world, where investment in any period is shaped by past experience (which provides the only basis for the formation of expectations about the future), there is no reason why growth should occur at all, why the economy should not sink into a state of simple reproduction. In fact, if investment is governed entirely by endogenous stimuli as Harrod had assumed, in other words that investment occurs because, and to the extent that, growth had been occurring in the past, then the only stable trend (ignoring cyclical fluctuations) that a capitalist economy can experience is a zero trend. This was demonstrated by Kalecki (1962). The warranted rate of growth which represents a second possible solution for steady growth, is, by its very nature as Harrod had recognised, an unstable trend. Thus far from converging to the warranted rate of growth, the system as stylised by Harrod would converge to a stationary state and may oscillate around it.

To illustrate the point, let us consider a simple model which is Harrodian in spirit, though not formally identical with Harrod's. Suppose investment behaviour in the economy is such that net investment in the aggregate, or addition to capacity, which is denoted by i_t for period t, is given by

$$i_t = (K_t/K_{t-1})[i_{t-1} + b(u_{t-1} - u_0)i_{t-1}], \qquad (2.1)$$

where K refers to the capital stock at the beginning of a period, u refers to the degree of capacity utilisation (a pure number equalling the ratio between actual and potential output, the latter identical with $K\beta$ where β is the technological output–capital ratio), and u_0 refers to the desired degree of capacity utilisation. If capital decay is assumed to be of the 'radio-active' kind, so that a constant fraction d of capital stock goes out of use in any period, then the investment function (2.1) can be re-written in terms of gross investment I as follows:

$$I_t/K_t = I_{t-1}/K_{t-1} + b(u_{t-1} - u_0)(I_{t-1}/K_{t-1} - d). \tag{2.1'}$$

This investment function merely states that the proportionate change in the rate of growth of capacity depends upon how the actual degree of capacity utilisation compares with the desired degree; it is zero when the two coincide.

Now suppose total consumption in the economy depends partly upon wealth, i.e. K (this would be true of the capitalists) and partly upon output (we can assume the distribution between wages and profits to be given, all wages to be consumed and a fixed proportion of profits to be additionally consumed by the capitalists, apart from their wealth-induced consumption); then

$$C_t = cO_t + \alpha K_t, \tag{2.2}$$

where c and α are constants. In such a case, since

$$O_t = C_t + I_t, \tag{2.3}$$

$$u_t = O_t/K_t \beta. \tag{2.4}$$

The system (2.1')-(2.4) gives two possible solutions for steady growth, namely

$$I/K = \beta u_0(1 - c) - \alpha$$

and

$$I/K = d,$$

corresponding to which the rates of growth of the system will be

$$i/K = \beta u_0(1 - c) - \alpha - d$$

and

$$i/K = 0.$$

The first of these, which simply equals net savings per unit of capital stock at the desired level of capacity utilisation, is nothing else but Harrod's warranted growth rate. The second represents simple reproduction of the system. What is more, it is only the second solution that has the property of stability, which the first lacks, in the sense that, first, if the economy is at simple reproduction, a sudden departure from this state would bring the economy back to simple reproduction, while if it is at the warranted rate of growth, a departure would not bring it back to the warranted growth rate, and, second, starting from any arbitrary initial rate of growth which is non-negative and lies between simple reproduction and the warranted growth rate, other than the warranted rate itself, the economy would converge to simple reproduction.

This result is not specific to the investment function (2.1') assumed here; indeed Kalecki who demonstrated such a result, arrived at it by taking a whole class of investment functions different from the one assumed above. The result therefore is not just a formal curiosum. It points to an important economic phenomenon, that if accumulation were dependent exclusively upon endogenous stimuli, in other words if the occurrence of growth were a result exclusively of past growth, then we would never be able to explain sustained growth.

1. ROSA LUXEMBURG'S THEORY

This of course was precisely the point that Rosa Luxemburg had made. She argued that postulating that the unconsumed surplus value in any period is realised through accumulation and that the still larger surplus value of the next period is realised through still larger accumulation, and so on amounted to 'going round and round in circles'. In other words, she rejected the view that accumulation derives its stimulus from accumulation itself, and underscored the point that there had to be some 'outside demand' for capitalist produce (so that accumulation was impossible in a closed capitalist economy). The essence of this argument was that the stimulus for accumulation could not be an endogenous one. Not surprisingly, her critics could not appreciate the point she was making. Since she posed the problem in terms of realisation, they only re-asserted that accumulation would enable capitalists to realise each other's unconsumed surplus value. And numbers were produced for Marx's reproduction schemes on the assumption that the unconsumed surplus value was accumulated to show how the realisation problem posed by her vanished into thin air.

The point at issue however was not whether realisation of full capacity output was logically possible or not, but whether it could occur if we made plausible assumptions about investment behaviour. What her critics had to produce was not an arbitrary set of hypothetical numbers, but a demonstration that these numbers were precisely the ones that would be thrown up by plausible aggregate investment behaviour. (See in this connection Lange 1964.) To assume that unconsumed surplus value was automatically invested was to assume away the problem of demand altogether, a precursor of what later neoclassical growth theory was to do; it was to criticise her by refusing altogether to see her problem.

To be sure, capitalists do not undertake investment decisions as a class, although Rosa Luxemburg's mode of expressing herself often suggested that they did. And insofar as aggregate investment is simply the outcome of a host of individual investment decisions, each spurred on by the undeniable fact of competition between capitals, there was a legitimate question to be asked, which Bukharin did (see Tarbuck 1972): why do we have to look for some special inducement to invest? Hadn't Marx himself said: 'Accumulate, accumulate, that's Moses and the Prophets!' But in asking this question, a distinction between accumulation and what is generally called investment, was slurred over (though it figures in Sweezy 1942). In the process of its reproduction, capital assumes a multiplicity of forms.

Even if it is the case that capitalists are driven on by competition to accumulate capital, this desire to accumulate need not always mean an immediate addition to physical productive capacity. While capitalists would always wish to accumulate capital in money form, they need not always wish to invest forthwith this accumulated money capital in the form of larger productive capacity; for the timing of the latter, expectations of market growth are important. Indeed a capitalist who rushes ahead with investment plans at a time when the overall market is shrinking would find himself at a competitive disadvantage *vis-à-vis* more prudent rivals. Once this is granted, the necessity for separately investigating the inducement to invest, notwithstanding the fact of competition between capitals, becomes clear once again, and the problem of realisation again comes into its own. This problem arises from the fact that even though capitalists are impelled to accumulate capital, as long as a part of accumulation is sought to be held in money as opposed to physical form, this part would remain unrealised, so that the capitalists would not even succeed in accumulating in money form. The fact of competition between capitals and the consequent drive to accumulate does not by any means therefore render her problem irrelevant, or nullify the significant conclusions she arrived at, which, as Mrs

Robinson rightly says, were to anticipate a good deal of post-war discussion.

The real problem with Rosa Luxemburg's theory lies elsewhere, namely in her belief that a closed capitalist economy cannot throw up exogenous stimuli to keep a positive rate of accumulation going, even when left to its own devices. I have suggested above that her argument that postulating production for production's sake amounts to 'going round and round in circles' can be interpreted to mean that a sustained process of investment in a capitalist economy cannot be explained purely on the basis of endogenous stimuli. From this which is a valid argument, she deduced however that expanded reproduction was altogether impossible in a closed capitalist economy. She saw incursions into pre-capitalist markets and armaments expenditure by the State, the two being related phenomena, as being essential for expanded reproduction, a proposition that does not follow. Even if endogenous stimuli cannot explain expanded reproduction as a sustained process, surely a certain amount of investment, and hence a certain rate of expanded reproduction, would always occur even in a closed capitalist economy, without bringing in the State and pre-capitalist markets, because of exogenous stimuli which are also inherent in such an economy.

The most important of the exogenous stimuli, which Schumpeter was to focus on in his altogether different theoretical system but which Kalecki also emphasised in his own theory that systematically incorporated the problem of effective demand and markets, are innovations in the broadest sense of the term. The sheer availability of new processes, new products, new sources of raw materials and so on, entail, in a milieu where capitals compete against one another, a certain amount of investment occurring quite independently of the expected growth of the overall market, by virtue of each capitalist wishing to steal a march over his rivals. If this happens as a more or less continuous process because new processes and new products keep arriving in a stream (not necessarily a steady one), then there would be an autonomous element of investment which would impart a positive trend to the system.

To illustrate the point, consider a simple variation of the system analysed above. Suppose the adoption of innovations does not affect *ex post* any of the parameters of the system, namely, the capital–output ratio, the profit share, the consumption behaviour, and the rate of decay of capital equipment. But the availability of innovations implies not only that all net investment takes the form of new equipment rather than old, but also that there is an additional amount of net investment undertaken in every period, which (for simplicity) is proportional to the magnitude of capital stock existing at the beginning of the period. The investment function then becomes:

$$I_t/K_t = I_{t-1}/K_{t-1} + b(u_{t-1} - u_0)(I_{t-1}/K_{t-1} - d) + e, \qquad (2.2'')$$

where the last term represents the additional investment brought about by innovations. This new system would, as before, have two steady growth solutions, the larger, unstable, one of which would be smaller than in the earlier case, while the smaller, stable, one will be larger than in the earlier case (see Figure 2.1). In the new situation with $e > 0$, the stable rate of gross accumulation I/K will exceed d, so that the system which earlier was in simple reproduction will now have a positive trend. (The rate of growth, it should be noted however, will not in general simply be e.)

To be sure, it has been argued, e.g. by Steindl (1952), that innovations only alter the form of investment, but not its magnitude. This argument is not without a degree of intuitive plausibility. Even if an innovation lowers the unit prime cost, for example by reducing for a given money wage the labour requirement per unit of output, in an

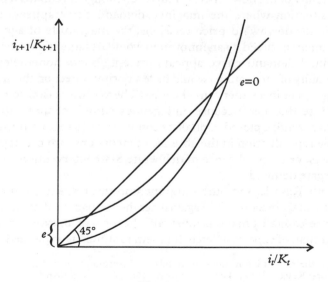

Fig. 2.1.

oligopolistic setting, where each capitalist's imagined demand curve is price-inelastic for a downward revision of price relative to its prevailing level, enlarging sales at the expense of rivals appears unpromising. Each oligopolist then would introduce the new process only by incorporating his gross investment in the form of the new equipment. If so, then innovations cannot introduce any positive trend.

This argument however clearly overstates the case. Its applicability is clearly limited in the case of product innovations: each oligopolist in turning out a new product can surely believe that even at the prevailing price, to the extent that his product is new, he can attract buyers from his rivals who are slower at product innovation; and this is precisely what happens in reality. Even in the case of process innovations, which in reality in any case can scarcely be separated from product innovations, since advertisement and sales effort play an important role in altering market shares, each oligopolist, in introducing a new process with lower unit prime costs, which he believes will give him a larger amount of profit than before even at existing market shares, will feel capable of sustaining a larger sales effort and enlarging somewhat his market share itself. In short, he would undertake a larger amount of investment on account of the availability of the new process. Thus even though it remains true that in a situation where the imagined demand curve appears price-elastic for downward price revisions, the magnitude of aggregate investment induced by an innovation would be larger than where the imagined demand curve appears price-inelastic, nonetheless the availability of innovations would have a positive effect on the amount of aggregate investment in all cases.[2] There is no reason to believe therefore that just because endogenous stimuli cannot explain a positive trend, a closed capitalist economy would remain trapped in simple reproduction in the absence of incursions into pre-capitalist markets, or in the absence of deliberate State intervention to boost aggregate demand.

While Rosa Luxemburg's argument in this respect is not a valid one, a usual objection cited against her theory, namely that incursions into pre-capitalist markets must take the form of an export-surplus, rather than of exports as such, for them to stimulate expanded repro-

---

2 On the role of innovations in stimulating investment, there has been a large literature: Kalecki 1968; Baran and Sweezy 1966, ch. 4; and Joan Robinson 1956, 407, apart from Steindl 1952.

duction, is without any basis (see P. Patnaik 1972*a*). This objection however has been raised by a host of distinguished writers, from Bukharin to Kalecki (1971), Dobb (1972), and Sweezy (1942). The fact that an export surplus from the capitalist to the pre-capitalist sector, which must necessarily be financed through capital exports, plays a role similar to internal investment within the capitalist sector, or a budget deficit which is but a form of domestic capital exports to the State, in boosting aggregate demand and easing the problem of realisation of surplus value, is of course obvious and undeniable. What is questionable is the parallel proposition that exports balanced by equivalent imports in the trade between the capitalist and pre-capitalist sectors have no favourable effects for the realisation of surplus value.

Starting, let us say, from a position of simple reproduction, if trade opens up with the pre-capitalist sector, even though this trade may be balanced, it would have some effect in the shape of stimulating domestic investment. The expansion of exports on the one hand and the contraction of import-competing activities on the other would have asymmetrical effects upon domestic investment, the positive effects of the former being larger than the negative effects of the latter, if for no other reason then at least for the obvious fact that gross investment in any sector cannot fall below zero. The overall net expansionary effect of balanced trade upon aggregate domestic investment would then mean an expansion of aggregate demand for domestic output in the capitalist country, and hence an alleviation of the realisation problem. So far, however, we have talked of the single-period effect of the act of opening up trade. If we are talking about a continuous process of export expansion into the pre-capitalist economy, even if exports in every period are balanced by imports, clearly the economy cannot settle down into a state of simple reproduction; a positive trend would emerge even with balanced trade. In an extreme case, we can visualise the very availability of external markets stimulating investment to a point where the entire unconsumed surplus value at full capacity use is invested in every period. Trade remains balanced and merely changes the composition of commodities domestically available. Yet the stimulus for this dynamism arises without doubt from the confident expectations of the capitalists that as long as pre-capitalist markets are available, demand cannot possibly act as a constraining factor. This is the picture of Luxemburg's model put forward in Robinson 1963.

When we come to the further objection to Luxemburg's argument that export-surplus from the capitalist world has historically not played an important role in the trade with pre-capitalist economies, the critics' position becomes even more questionable. Export surpluses from the capitalist sector are not only theoretically unnecessary, but also must not be confused with export surpluses from the developed to the under-developed economies; even with balanced trade between the latter two entities, it may still be the case that imports from under-developed pre-capitalist economies are used to replace domestic pre-capitalist producers within the developed capitalist economy. Balanced trade between two economies in other words is perfectly compatible with export surpluses from the capitalist to the pre-capitalist sector: as Rosa Luxemburg put it, the crucial distinction is not between geographical territories, but between social entities. While she may be guilty of the error of underestimating the dynamism which even a closed capitalist economy may possess because of its internally generated exogenous stimuli, she certainly cannot be accused of the elementary logical errors which her critics have often attributed to her.

2. THE TREND AND THE NATURAL GROWTH RATES

It remains true nonetheless that even though the spontaneous operation of a capitalist economy in isolation would generate a positive trend on account of innovations, the growth rate so generated would have no reason to equal the natural rate of growth. No mechanism is provided by the market which would make the trend rate of growth, thrown up by capitalists' investment behaviour, adjust to the natural rate of growth, and hence make the growth of labour demand over time adjust to the growth of labour supply. Since this assertion runs contrary not only to neoclassical theorising (which in any case assumes a multiplicity of techniques, movements along an (as if existing) aggregate production function, and the absence of even single-period involuntary unemployment), but also to a good deal of Marxist theorising, it perhaps deserves examination at some length.

If the trend growth rate fell below the natural growth rate, there will be a secular increase in the unemployment rate. Goodwin, following a strand of Marx's thought, argues that this would exert a downward pressure on real wages, and even with given techniques, raise the share of profits and hence investment. With a larger share of investment in output, the trend growth rate will rise until it equals the natural growth rate. The converse process operates if the trend growth rate happens to exceed the natural growth rate. The long-run tendency of a capitalist economy therefore is for the trend growth rate to adjust to the natural growth rate, and for the unemployment rate to be stable (see Goodwin 1967). The problem with Goodwin's argument in this instance is the assumption that all savings are invested: there is no independent investment function. As the discussion of the previous sections has shown however the dynamics of a capitalist economy turns out to be quite different once we recognise that capitalists' investment behaviour assumes more complex forms than a mere reinvestment of savings.

Even with an independent investment function, of the sort for instance we have discussed above, the following argument, derived from another strand of Marx's thought, may be put forward to show that the unemployment rate tends to be stable in the long-run. The natural rate of growth is the sum of the rate of growth of the labouring population and the rate of growth of labour productivity. Even if the first of these rates is given, a change in the second would alter the natural rate of growth. Now, if there is a secular rise in the unemployment rate, and a consequent downward pressure on real wages, this would, it may be argued, induce more labour-using technological progress, so that the rate of growth of labour productivity would decline, reducing the natural rate of growth until it equals the trend rate of growth, and the unemployment rate stabilises.[3] Conversely, if the trend growth rate exceeds the natural rate of growth, the upward pressure on real wages would induce technological progress involving a higher rate of growth of labour productivity, which once again would bring the two rates together. To be sure, this mechanism of adjustment has to be rigorously theorised, but such a mechanism is clearly conceivable and was mentioned by Marx.

The problem with it, which is shared by the Goodwin model as well, is that the wage is bargained in money terms rather than real terms. Real wages are a resultant of movements in money wages and prices. In a world with conglomerate decision making in the sphere

[3] For a modern discussion of the effect of distributive shares upon the nature of technological progress, see Kennedy 1964.

of prices, a rise in unemployment need not exert a downward pressure on real wages. At best, it may exert a downward pressure on money wages, and even this if it happens comes about through complex mediations, via its adverse effect on trade union strength. A downward pressure on money wages however need not mean a downward pressure on real wages. Unless the capitalists' strength and cohesiveness in fixing prices is enhanced the profit margin need not change with changes in money wages, in which case the real wages may remain unchanged even with a rise in the unemployment rate. If profit margins for instance are taken to be dependent upon the degree of capacity utilisation, as a first approximation to capitalists' cohesiveness, then as long as this remains unchanged, a rise in the unemployment rate would not alter the real wage but only the trajectory of money wage and price movement. And with a flexible monetary system where the supply of money adjusts to the demand for it, even this alteration in the trajectory of money wage and price movement would have no equilibrating effects via its influence on investment decisions. Marx's well-known proposition that money wage movements result in real wage movements in the same direction, so that trade union action can raise the share of wages, which he elaborated in opposition to Citizen Weston in his booklet *Wages, Prices and Profits* (reprinted in Marx–Engels 1970), is advanced in the context of a commodity money system, and does not retain its validity in a world with paper money. Consequently, the feed-back effect of a rise in unemployment rate, if the trend growth rate falls short of the natural rate of growth, may not operate in the direction of closing the gap between the two.

Even if this is conceded, the question may be asked: what about the converse case? The trend rate of growth cannot after all exceed the natural rate of growth ad infinitum. When labour shortages appear, unless one postulates an accelerator mechanism (which we have not), the trend rate of growth would surely get pegged to the natural rate of growth. The economy would 'crawl along the ceiling', exhibiting at best minor downturns from it which would get quickly reversed, since the stream of innovations would keep pushing investment up from such downturns. Looking at it differently, the very factors which make for the stability of the trend growth rate would ensure that, unlike in the case of the unstable warranted growth rate, a downward movement of the economy would be temporary and would reverse itself, even though its upward movement gets periodically arrested by labour shortage. In other words, if the trend rate is higher than the natural rate, this should not pose any serious problems for the functioning of the system, unlike in the case where it is lower.

The problem with this is that when labour shortages appear, we are in effect in a situation of rationing, in which the distribution of the labour force across sectors can be quite arbitrary. It is not the case that each sector receives a uniformly smaller proportion of its labour requirements, but some sectors may receive their entire labour requirement while others go desperately short. In this situation, not only do the parameters of our model change, but they change in an arbitrary manner, so that the behaviour of the system can be wildly unpredictable and erratic. It is quite possible that the system may show violent oscillations, rather than peacefully 'crawling' or 'hopping' along the ceiling. Let us take an example. Suppose in the period when labour shortages appear, the investment goods sector is not affected by these shortages whose entire impact falls on the consumer goods sector. The latter even though it adds to its capacity as planned for the period, because its investment orders are being fulfilled, experiences a drop in the level of utilisation of existing capacity. In deciding upon the investment orders for the next period, it would not behave as in eqn. (2.1''), nor necessarily in some manner which is a minor modification of eqn. (2.1''); it may well decide not to place any investment orders for a while, in which case the economy would move sharply downwards. In other words the effect of the unemployment rate upon investment decisions could well be sharply discontinuous: being negligible as long as unemployment rate is at all positive or above some critical minimum level (in which case (2.1'') holds), and being quite sharp when it drops to zero or below the critical level. The equilibrating influence of the market in reducing the trend growth rate, if it happens to exceed the natural rate, to the level of the latter, is thus as dubious as its equilibrating influence in the opposite case.

To say this is not to make the absurd claim that capitalist economies do actually witness secular increases in the unemployment rate or sharp oscillations on account of labour scarcity, nor to assert that the absence of such pathological behaviour has nothing to do with the functioning of the market mechanism, but merely to underscore the fact that the market functions in a milieu altogether different from what traditional theory has supposed. The rate of growth of the labouring population available to the capitalist sector, far from being a given magnitude to which other variables in the system adjust, has itself tended to adjust to the requirements of the capitalist sector. Let us see how.

3. THE IRRELEVANCE OF THE NATURAL GROWTH RATE

The idea that the rate of growth of the labouring population under capitalism adjusts to the rate of accumulation is of course as old as classical political economy. But Ricardo (1951), the most rigorous exponent of this view, relied on the Malthusian theory of population to defend it. Quite apart from the analytical problems it poses for classical dynamics, problems arising from the fact that the time lags between wage movements and the population movements which they supposedly give rise to are bound to be inordinately long, the Malthusian theory of population, which Marx called 'a libel upon the human race', has too shaky an empirical foundation to provide adequate support to Ricardo's theoretical structure. By relying on Malthus's theory however Ricardo lost sight of the far more important and basic mechanism by which the supply of the labouring population adjusts to demand under capitalism, namely migration.

By migration I mean the migration of the labouring population between the pre-capitalist and the capitalist sectors, as well as that part of the migration of capital which is but a substitute for the migration of labour. The labouring population within the capitalist sector in any period consists of that segment which is employed and that which in a discernible sense is unemployed or underemployed. The assumption made in economic theory including in a good deal of Marxist theory is that it is this second segment alone which constitutes the labour reserve available to capitalism. The growth of this labouring population, consisting of both segments, is then seen to constitute the profile over time of the maximum labour force available to capital. As a matter of fact however the entire labouring population engaged in the pre-capitalist sector, not only within a country but even abroad, constitutes a potentially tappable reserve labour force for capital. In situations where the internally available labouring population within the capitalist sector is insufficient for the needs of capital this immense reservoir of labour force available in the pre-capitalist sector is drawn upon. On the other side, when the internal reserve army has become too large, the migration of a part of the internal labouring population into pre-capitalist territories has acted as a kind of 'safety valve'. Of course the two kinds of migration have not been symmetrical. Inward migration of workers from pre-capitalist territories has not put these workers on a par, socially and economically, with the domestic workers within the capitalist sector. On the other hand, outmigration of workers from the capitalist sector has resulted in such workers driving out the 'natives' from their lands in the pre-capitalist territories and acquiring positions of social and economic dominance in their new environments. However, this aspect, the world-scale racial discrimination unleashed by capitalism, does not concern us at the moment. The important point is that the so-called 'natural rate of growth' as an independently given entity is a meaningless concept in capitalist conditions.

In retrospect it is amazing that when the entire history of capitalism is replete with episodes of enormous shifts of population across the globe to serve the needs of capital, of thousands of African slaves transported across the Atlantic to the Caribbean and the American colonies to work on the plantations, of thousands of Indians taken as indentured labourers to work on the mines and plantations in Africa and the Caribbean, of thousands of Chinese likewise shipped to various parts of the globe, and on the other side, of thousands of Europeans migrating to colonies in the temperate zones of the world and often setting up as independent petty producers on land hitherto held by the 'natives', economic theory should be propounding the view that the rate of capital accumulation is limited by the 'natural rate of growth' of the labour-force internal to the capitalist sector.[4] It is like an analyst of *Hamlet* who thinks that the play is about the life of the grave-diggers!

The instruments through which capital has always commandeered an adequate labour-force for itself include a strong element of coercion. But coercion and the pull of the market are in this instance

---

[4] W. Arthur Lewis (1978, 14) wrote: 'The development of the agricultural countries in the second half of the nineteenth century was promoted by two vast streams of international migration. About fifty million people left Europe for the temperate settlements . . . About the same number—fifty million people—left India and China to work mainly as indentured labourers in the tropics on plantations, in mines, or in construction projects.'

not antithetical. While a Bihari worker may have been coerced into making the trip to Mauritius, or an African worker simply grabbed and packed off to the West Indies, those who did the coercing and the grabbing were responding to market opportunities. Let us therefore ignore the element of coercion, which though extremely important does not concern us here. Market signals from the capitalist sector, no matter whether mediated through coercion or not, influence the magnitude of inward or outward migration, and thus adjust the growth of the labouring population available to capital with the growth of its requirements for labour. But while the market in this sense does work, this is not because of the virtues of some invisible hand, but because it operates in a situation where the capitalist economy has as its substructure a vast pre-capitalist universe, which it dominates. The market therefore is neither a mechanism for mutual contracting, to the satisfaction (Pareto-wise) of all, among a group of symmetrically placed, free and atomistic individuals; nor even a forum where organised groups come face to face, bargain, take signals for their conglomerate or individual decision-making, and in their aggregate behaviour produce a relatively smooth evolution of an economy which thereby becomes intrinsically durable. It requires for its smooth operation the milieu of a pre-capitalist sector providing nourishment to the capitalist sector.

Let us however proceed with the argument. As a stylisation, the obvious market signal in response to which migration flows would occur, and which therefore can be said to influence the behaviour of the 'natural rate of growth' (no longer a constant) is the unemployment rate. If the growth rate of the working population which depends both on natural increase as well as on migration is denoted by g^k, the growth rate of labour productivity by g^p, the natural rate of growth by g^n, and the trend rate of growth by g, then it follows from the above that g^k is a function of the rate of unemployment v witnessed in the recent past.[5] We can use a simple function,

$$g_t^k = m - nv_{t-1}, \tag{2.5}$$

to capture this, where m and n are constants. By definition

---

[5] It should be noted that this is *not* the same as the hypothesis of Todaro (1969). We are talking about a situation where migration is not spontaneous, but is controlled; but the signal on the basis of which immigration into the capitalist metropolises is tightened or loosened is the unemployment rate.

$$g_t^n = (1 + g_t^k)(1 + g_t^p) - 1. \tag{2.6}$$

It would also be the case that the rate of growth of labour productivity, as Kaldor (1978) has emphasised repeatedly, would depend on the trend rate of growth itself and hence can be taken to be a constant for a particular g, i.e.

$$g^p = g(g). \tag{2.7}$$

Now, if g exceeds g^n, since the labour requirement in efficiency units per unit of output remains unchanged, v falls over time, which by increasing g^k and hence g^n has an equilibrating effect; and likewise when g falls short of g^n. Looking at it closely, suppose the economy is growing at the rate g; its labour productivity is growing at the rate g^p given by (2.7). If $g^n > g$, then $(1+g)/(1+g^p) < (1+g^k)$, so that $v_{\{t-1\}} < v_t$. This happens as long as $g^n > g$; but by (2.5), $v_{\{t-1\}} < v_t$ implies that $g_{tk} > g_{\{t+1\}k}$. Thus as long as $g < g^n$, g^n keeps falling. There would therefore be a unique level of unemployment rate $\bar{v}$, at which the economy would experience steady growth with $g = g^n$. This is given in Figure 2.2. The condition for a positive $\bar{v}$ less than 1 is that

$$(m - n) < (1 + g)/(1 + g^p) - 1 < m.$$

Thus a capitalist economy can experience not only steady growth, but also steady growth at a rate equal to the 'natural rate of growth'. But the mechanism through which this can be achieved is neither the neoclassical one of Solow and Swan, nor what is suggested in Marx-inspired models like Goodwin's, in both of which it is the trend rate that adjusts to the natural rate of growth, but rather a

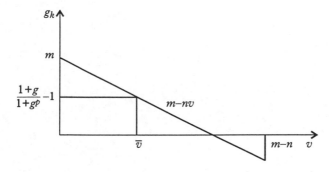

Fig. 2.2.

mechanism through which the natural rate adjusts to the trend rate
by means of migrations between the capitalist and the pre-capitalist
sectors. For this however the pre-capitalist sector must be suitably
'tailored' so that it responds appropriately to the signals thrown up
by the capitalist markets. In short, it is only given the milieu of a
suitably 'tailored' pre-capitalist environment that the capitalist sector can achieve a smooth performance of both output and employment, in the sense of having a sustainable trend rate of output growth
equal to the rate of growth of the labour force in efficiency units. The
invisible hand operates effectively only when there are visible
pre-capitalist surroundings.

But the role of pre-capitalist surroundings in ensuring smooth
functioning in the capitalist sector does not end here. Indeed, this
'reservoir' of labour role which we have attributed to the pre-
capitalist sector is if anything of subsidiary importance. The problem
of a capitalist economy does not consist solely in achieving a smooth
performance of output and employment. There is also the crucial
question of price behaviour. Even assuming that the capitalist sector
is growing at a uniform, steady trend rate of growth, even assuming
that this is accompanied by a constant rate of unemployment, the
question arises: do prices also exhibit a steady growth? I take up this
question in the next chapter where I argue that the spontaneous
tendency of a capitalist economy which is experiencing steady output and employment growth is to have a non-steady growth of
prices.

3

Steady Growth and Price Instability

1. THE GENESIS OF PRICE INSTABILITY

The basic objective of each price-making conglomerate agent is to tilt the distribution of income in its favour. The distribution of income is an area of struggle between different social groups, or classes, and the price that each charges for the commodity that it sells is a weapon in this struggle. This fact is completely obscured by the Walrasian picture of a large number of price-taking individual agents contracting on the market.[1] To be sure, the ability of each group to fix the price on the commodity it sells is not absolute; this ability itself is conditioned by a host of factors. Likewise since the actual or *ex post* income distribution is a result of the configuration of prices fixed by the conglomerate agents representing different social groups, what a particular group thought it would get when it fixed its price and what it actually gets, namely its *ex ante* claim and its *ex post* claim, need not coincide: there is no auctioneer who brings about a reconciliation of claims through a one-shot fixing of all prices to everybody's agreement. This is not a bargaining equilibrium arrived at between different social groups. On the contrary, the divergence between *ex ante* and *ex post* claims of particular groups influences the movement over time of their *ex ante* claims themselves, and gives rise to a price dynamic. Any single period therefore must be seen not as being characterised by a price equilibrium, but as merely describing a hypothetical and temporary state of rest in a dynamic sequence, where each group is not necessarily satisfied with

---

[1] For a discussion of the literature where prices and distribution have been looked at in this perspective, see Mitra 1977.

the price that it gets, relative to the others, in the period in question.[2] In analysing price-dynamics, no less than in analysing output-dynamics, we eschew the concept of a moving equilibrium, as being essentially unrealistic under capitalist conditions.

In any given period, there are four obvious claimants for the total output produced in the capitalist sector: the workers who obtain a part of it as their wages, the capitalists who lay claim to a share in it as their profits, the State which takes away a part as indirect taxes, and the 'outside', the pre-capitalist producers who claim a part of it in exchange for the primary commodities they sell which are embodied in the final product. The claimants do not however just take a bit of the final product, each bit for given technological conditions depending on the ratio of their respective prices to the final price of the commodity, and then retire home to dispose of their bits in whatever way they like. They also enter into complex mutual relationships. The workers for instance may exchange a part of their claim upon the final product against other commodities such as food imported from the pre-capitalist sector; the State in addition to its indirect taxes, which are mediated through prices, also levies direct taxes on some of the claimants, and so on. These latter kinds of direct relations between the claimants also have a bearing on the claims they put in on the final output. Before getting into these complexities however, we shall in this chapter ignore two of the claimants, the State and the pre-capitalist producers, whom we introduce in subsequent chapters and concentrate only on two of the claimants, the workers and the capitalists. This simplifies analysis not only by restricting its scope, but also because the possibility of the workers, or the capitalists, re-exchanging their share in the final output against some 'outside' commodities is ruled out. By implication, we are assuming the capitalist sector to be self-sufficient. Let us also abstract from changes in the composition of output, so that in effect we concentrate on a one-good model for the time being, and let us

---

2 There is an essential ambiguity about the concept of the 'degree of monopoly', which consists in the fact that 'degree of monopoly' as a resultant, *ex post*, of competing claims between workers and capitalists that characterise a disequilibrium situation, is altogether different from 'degree of monopoly' as an equilibrium concept where the claims are reconciled by each class in some sense considering the response of the other in putting forward its own claim. In the latter case there is no continuous inflation. Kalecki uses the concept only in this latter sense, which is why he argues that strong trade unions reduce the degree of monopoly. For the distinction between the two concepts see P. Patnaik 1988.

also assume that both workers and capitalists are organised respectively into unions and, implicitly or explicitly colluding price-fixing firms. The money wage rate which the workers succeed in obtaining in any period is such as would give them, at the expected price, command over a certain real wage bundle. The magnitude of this real wage bundle relative to their productivity depends upon their bargaining strength, the most important proximate determinant of which is the unemployment rate. To put it differently, the *ex ante* share of wages in output which the unions succeed in obtaining is dependent on the unemployment rate. In other words

$$w_t = p_t^e \overline{w}_t \tag{3.1}$$

and

$$l_t \overline{w}_t = F(v_t) \qquad F' < 0, \tag{3.2}$$

where w refers to the money wage rate, $\overline{w}$ to the real wage rate, l to the labour coefficient per unit of output (the reciprocal of labour productivity) and p^e to the expected price.

The capitalists fix a price which is a mark-up over the unit prime cost, that in the current context, where production is assumed to be vertically integrated, with the capitalist sector being entirely self-sufficient, is identical with the unit labour cost. The magnitude of the mark-up depends on the degree of unity among the capitalists, an important determinant of which should be the level of capacity utilisation. To keep things simple however we shall take the mark-up as a constant. Therefore

$$p_t = w_t l_t \mu. \tag{3.3}$$

No mention has been made above of money supply upon which, according to an important tradition in economics, the level of prices is supposed to depend. The assumption here is that the supply of money is endogenous, adjusting to the demand for it. We can conceptualise it as follows: banks are willing to hold an unlimited amount of 'safe' private debt at a fixed real rate of interest, and other 'non-safe' debts on terms which reflect their relative degree of unattractiveness compared to 'safe' debt, where a 'safe' debt is one which carries no risk of default and on which the nominal interest rate is a variable one indexed in each period to the magnitude of price increase. Suppose for instance that the real rate of interest at which the banks are willing to hold an unlimited amount of 'safe' private debt is 5 per cent. Then a 'safe' debt of $100 is one which not only carries zero risk of default, but upon which the banks are paid back $107 at the end of the period if the price rise during the period is 2 per cent, and $110 if the price rise is 5 per cent. It should be noted that the assumption of a perfectly elastic money supply in this sense does not mean that the principle of increasing risk does not hold for individual borrowers, since the more an individual borrows from banks the greater is the risk of default on his debt, and hence the higher the real rate of interest that he would have to pay at the margin. Hence individual borrowers would still be concerned with the danger of becoming illiquid even though the supply of money is endogenous.

The endogeneity of money in this sense is an assumption which may be objected to. It even differs in at least two ways from what the proponents of endogenous money in the literature usually assert. First, they postulate that it is the nominal, rather than the real, rate of interest which is fixed at any time, and at which money supply is elastic. Second, they recognise that this administered interest rate is altered from time to time.[3] By contrast, we have assumed the real rate to be fixed, and that too for ever. Surely, it may be said, if the rate of inflation accelerates, this administered rate would be jacked up. As a matter of fact, the effect of changes in the administered rate will be discussed in the next chapter, so the present assumption is not a final one. Nonetheless, there is some intrinsic merit in discussing the price-output dynamics of a system with a fixed real interest rate for the following reason: if money supply is endogenous in our sense, then in conditions of steady growth, assuming a given income velocity of circulation of money and assuming money to be the only financial asset held by individual wealth-holders, the distribution of total profits between the capitalist entrepreneurs and the banks remain unchanged, no matter how prices move over time.

Investigating the dynamics of the system where this distribution is given in steady state is therefore analytically important, especially since altering this distribution would inevitably have serious political implications. This is a matter which we shall come back to later in the course of this chapter.

---

[3] There are of course differences among theorists of endogenous money. See Pollin 1990 and Moore 1989 for a discussion. The view referred to here is what is found for instance in Kaldor 1964.

Finally, let us assume that the current period's expected price is simply the previous period's actual price projected into the current period at the previous period's actual rate of inflation, that is:

$$p_t^e = p_{t-1}(p_{t-1} / p_{t-2}).$$ (3.4)

This assumption may appear too tame at a time when 'rational expectations' are so much in vogue. But the concept of 'rational expectations' is closely tied to the concept of a Walrasian equilibrium. And since we question the relevance of the latter concept itself, 'rational expectations' are totally meaningless for us. Even so, it may be argued that eqn. (3.4) provides no scope for learning from past experience, by postulating a mechanical rule for expectation formation. But quite apart from the fact any formal stipulation of expectation formation, in the form of an equation, would necessarily invite the charge of being mechanical, it is also the case that incorporating 'learning' into the formation of expectations about price will only accentuate the problem of price instability to which we draw attention below, only strengthening our argument. Equation (3.4) has the merit from our point of view of deliberately understating our case.

Now, from equation (3.1) to (3.4), it follows that

$$p_t / p_{t-1} = (p_{t-1} / p_{t-2})F(v_t)\mu.$$ (3.5)

A condition for steady inflation therefore is that v must have such a value that $F(v)\mu=1$, which means that the unemployment rate v must have a value v^* where $v^*=F^{(-1)}(1/\mu)$. Now v^* is nothing else but the 'non-accelerating inflation rate of unemployment' (NAIRU). On the steady growth path, however, the unemployment rate which would be maintained, and at which the natural rate of growth would equal the rate of increase of capital stock is, as we have seen in the last chapter, given by $\bar{v}$. There is no reason why v^* should equal $\bar{v}$. There is no reason in other words why along the steady growth path, there should also be steady inflation. If $v^*>\bar{v}$, then the steady growth path would witness accelerating inflation and if $v^*<\bar{v}$, then the steady growth path would witness decelerating inflation. There does not seem to be any way that both steady growth and steady inflation can be combined in the performance of the economy.

2. PRICE INSTABILITY AND INVESTMENT

It may be objected, however, that this result is due to the absence of a mechanism whereby price instability (in the sense of accelerating or decelerating inflation) can react back on the output system. Or, what comes to the same thing, we have not recognised the possibility that unsteady inflation can also influence investment behaviour, which constitutes the key to the behaviour of the output system. The issue here, it should be noted, is the effect of money variables on the real system. Whether inflation is accelerating or decelerating, and whatever its rate, our assumption that the profit margin remains unchanged means that inflation has no effect on income distribution, nor therefore upon consumption behaviour, nor, via this channel, upon capacity utilisation rates, and so on. Direct effects of nominal price increases upon real investment behaviour (unmediated through the usual real channels) are generally supposed to operate through the interest rate. If all prices, including money wages, increase while money supply does not, then interest rates are supposed to rise, exercising an adverse impact on the magnitude of real investment. But this particular avenue is also blocked in our case since money supply is assumed to be endogenous and real interest rates fixed.

There exists nonetheless another channel through which the rate of inflation affects investment decisions. Its significance of course gets lost in a one-good model such as we are examining. But since the one-good model is just for convenience, there is no reason why some real phenomenon existing outside of it should not be incorporated into it. The idea, first suggested by Fritz Machlup, was incorporated by Schumpeter (1930, vol. 1, 135–6) to explain the end of the boom in his model and endorsed by Oskar Lange (1941) in his review of Schumpeter's work. When prices are rising, since they are not necessarily rising in tandem, the prediction of profitability becomes difficult, so that the risks associated with investment increase, exerting a restraining influence on the magnitude of investment. It follows that stable prices provide the best environment for investment decisions. There is no reason however why what was said then about stable prices should not hold equally well for a steady rise in prices. If all prices are rising at more or less the same rate over time, there should not be much problem in predicting profitability. But if inflation is accelerating—and this is typically associated with a greater variance in the rates of inflation across commodities during any given period—then the risks associated with investment will be larger. The greater the degree of acceleration in overall inflation, the greater the adverse impact on investment decisions.[4]

To be sure, the effect upon investment of one deceleration in the inflation rate is not necessarily identical to that of another. Even if deceleration over a certain range, involving for example absolute declines in prices, affects investment adversely, deceleration in all circumstances cannot be held to have a similar effect. What is more, the magnitude of the adverse effect of a deceleration in the rate of inflation would by no means be the same as that of a corresponding acceleration. Notwithstanding this, we shall assume that both acceleration and deceleration in inflation have identical adverse consequences for investment. This drastic assumption is made here partly for simplicity, partly because it does not vitiate the conclusions of this chapter, and partly because deceleration is less likely in practice than acceleration. A modification of the investment function (2.1″) of the last chapter which takes into account the adverse impact of accelerating or decelerating inflation upon investment decisions is given by:

$$i_{t+1} = (K_{t+1} / K_t)\{i_t + b(u_t - u_0)i_t - \varepsilon[(p_t / p_{t-1})(p_{t-2} / p_{t-1}) - 1]^2 i_t\}$$
$$+ eK_{t+1}. \tag{3.6}$$

The only new element in eqn. (3.6) compared to eqn. (2.1″) is the third term within the angled brackets. This states that if the rate of inflation in the current period is higher or lower than in the previous period, then this has an adverse effect upon investment decisions of the current period, and hence upon the actual investment of the next period, the magnitude of the effect depending on the level of investment. Since both acceleration as well as deceleration of inflation are assumed *ex hypothesi* to have adverse effects which are symmetrical, we have introduced a squared term.

Now let us consider a system whose investment behaviour is given by eqn. (3.6), and whose other behaviour is captured by equations (2.2) to (2.7) of the last chapter and equations (3.1) to (3.4) of the

---

[4] It can be argued that even with steady inflation, a higher *rate* of inflation will involve greater risks for investors for this reason than a lower *rate*. But even if this argument is accepted, the difference between the risks associated with these cases is likely to be smaller than the difference between the cases of steady and accelerating inflation, which is why we have ignored it here.

current chapter, and examine whether steady output growth and steady price growth are both possible in such a system. This is an extremely simple stylisation of an economy in which the price dynamic is a result of competing claims between the workers and the capitalists, where output is demand-determined, and where investment, the main autonomous component of demand, depends upon the pace of innovations and the level of capacity utilisation, with a negative feed-back effect of accelerating or decelerating inflation acting on it.

The results, derived in the appendix to this chapter, show once again that none of the possible steady-growth configurations that the economy can accomplish is, except by some freak coincidence, associated with steady inflation. The hypothetical steady-growth configuration, which would ensure steady inflation, is unachievable owing to the nature of the investment behaviour. Though important, we are not concerned here with questions of stability, whether an economy conforming to our stylisation would actually converge to steady growth starting from some arbitrary initial state, or whether, if it is disturbed from a steady growth configuration, it would tend to return to it. The point here is simply that there is nothing in the spontaneous working of a capitalist system, as stylised here, which can enable it to achieve both steady growth and steady inflation.

Our model of course relies on a very specific investment function. But the conclusion it throws up is robust enough to survive the substitution of this particular investment function by some other one. Indeed the problem which the model illustrates arises not from some peculiarity of the model; it goes deeper. Let us turn to a discussion of it now.

3. NEOCLASSICAL AND OTHER STORIES OF STABILITY

Let us begin with an analytical contrast of our conclusions above with those reached by much of what is taught as macro-economics today. Monetarism believes that there is a 'natural rate of unemployment', which for all practical purposes is synonymous with full employment, at which the economy maintains not only steady growth but also a steady rate of inflation determined by the difference between the exogenously given rate of growth of money supply and the natural rate of growth (for a constant income velocity of circulation of money). More generally, to the extent that the income velocity of circulation of money itself grows over time at some independently determined rate g^c, the steady rate of inflation is given by $g^m + g^c - g^n$, where g^m and g^n refer respectively to the exogenously given rate of growth of money supply and the exogenously given natural rate of growth. It follows then that all that is necessary to reduce the rate of inflation is to reduce the rate of growth of money supply. While such a reduction in the rate of growth of money supply may have transitional effects, at best, upon employment and the growth rate, its long-run effect will be exclusively upon prices, since the real system would move back into equilibrium, with employment and the growth rate reverting back to their 'natural' levels. In short, there is a homogeneity postulate underlying monetarism, according to which any money supply increase spends itself eventually and exclusively upon a corresponding price increase, leaving the real system, which has built-in equilibrating mechanisms, pegged at the natural rate of unemployment, a concept which incidentally precludes Keynesian involuntary unemployment. The proponents of 'rational expectations' would even deny, quite categorically, the possibility of transitional disruptions of the equilibrium state.

The specific monetarist dogma which even denies the possibility of involuntary unemployment has been widely attacked. But the monetarists' general belief that a capitalist economy in its spontaneous operation can combine steady output growth at a constant rate of unemployment with a steady rate of inflation, that it can combine both output and price stability would be shared by many who are ideologically distant, and even hostile, to monetarism. The concept of a NAIRU, for instance, which may entail considerable involuntary unemployment, but at which a capitalist economy in its spontaneous operation can settle, figures even in the non-monetarist literature. To take an example from the very opposite end of the ideological spectrum, Rowthorn's (1977) paper setting out a conflict model of inflation, which we ourselves have drawn upon above, concludes not only that, once inflation has begun to be anticipated, a steady rate of inflation can be achieved in a capitalist economy only at the expense of considerable unemployment, but also that the economy can stabilise itself at the NAIRU. It would grow at the natural rate of growth, maintaining this steady rate of unemployment, with inflation steady at a rate equal (for $g^c=0$) to the excess of the rate at which the monetary authorities expand money supply over the economy's natural rate of growth. A capitalist economy according to this view can combine, through its spontaneous operation, both output and price stability at the NAIRU. Rowthorn's view differs from monetarism in its claim that the NAIRU itself may entail considerable involuntary unemployment; it is an altogether different animal from the monetarists' 'natural rate of unemployment'.

The most obvious reason for the difference between this view and ours lies in the fact that it does not, unlike ours, account for investment behaviour. First, it postulates no independent investment function. The question is not asked: if the level of NAIRU is high, would the capitalists have the inducement to invest in any period the entire amount of savings generated out of the output obtained by the maintenance of NAIRU in that period? Second, even assuming that they invest the entire savings generated out of the NAIRU output in a particular period when the NAIRU has been established, what ensures that the NAIRU would be sustained in the next period or in subsequent periods? Given the savings ratio and the technological capital–output ratio, if the percentage increase in output in the next period over its current level happens to be higher than the percentage increase in the work-force (which is exogenously given)[5] can sustain, then clearly either the unemployment rate must fall below the NAIRU in the next period, or the degree of capacity utilisation must fall below its current level in the next period. If it is the former, then clearly the NAIRU is not being sustained. If it is the latter, then surely this very fact would have some impact upon investment behaviour. It makes no sense to assume that when capacity is growing faster than the work-force, with the NAIRU being maintained, so that the degree of unutilised capacity is increasing from one period to the next, the capitalists are nonetheless continuing to invest the entire amount of savings generated from the NAIRU output in every period. Once we introduce an independent investment function, however, which eschews the assumption that all savings out of the NAIRU output are being invested in every period, and instead make investment decisions sensitive to the degree of capacity utilisation, then we are

---

[5] In the discussion which follows the growth of 'work-force' always refers to growth in efficiency units and this is assumed to be given by all those who talk in terms of the 'natural rate of growth'.

in a world such as the one stylised in our model, and the conclusion that a capitalist economy can spontaneously maintain both output and price stability no longer holds.

The neoclassical model can claim formal invulnerability to this criticism. If the capital stock is growing faster than the work-force, with a constant rate of unemployment (usually zero) being maintained, then it is not capacity utilisation that keeps declining but the degree of capital-intensity of the methods of production. With all savings being invested in every period, if the rate of capital accumulation exceeds the rate of work-force growth, then full-capacity use of capital stock is not abandoned, but the capital stock changes form like jelly in such a way that it is operated with less labour. The rise in the capital–labour ratio that must occur over time in such a situation is brought about not by a decline in the degree of utilisation of the capital stock, but by the same capital being operated with less labour. And, it may be argued, since full capacity is always used, why should the capitalists not go on investing the entire savings generated by such use in every period? This however is merely an arbitrary construction. To believe that when the rate of capital accumulation exceeds the rate of growth of the work-force capacity-utilisation does not change at all but only the methods of production do, amounts merely to pushing one's point by assumption rather than constructing a plausible argument in favour of it.

A neoclassical story can of course be told, and has been told, not in terms of 'capital-as-jelly', but in terms of different 'vintages' of capital. The available work-force, when fully employed (or at a constant rate of unemployment), determines the 'marginal' vintage which can be used. The average product of labour on this vintage (labour being the only current input) determines the real wage. The savings generated from the output produced on those vintages which are in operation in any period are assumed to be invested, as in the standard neoclassical case. The problem with this route of rescuing the neoclassical paradigm, however, lies in the assumption that all agents act merely as price-takers. If the workers insist on obtaining a *minimum* money wage and the capitalists also pursue an independent pricing rule (a plausible example of which would be a *minimum* mark-up charged by a price-leader, who is among the efficient producers, over his unit prime cost) then once again the question of unutilised capacity on account of labour shortage, in the sense of potentially profit-earning productive capacity lying idle owing to the

non-availability of labour, arises with all its other implications that
we have discussed.

There is however one particular mechanism which the proponents
of the 'spontaneous stability' view can fall back upon, which does not
depend on the neoclassical multiplicity of techniques. It is perhaps
this mechanism which many of them, such as Rowthorn, have in
mind when they ignore the need to postulate an independent investment function. If money supply grows at a steady exogenous rate,
since any deviation of the economy from the NAIRU would cause accelerating or decelerating inflation, sooner or later a divergence must
arise between the demand for money and its supply. This must affect
interest rates and hence investment, if not savings, behaviour until
the economy's deviation from the NAIRU is rectified. In the example
discussed above, if in a particular period the NAIRU is maintained,
and all savings are invested, and if the rate of accumulation so
achieved exceeds the rate of growth of the work-force, then in the
next period the unemployment rate would fall below the NAIRU. This
must immediately or over time raise interest rates and affect investment until the NAIRU is re-established. And if the economy must remain pegged to the NAIRU then the rate of accumulation must adjust
to the rate of growth of the work-force. In equilibrium, since investment must equal savings out of NAIRU-output (for otherwise the
NAIRU would not obtain), and since the rate of accumulation must
equal the rate of growth of the work-force, the degree of capacity
utilisation, and the interest rate would have to have such values as to
make both these things happen.[6]

We do not, in other words, need the neoclassical multiplicity of
techniques to ensure steady-state growth with steady inflation. Nor
do we need to postulate explicitly an independent investment function, since as long as investment is sufficiently sensitive to the interest
rate its amount as well as the rate of accumulation in any period
along the equilibrium path would have to take on specific values
through the maintenance of an appropriate level of the interest rate.[7]

[6] It should be noted that it is the real rate of interest which should keep changing,
and sufficiently in each period, to ensure the working of the equilibrating tendency.

[7] This depiction is different from that of Sen (1965), who introduced the real interest rate as a possible equilibrating mechanism in the context of a *neoclassical* model.
He took the money rate of interest as exogenously given (not the money supply) and
assumed a neoclassical production function where all savings in any period were
automatically invested. Because of the neoclassical setting he drew the conclusion
that a rise in the real interest rate would *increase the rate of accumulation*: since in

We shall come back to this proposition in the next chapter, but it is worth noting here that this proposition is inconsistent with the view that the distribution of income is an area of struggle between different social groups in a capitalist society. If one believes that workers and capitalists struggle over the distribution of output between wages and profits, then it seems inconsistent not to believe that a similar struggle over distribution takes place between the rentiers and the entrepreneurs among the capitalists. To be sure, unlike other price-fixers the rentiers themselves do not fix the interest rate. Since this rate depends upon the monetary policy pursued by the State it clearly is not directly within the province of action of the rentiers. But the fact that the State pursues a monetary policy which fixes the interest rate does not mean that the State is at liberty to pursue any monetary policy. The conflict between the rentiers and the entrepreneurs is mediated through the State;[8] and the monetary policy of the State, instead of being the original act from which other consequences, such as distribution between rentiers and entrepreneurs, follow, itself gets tailored so as to ensure a certain distribution between these two groups. Once we go beyond the Walrasian framework of a multitude of price-taking individuals, interacting, each in its isolation, with one another on the market, it cannot be maintained that money supply is exogenous. The level of money supply and how it changes are derived from the need through State action to maintain a certain distribution between entrepreneurs and rentiers, which means a certain real interest rate.

This is not to argue that the real interest rate is always a constant through time. It certainly changes in response to events, and above all in response to pressures, though over long stretches of history it

equilibrium the real rate of interest must equal the rate of profit, a rise in the real rate of interest would raise the rate of profit through movements along the production function. Since all savings are invested, such a rise in the rate of profit, quite obviously in the case of a classical savings function but less obviously though equally certainly in the case of a proportional savings function, would raise the rate of accumulation. Now a reduction in the unemployment rate below its equilibrium value (say the NAIRU, though this postdates Sen's paper) would on this argument *lower* the real rate of interest (owing to inflation) and hence the rate of accumulation. The ultimate conclusion, namely that at low levels of unemployment the rate of accumulation comes *down*, though reached differently, is the same as Rowthorn 1977; the route, however, is as questionable as its basic neoclassical setting.

8 For an interesting analysis of the effects upon State policy of the pressure of the rentier interests in post-War capitalism, see Steindl and Bhaduri 1984.

has been far more steady than a belief in exogenous money would suggest.[9] But even if the real interest rate changes from time to time, the supply of money can be taken to be elastic at each level. In the next chapter we shall examine the effects of such changes, which are by nature parametric. Given the politico-economic factors underlying such changes, which entail distributional shifts, a preliminary stylisation of a capitalist economy as one where the real interest rate is fixed and the supply of money adjusts to the demand for it seems more appropriate than taking money supply as exogenous. It is investment behaviour which is the crucial exogenous factor and not money supply.

This was the Keynesian contention, though Keynes himself, confining his attention to the single period, took money supply as given. The endogeneity of money supply, as a good deal of empirical work shows, is an essential ingredient of the institutions we live under. And this is also what is logically entailed in focusing attention on investment behaviour as the autonomous element in the picture.

If investment is autonomous then the problem of the impossibility of combining price with output stability through the spontaneous operation of a capitalist system must necessarily arise. This is not because of a sleight of hand such as the specification of a particular kind of investment function, but due to a more fundamental reason, the autonomy of the investment decision. With autonomous investment the level of activity in the economy is determined *inter alia* by the aggregate of investment decisions. At this level of activity if the competing claims of workers and capitalists cannot be reconciled there would be price instability, the feed-back effects of which upon investment may not be sufficient to nullify it.

Interestingly, the possibility of this instability was anticipated by Keynes himself. In chapter 17 of *The General Theory*, referring to Pigou's presumption 'in favour of real wages being more stable than money wages', Keynes wrote: 'If indeed some attempt were made to

---

[9] A comparison of price movements with those in the long-run rate (the average yield on Consols) for the British economy suggests that over the period 1880–1914, for instance, the real rate of interest did not rise in the boom nor fall in the slump. The nominal rate which was 3.21 per cent during 1880–94 fell to 2.38 per cent during 1894–1900 and rose to 3.27 per cent during 1910–14. The first period however saw a faster rate of price decline and the second period a faster rate of price increase. Over the entire period 1880–1914 the cost of living index did not change; nor for that matter did the nominal rate of interest. The nominal rates are taken from Kalecki 1954 and the price data from Lewis 1978*b*.

stabilise real wages by fixing wages in terms of wage goods, the effect could only be to cause a violent oscillation of money prices. For every small fluctuation in the propensity to consume and the inducement to invest would cause money prices to rush violently between zero and infinity. That money wages should be more stable than real wages is a condition of the system possessing inherent stability.' Keynes here was clearly thinking in terms of endogenous money. With endogenous money, if real wages are fixed, any tendency for economic activity to increase, insofar as this is impossible without some reduction in real wages, would simply push money wages and prices to infinity. The fixity of money wages, by allowing prices to vary relative to money wages, permits fluctuations in economic activity without the price system exploding. Keynes however was thinking in the context of a single period. If trade unions' money wage claims, fixed during the single period, are jacked up over time to compensate for the real wage decline, then inflation would be continuous; and if inflation begins to be anticipated, then it would be accelerating.

In other words, the maintenance of any level of activity at which the *ex post* real wages of workers are lower than the *ex ante* real wages that they can enforce for that level of activity, is accompanied by accelerating inflation; the opposite happens when the level of activity is on the lower side. The conclusion about the impossibility of combining price and output stability follows directly from this. These two kinds of stability can be combined only if there is a social class whose *ex ante* claims are squeezeable—one which can act as a shock-absorber. Keynes thought that the workers constituted such a shock-absorbing class. But if the workers are organised enough to prevent their *ex ante* claims from being squeezeable, then there are no such shock-absorbers and the two kinds of stability cannot be combined.

4. A METHODOLOGICAL CLARIFICATION

A methodological point should be clarified here. It may well be asked: 'surely if an economy is experiencing accelerating inflation (or its opposite), a time must come when the postulated behaviour pattern in our system of equations would cease to be valid. What is the point then of deriving a conclusion that there would be accelerating inflation on the basis of a behaviour pattern which itself gets subverted by the fact of accelerating inflation? And isn't this subversion but another mechanism that would terminate accelerating inflation?' In other words, is not the conclusion about price instability merely a result of our postulating certain rigid behaviour patterns? Are we not attributing to the capitalist system characteristics which arise only from extremely simplistic, and hence bad, theorising?

A distinction between 'smooth stability' and 'catastrophic stability' should be drawn here. No actual system can forever experience explosive inflation. Something is bound to happen to upset the trajectory of its movement. That something could be street demonstrations, a political crisis, a collapse of economic confidence, or an abrupt cessation of investment activity. Some of these could even bring explosive inflation to an end, in which case the system can be said to possess a kind of stability. But this kind of stability induced by 'abnormal' behaviour, by a change of state, is quite different from the inherent stability based on 'normal' behaviour which is claimed in economic theory for the functioning of the capitalist market system. The former kind of stability could be called 'catastrophic stability' and the latter 'smooth stability'. All that has been said until now relates to the concept of 'smooth stability'. Until now it has been argued that a capitalist system, in which organised workers face organised capitalists and investment decisions are autonomous, lacks smooth stability, in the sense that it cannot combine steady growth with steady inflation on the basis of 'normal' behaviour. It may possess catastrophic stability, but the latter by its very nature is unpredictable and should not be confused with inherent regularity. We cannot assert with any degree of confidence that a movement in a particular direction would necessarily reverse itself through abnormal behaviour (it could for instance lead to an end of the system itself), nor that, even if it does so, the consequences of such reversal through extraordinary means would themselves necessarily be predictably reversible, and so on. 'Normal' and 'abnormal' behaviour are qualitatively different; the former is not to be confused with the empirically average state of affairs in a system lurching from one extreme state to another.

Even if the legitimacy of the distinction between two kinds of stability of the system, one based on 'normal' behaviour, and the other a possible result of 'abnormal' behaviour, is granted, the question still remains: what is 'normal' behaviour? Surely, what we have captured in our model so far are some simple and rigid patterns of behaviour which cannot possibly exhaust the corpus of 'normal' behaviour. Economic agents adapt their behaviour to changing circumstances; what then is the status of our conclusions derived from postulating rigid behaviour patterns?

The problem however has nothing to do with 'simple' versus 'complex', or 'rigid' versus 'flexible'. Normal behaviour responses are worked out keeping a range of normal circumstances in mind. Economic theory believes that the aggregate outcome of such normal behaviour is to preserve the prevalence of 'normal' circumstances. It is this proposition which our argument challenges. What it says is stronger than appears at first sight. No matter how complex our 'normal' behaviour postulates, derived from observing behaviour in normal circumstances, we cannot explain the prevalence of 'normal' circumstances on the basis of these postulates. The fact that this argument is sustained by some simple behaviour postulates is of little significance. No matter how complex we make normal behaviour, as long as it is behaviour shaped under the prevalence, within a range, of normal circumstances, it cannot itself explain such prevalence.

This does not mean that normal circumstances do not actually prevail most of the time. It does means that this prevalence cannot be explained as a result merely of the inner working of the system. If capitalism has been a robust and durable system, it is not the virtues of the 'invisible hand' which are responsible for it. If capitalism over long stretches of time has managed to combine price with output stability (apart from cyclical fluctuations which themselves hold little threat for the system), this is not because it is an inherently stable system. The reason lies elsewhere as we shall see in subsequent chapters.

No doubt there is an identification problem here. When we observe a dog standing on its hind legs supporting itself on some object, we can theorise either that the dog is a biped animal, or that it needs a support to be able to stand up. If our experience of dogs was confined entirely to dogs which were standing in this way, there would be a genuine problem in deciding between the theories. Our experience of social systems is rather like that. Not only has capitalism been around for a comparatively short time; it has also never been observed in a situation where it does not have the crutch of external support, of pre-capitalist economies. This gives rise to a problem of deciding between theories. We have to fall back upon

internal evidence, such as the degree to which behaviour observed in
a stylised manner in this 'normal' position can explain the position
itself. In the case of the dog, for instance, we can attempt to find out
from its muscular development and muscular effort, as observed in
the standing position itself, whether it is these alone which contribute to its standing position. But there is no reason why, observing
the dog standing, we should necessarily conclude that it is inherently
stable on two legs, nor rule out any questions regarding its need for
external support. Yet this is what economic theory has done
systematically for decades.[10]

10 It may be thought that a distinction was necessary here. Even if it is the case that
capitalism uses pre-capitalist economies for support, when such support is available,
does it follow that such support is necessary? From its functioning when such support
is available, would we be justified in concluding that such support is necessary without postulating what its behaviour *would be* when such support is not available? This
is a question which I do not consider to be of any great practical significance. It is
enough for us to show that in conditions of availability of such support it is necessary.
What would happen in its absence is a question which belongs to that realm of
speculative theorising which is irrelevant in a historical science such as economics.

Appendix

The complete system of equations describing the behaviour of consumption, population and productivity movements as given in Chapter 2, and of price and money wage movements as given in Chapter 3, together with the investment function which incorporates a negative feedback effect of accelerating or decelerating inflation on accumulation is given below. We shall refer to this set of equations as System 1.

$$i_{t+1} = (K_{t+1} / K_t)\{i_t + b(u_t - u_0)i_t - \varepsilon[(p_t / p_{t-1})(p_{t-2} / p_{t-1}) - 1]^2 i_t\}$$
$$+ eK_{t+1} \tag{i}$$

$$C_t = W_t + c_2 P_t + \alpha K_t \tag{ii}$$

$$O_t = C_t + i_t + dK_t \tag{iii}$$

$$u_t = O_t / \beta \bullet K_t \tag{iv}$$

$$P_t = i_t + dK_t + c_2 P_t + \alpha K_t \tag{v}$$

$$W_t = O_t l_t w_t / p_t \tag{vi}$$

$$w_t = p_t^e \overline{w}_t \tag{vii}$$

$$\overline{w}_t l_t = F(v_t), \qquad F' < 0, \tag{viii}$$

or, in an explicit form,

$$\overline{w}_t l_t = q - r v_t,$$

where q and r are constants.

$$v_t = 1 - (O_t l_t / L_t) \tag{ix}$$

$$L_{t+1} / L_t = 1 + m - n v_t \tag{x}$$

$$l_{t+1} / l_t = 1 / (1 + g_t^p) \tag{xi}$$

$$g_t^p = g(i_t / K_t), \qquad g' > 0, \tag{xii}$$

or, in an explicit form adopted for convenience,

$$g_t^p = [(1 + i_t / K_t) / (1 + \gamma i_t / K_t)] - 1, \qquad 0 < \gamma < 1$$

$$p_t = w_t l_t \mu \qquad\qquad\qquad (xiii)$$

$$p_t^e = p_{t-1}(p_{t-1} / p_{t-2}) \qquad\qquad\qquad (xiv)$$

$$K_{t+1} = K_t + i_t \qquad\qquad\qquad (xv)$$

The symbols and the equations have already been explained in the text (apart from certain definitional equations which are self-explanatory). There are fifteen equations altogether in this system and twenty-one variables, which are as follows: $i_t, i_{\{t+1\}}, K_{\{t+1\}}, K_t, u_t, p_{\{t-1\}}, p_t, C_t, W_t, P_t, w_t, \bar{w}_t, p_{\{t-2\}}, p_t^e, l_t, v_t, L_t, L_{\{t+1\}}, g_t^p, l_{\{t+1\}}$, and O_t. Of these, six are given in any period, namely, $K_t, i_t, p_{\{t-1\}}, p_{\{t-2\}}, L_t$, and l_t. The remaining fifteen are determined by the fifteen equations, which in turn bequeath for the next period another six variables.

Let us now look at possible steady-state solutions of the system. In steady state i/K will be constant and equal to, say, g; $L_{\{t+1\}}/L_t$ will equal $1 + \gamma g$ and the unemployment rate $\bar{v}$ will equal $[m/n - \gamma g/n]$. The degree of capacity utilisation will also remain steady at some level $\bar{u}$. From equations (i), (vii), (viii), (xiii), and (xiv), it follows that in steady state, we must have

$$[e + b(\bar{u} - u_0)g] - \varepsilon g(q\mu - rv\mu - 1)^2 = 0. \qquad (A1)$$

On the other hand, from (ii),(iii),(iv),(v),(vi) and (xiii), it follows that

$$\bar{u} = (g + d + \alpha) / \beta s, \qquad (A2)$$

where $s = 1 - 1/\mu - c_2(\mu - 1)/\mu$.

Now if g is negative, then, from (A2), $\bar{u} < (d+\alpha)/\beta s$. But since it must necessarily be the case for the system to be meaningful that the desired level of capacity utilisation exceeds what is required for meeting the capitalists' autonomous consumption and depreciation requirements, namely that $u_0 > (d+\alpha)/\beta s$, it follows that if g is negative, then the left-hand side of (A1) would be positive. The system therefore cannot have negative roots.

The possible values of g are given by the roots of the following equation which is derived from (A1) simply by substituting the steady-state value of v:

$$g^3 + Ag^2 + Bg + D = 0, \qquad (A3)$$

where

$$A = (n^2 / \varepsilon^2 r^2 \gamma^2 \mu^2)[2\varepsilon(q\mu - 1 - mr\mu / n)r\mu\gamma / n - b / \beta s],$$

$$B = (n^2 / \varepsilon r^2 \gamma^2 \mu^2)[-b(d + \alpha) / \beta s + bu_0 + \varepsilon(q\mu - 1 - mr\mu / n)^2], \text{ and}$$

$$D = -en^2 / \varepsilon\gamma^2\mu^2 r^2.$$

Now, D is obviously negative. Since, as we have seen, the system cannot have negative roots, it must have either three positive real roots or one positive real root and complex roots. In Figure 3.1 we have plotted what the curves corresponding to the two parts on the left-hand side of (A1) would look like; adding the two curves we would get the curve corresponding to the polynomial in (A3). Real roots exist when it intersects the x-axis three times, and complex roots when there is only one intersection.

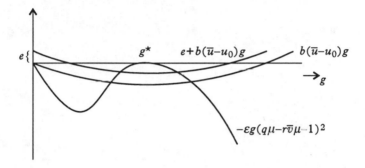

Fig. 3.1.

The point g^*, where the curve representing the second term on the left-hand side of (A1) touches the x-axis (it can only touch), corresponds to that hypothetical rate of steady growth which if it obtained would ensure a steady rate of inflation, but it would not obtain because there is an additional term in square brackets on the left-hand side. In other words a steady-state path with steady inflation would only exist if the curve representing the first term in square brackets also happened to intersect the x-axis precisely at g^*. But this can happen only by a freak accident. Thus given the investment behaviour of the economy, the possible steady growth configurations would not, except by sheer accident, be accompanied by steady inflation.

II

State Intervention and Stability

4

Monetary Policy as an Instrument of Stabilisation

In the last two chapters the possibility of State intervention was not considered. The only way that the State came into the picture was through the assumption that it helped to maintain a certain fixed real rate of interest at which money supply adjusted to the demand for it. And in such a case it was argued that the maintenance of steady output growth together with a steady rate of inflation was impossible through the spontaneous operation of a capitalist economy. But then, it may be asked, why talk about the spontaneous operation of the system? The capitalist system from its very inception has been characterised by State intervention, not only in its external relations, but also directly in its internal functioning. No doubt the scope of State intervention has varied over time, but it has been there all along. Through State intervention surely the problem of instability mentioned earlier can be overcome, even if the spontaneous operation of the system cannot remove it. In other words, the more or less successful functioning of the capitalist system, which explains to a large extent its historical durability, can surely be ensured by, and attributed historically to, judicious State intervention. The purpose of the present chapter, and the following one, is to examine briefly the nature of and the constraints upon State intervention. The present chapter deals with monetary policy while the following one is concerned with intervention through fiscal means.

1. THE STABILISING POTENTIAL OF
EXOGENOUS MONEY

Before analysing the potential of monetary policy for stabilising a capitalist economy, however, let us briefly go back to the argument mentioned in the previous chapter. If the State ensured a constant exogenous rate of growth of money supply, then the problem of instability discussed above would automatically disappear. We have already seen that this argument unrealistically assumes that rentier interests have no influence on State policy. In addition however it is logically faulty, and it is this latter aspect which we discuss below.

To incorporate the effects of money-supply growth, and indeed of any monetary policy, on the economy, we have to make investment decisions sensitive to the interest rate. In a world in which the wage unit itself is changing it is the real interest rate rather than the nominal interest rate that would influence investment decisions. The simplest way of doing so would be to make e, which is a constant in eqn. (i) of equation system 1 (see the appendix to Chapter 3), a function of the real interest rate j, so that

$$e_{t+1} = e(j_t), \qquad e' < 0 \tag{4.1}$$

and

$$j_t = (1 + j_t^n)/(p_t/p_{t-1}) - 1. \tag{4.2}$$

The nominal rate itself can be taken to be determined by the supply of and the demand for money in the following manner. Given the money income in any period, if the total quantity of money available is to be held, the interest rate must adjust to make this happen. So much is standard liquidity preference theory; in addition however the position of the liquidity function would also be influenced by the prospective yield on the capital asset. The lower this prospective yield, the higher would be the demand for money for any given rate of interest and nominal income. In other words, the choice between money and bonds cannot remain unaffected by the prospective yield on the capital asset since bonds represent, however indirectly, claims upon the capital asset. Taking this into account and assuming that the estimate of this prospective yield depends upon the sum of the current rate of profit and the current rate of inflation (since this inflation also raises the value of the capital asset), we can state:

$$j_t^n = j(p_t O_t / M_t; P_t / K_t + p_t / p_{t-1} - 1), \qquad j_1 > 0, j_2 < 0. \qquad (4.3)$$

Finally, we assume that money supply grows at the rate ρ, so that

$$M_{t+1} = M_t(1 + \rho). \qquad (4.4)$$

With the fifteen equations of system 1 (from the appendix to Chapter 3) with e in (i) there now having a time subscript $t+1$, and the above four equations we have altogether nineteen equations and twenty-seven unknowns, the latter now including j_t, j_t^n, $e_{\{t+1\}}$, M_t, $M_{\{t+1\}}$, and ρ, of which M_t and ρ would be given in any period in addition to the six already assumed there to be given. We thus have a complete determination of the single-period configuration. What can we say about the steady-state possibilities of the new system?

It can be checked that the system is capable of a steady growth–steady inflation equilibrium, along which the nominal and the real rates of interest remain constant, and steady inflation occurs at a rate equal to $(1+\rho)/(1+g) - 1$. But this equilibrium is not necessarily a stable one. A necessary condition for stability is that whenever the rate of growth of the economy happens to be less than the equilibrium rate of growth, the real rate of interest which provides the equilibrating mechanism must remain below the equilibrium real rate. This condition however is not necessarily satisfied here.

The reason for this, indeed the reason why simply letting the money supply grow at an exogenous rate would not necessarily bring the economy back to the equilibrium path, can be explained as follows. Suppose the economy is on the equilibrium path to begin with, and suppose for some reason investment drops in a particular period. Now this drop does not affect the real rate of interest directly, since the latter is dependent on two different entities, the nominal rate of interest and the rate of inflation. While a reduced level of activity owing to the investment drop would pull down the rate of inflation, what happens to the nominal rate of interest would depend on whether the greater desire for liquidity owing to reduced yields on capital assets is counterbalanced by the greater availability of liquidity owing to reduced nominal income. Even if the nominal interest rate falls it does not follow that the real rate would fall as well.

Suppose however that the real rate also falls. But then its effect on investment in the next period may not be large enough to offset the retarding effect of the current period's decline in activity. If under these circumstances the activity decline continues for some time, the rate of inflation would continue to decline until it becomes negative. Since the nominal rate can never fall below a certain minimum positive level compensating for lender's risk, the real rate would start rising from then on, and if equilibrium has not been achieved by then it would never be achieved thereafter.

It can of course be argued that negative inflation is an unrealistic assumption. This however does not affect our argument. If we put a lower bound of zero on the rate of inflation, so that money wages and prices can in the extreme case remain constant but would never actually fall, even then the nominal interest rate (which would be identical to the real rate with zero inflation) may settle at some floor level, because of increased liquidity preference arising from the decline in the prospective yield on capital assets, that is still higher than the equilibrium real rate. In such a case the decline in activity can never be reversed. And if with declining activity it is only the rate of price increase that has a zero lower bound while money wages can fall in absolute terms (the degree of monopoly increases), then of course our argument about the failure of the equilibrating mechanism is even further strengthened.

It might be objected that it is not exclusively through the channel of investment decisions that a relative abundance of money supply compared to money income makes itself felt, but also through the channel of consumption. But since we are assuming until now that all money is issued against private debt, there cannot be any wealth effects upon consumption induced by changes in any of the variables in the model: the real wealth of the private sector is nothing else but the total capital stock. As regards the possible effects of the changes in variables upon the savings propensities out of current income, it is hardly likely that in a period of declining activity, as long as activity is expected to decline further, even if consumption as a proportion of income rises somewhat, it would rise to an extent that altogether reverses the activity decline.

Certainly, on the other side of the equilibrium, when the economy is pushed off the equilibrium path through an increase in investment so that the activity level rises and the rate of inflation accelerates, a constant rate of growth of money supply is likely to act as a constraint that eventually acts in an equilibrating direction. The excess demand for money for transaction purposes will raise the nominal interest rate sufficiently such that the real interest rate rises, which lowers the employment rate and hence checks accelerating inflation. But this in itself is of little consolation. Unless an exogenous growth in money supply can be relied upon to call forth an automatic equilibrating mechanism *in the face of both rising as well as falling rates of inflation*, we are back with the problem that a steady growth-cum-steady inflation path cannot be attained spontaneously through the functioning of the capitalist market-system. The fact that an equilibrating mechanism may exist for movements in one direction is of little consequence unless a similar mechanism exists for movements in the other direction.

2. STATE INTERVENTION THROUGH INTEREST RATES

If the State directly influenced the real rate of interest, and was free to move it to any level, then of course stabilising the economy on a steady growth–steady inflation path becomes possible. With investment dependent on the real interest rate (eqn. (i) of system 1 of the appendix to Chapter 3 having now a time subscript $t+1$ attached to e and eqn. (4.1) added to the system) and the real interest rate taken as a policy variable, the State just has to maintain it at an appropriate level to keep the economy on an equilibrium path, and jiggle it up or down whenever it is off such a path to bring it back. There would nonetheless be a problem arising from the distinction between logical and historical time, on which more later, but, leaving this aside for the time being, equilibrium could be achieved.

The State intervenes however through the nominal rate of interest. Even in such a case as long as it is free to move the rate to any level, it can be argued that the economy can be stabilised on an equilibrium path. We just have to add eqn. (4.2) to the system of equations mentioned in the previous paragraph, and take the nominal rate as a policy variable to see the possibility of equilibrium with stability.

In principle, it can, therefore, be argued in contrast to the monetarist perception that a regime of endogenous money with administered interest rates is not prone to the problem of instability of the equilibrium discussed in the previous section. The fact that the State has discretion in changing the interest rate makes it possible for it to halt a downward cumulative slide of the economy. Of course once such a slide has gone beyond a certain point where prices have started declining perceptibly, the nominal interest rate which is the instrument of State intervention may no longer be capable of being pushed down to the level required for halting a further downward movement; but the State in principle can act early enough to prevent the economy's reaching this point. For instance, if as soon as the economy deviates downwards from the equilibrium position, the State lowers the nominal interest rate sufficiently to ensure that the real interest rate is reduced to a level adequate for giving a net boost to investment, there is no reason why the downward slide should continue or gather momentum. Thus, the arguments against the automaticity of adjustment should not be taken to mean that intervention through monetary policy is *per se* ineffective.

Before we discuss the problems with such intervention however a few clarificatory remarks about the nature of the equilibrium are in order. These remarks are obvious, but still bear repetition. (They would hold equally well even if a stable equilibrium could be attained, contrary to our argument in the previous section, through a steady exogenous growth in money supply). First, the basic mechanism through which monetary policy can stabilise the economy is through changes in the unemployment rate, brought about through changes in investment. In other words, any movement from accelerating to steady inflation is accompanied by an increase in the rate of unemployment.

Second, as already mentioned in earlier chapters, the real system in the above conception is not in a Walrasian equilibrium, owing to the existence of conglomerate agents. The level of unemployment at which the economy would experience steady growth-cum-steady inflation in equilibrium, if it were reached, would be v^*, which is not the natural rate of unemployment and does not constitute a state of de facto full employment as claimed by the monetarists. The level of v^* would depend upon the strength of trade unions in enforcing *ex ante* claims, and consequently at v^* there would be considerable involuntary unemployment.

Third, the rate of steady growth at v^* would not be an exogenously given 'natural rate of growth', since the natural rate itself is a function of the unemployment rate. The difference between a state of accelerating inflation and a state of steady inflation lies not only in the fact that the former has a lower level of unemployment, but also in the fact that the former has a higher rate of growth as well. Accelerating inflation is accompanied by a higher rate of growth, and in moving from accelerating to steady inflation the economy would have to make a sacrifice in terms of the growth rate, no matter how desirable such a move may be considered on other grounds. This is a phenomenon not recognised by the monetarists, though it has figured prominently in the literature on developing countries, where admittedly the line of argumentation is not identical with that adopted here. The Latin American structuralists, for instance, have always insisted that the process of curbing inflation through tight monetary policy is simultaneously a process which raises the rate of unemployment and lowers the rate of growth in the economy (Baer and Kerstenetzky 1964). No matter what one thinks of structuralist policy prescriptions, in this particular respect the validity of their position can hardly be doubted, and our model though stylising an altogether different context also reaches the same conclusion, though via a different route. Thus even if we assume that monetary policy works in stabilising the economy by achieving steady growth-cum-steady inflation, the equilibrium it would succeed in achieving is altogether different from what monetarist-type reasoning visualises.

3. PROBLEMS OF INTEREST RATE POLICY

The problem with stabilisation through State intervention via the interest rate arises for two reasons. First, what is true as a logical statement about what would have happened if the interest rate were higher or lower, is not necessarily true as a predictive statement over time about what would actually happen if the interest rate was to be increased or decreased. The very increase or decrease in the interest rate would alter the entire climate of expectations of the entrepreneurs and therefore alter the coefficients of the investment function, underlying which was the assumption of a fixed real interest rate. Even with unchanged coefficients it must be the case that finding an appropriate nominal rate of interest compatible with equilibrium would have to be a process of trial and error. The nominal interest rate would have to be moved about a good deal for the purpose of introducing dual stability into the system. If a result of such movements is also to alter the values of the coefficients, then it follows that stabilisation may become an even more elusive goal.

For example, if in response to accelerating inflation, the nominal interest rate is raised sufficiently to raise the real interest rate, this may take the economy not to v^*, but to a level of unemployment exceeding v^*. This would initiate a deceleration in the inflation rate. Now if the State brings about a lowering of the real rate of interest to reduce unemployment and raise the growth rate, investment behaviour may fail to respond adequately, at any rate for a considerable period of time, insofar as the very up-and-down movement of the real interest rate would have introduced a greater degree of risk into investment decisions. The economy is not a mechanical entity, the feeding of certain policies into which would always produce certain predictable results.

This is obvious. But if this is true of State intervention directly in altering the interest rate, it is much more true of a policy of controlling the rate of growth of money supply. Here the State is neither directly fixing the variable which influences investment behaviour, namely the real interest rate, nor is it fixing the nominal interest rate and thereby indirectly influencing the real rate, but is indirectly influencing the nominal rate itself. Even assuming that the growth in money supply can be controlled (which is itself doubtful, given the nature of the financial institutions we live under), and that money substitutes do not appear or disappear in response to shortages or abundance of money supply relative to the demand for it, control over money supply is basically a means of influencing the real system through its effect on interest rates. But what exactly the effect upon interest rates would be of a particular measure of control over money supply is itself unpredictable, so that an additional element of unpredictability is introduced, besides the unpredictability of the effects of changes in interest rate on investment and employment.

The second and more serious problem with the efficacy of monetary policy as a stabilising instrument arises from a point mentioned earlier, that the State does not have unconstrained freedom to move the interest rate. The constraints upon its actions arise from the interests of the rentiers. And by rentiers we mean not just the numerous so-called 'widows and orphans', but primarily the banks. Banks are the rentiers *par excellence* in a capitalist economy, a role that gets camouflaged in the entire discussion which looks upon them merely as financial intermediaries. Such intermediaries to be sure they technically are, but intermediaries which are so large that they constitute a powerful interest.

4. THE ROLE OF RENTIER INTERESTS

To highlight the nature of this interest, we shall assume for simplicity below that the banks are the sole rentiers in the sense of deriving an income from the activity of lending. The 'public' in other words is assumed to hold only money, which is the liability of banks, created against private debt. We shall also make the simplifying assumption that the nominal rate in any period, which is the administered rate, applies not just to the fresh loans contracted during the period, but to all outstanding loans. So all outstanding loans are recontracted in every period.

The real interest rate affects the distribution of profits (or surplus value) between entrepreneurs and rentiers. In the present model, where the 'public' is assumed to hold only one financial asset, money, the real interest rate affects the distribution of profits between the banks and the entrepreneurs, or between the capitalists engaged in finance and the capitalists engaged in production. It stands to reason then that different sections of capitalists would take action to prevent such changes in the real interest rate as would adversely affect their relative shares, or to insulate themselves against such changes. If for instance the real interest rate is raised, then the capitalists in production, who until now we have assumed simply to be protecting their share against the workers, would, *ceteris paribus*, find their post-interest share to be declining and would take action by raising their profit margin. In other words, one way in which the struggle over distribution among different sections of capital can be incorporated into the model is by making the capitalists engaged in production adjust their prices so as to obtain a fixed mark-up over unit costs which include not only the unit wage costs, but also a part of the unit credit charge.

But this only takes account of the entrepreneurs' side of the story. The banks too would naturally try to protect their share. They are in other words not automatons, or, what comes to the same thing, atomistic agents meekly adjusting their behaviour to the autonomous decisions taken somewhere within the State. They put on pressure to ensure that their interests are protected. And as a simple representation of their objectives, we shall postulate that λ which is their relative share in total income must remain above some λ^*. The banks' objective can be stated quite legitimately to be different from what we have specified. But our specification should do as a first approximation; and in any case the argument here does not depend on the precise objective.

Now let us consider an extremely simplified picture. Banks' assets are the loans they make to the 'public', which we take to be synonymous with the entrepreneurs in this context, and the reserves they hold. Their liabilities are the deposits, all of which are non-interest earning, which we take to be synonymous with money supply, and their debt to the Central Bank against which they obtain their reserves. The interest rate they pay to the Central Bank is a fixed fraction δ of the interest rate they charge on loans, which is not an inappropriate assumption since it makes banks in effect 'cost-plus' pricers, and simplifies the complex mechanism through which monetary policy works in practice without violating its essence. The money supply which is held in the economy is an amount which always bears a certain ratio to the total money income. (This follows from our assumption of endogeneity in this section.) Since all of it comes into the economy as loans to the entrepreneurs, who 'pass on' the interest cost through the price they charge, we take this ratio to be a constant independent of the interest rate. Likewise banks only hold as much reserves as are considered necessary (which need not be statutory), say a fraction R of their total liabilities, and use any excess to redeem their IOUs to the Central Bank. Finally, in order to keep things simple and avoid excessive simultaneity, we assume that the part of the unit credit charge which entrepreneurs pass on through prices in the current period is what they calculate to have actually obtained during the previous period.

Since loans are being assumed to be recontracted in every period, the total credit charge for the previous period is $M_{\{t-1\}}(1+j^n_{\{t-1\}})$, and the credit charge per unit of output is this figure divided by $O_{\{t-1\}}$. A proportion x of this is assumed to be included in the calculation of the base upon which a fixed mark-up is charged by them in the current period. Thus in lieu of eqn. (xiii) of system 1 we now have

$$p_t = \mu[w_t l_t + x M_{t-1}(1 + j^n_{t-1}) / O_{t-1}] \tag{4.5}$$

and, in addition,

$$M_{t-1} = kO_{t-1}p_{t-1}. \tag{4.6}$$

The share of output λ_t of the banks in any period t is simply equal to

$$\lambda_t = M_{t-1}[j^n_{t-1} - \delta j^n_{t-1}R / (1 - R)] / O_t p_t. \tag{4.7}$$

Our entire system of equations now consists of system 1, with eqn. (4.5) replacing eqn. (xiii) and e in eqn. (i) having a time subscript, together with equations (4.1), (4.2), and (4.6).

There are eighteen equations altogether and twenty-seven variables, including, in addition to the twenty-one of system 1, j_t, j^n_t, $j^n_{\{t-1\}}$, $O_{\{t-1\}}$, $M_{\{t-1\}}$, and $e_{\{t+1\}}$. Of these, in addition to the six mentioned in connection with system 1, $j^n_{\{t-1\}}$, j^n_t, and $O_{\{t-1\}}$ are given. The single period state therefore can be determined for this system.

This system, it can be demonstrated, is capable of yielding a steady growth-cum-steady inflation solution. We have already seen that system 1 itself is capable of yielding such a solution provided the State can alter the real rate of interest. The present system is essentially a variation on the same theme. Instead of directly administering the nominal rate of interest, the State here is, more realistically, assumed to be administering it through the rate of interest charged by the Central Bank (though we do not show this explicitly). The equilibrium which exists however does not give a unique value for the nominal rate of interest. This is hardly surprising: what we do get for equilibrium is a unique value of the real rate of interest, and depending upon what the precise value of the steady rate of inflation would be in equilibrium (which is not determined by the model) the nominal rate of interest would take on a corresponding value. The question of how and through what process, if at all, the State can intervene to bring the economy to equilibrium is a matter that we are not concerned with. Even assuming that the State can some how do so, there are three points about this equilibrium which are worth noting.

The first relates to the fact that the usual assumption that accelerating inflation can be cured through a rise in the real rate of interest is not necessarily true. Changes in the real rate of interest affect not only investment decisions but also the intensity of the distributional conflict. These two effects run counter to one another. A rise in the real rate of interest, by restricting investment decisions, has a stabilising effect on prices if inflation was accelerating to start with. But at the same time by reducing the share of real wages it has an aggravating effect upon accelerating inflation. This does not mean that an equilibrium does not exist; but the rule which has to be followed for achieving it is not necessarily the simple one usually prescribed. In the case for instance where the effect of the real interest rate upon investment is negligible, and the coefficient b (capturing the effect of capacity utilisation on investment) is also small, it could well be that to cure accelerating inflation the real rate of interest has to be lowered rather than raised which is the usual policy response. While this fact has received some recognition in the development literature (see for instance Taylor 1983), it has a relevance in a wider context as well. But, as stated earlier, let us assume that the State, no matter what problems it faces in adjusting policy through historical time, achieves equilibrium, pursuing, where necessary, measures which run contrary to the usual economists' prescriptions.

The second and more important point is that at this equilibrium there is no reason to believe that the banks' objective, of getting more than a certain minimum share of output will be fulfilled. From eqn. (4.7) it follows that in equilibrium the share of the banks in total output will be

$$\lambda = kj^n[1 - \delta R / (1 - R)] / (1 + g)(1 + g_v),$$

where g denotes the rate of steady growth of output and g_v the rate of steady inflation. It follows then that the equilibrium real rate of interest and the rate of steady growth determine between them the relative share of the banks. And there is no reason why this configuration should be such as would give the banks a share that satisfies their minimum requirement, in which case the banks would put pressure to prevent such a real rate of interest from obtaining.

It may of course be asked: what determines λ^*, the banks' minimum requirement? Why should we take some arbitrary value of λ^* and impose it as a constraint to show the impossibility of attaining equilibrium? This criticism however misses the point of the argument. Even if we assume that λ^* is nothing else but the share achieved during the past when, say, the economy was in a steady-growth–steady-inflation equilibrium, a parametric shift which leaves everything else, including λ^*, unchanged, but alters only one parameter, say $e(j)$ in a downward direction, would mean that no equilibrium need exist in the new situation. To be sure, we are not claiming that $\lambda > \lambda^*$ would not be satisfied at the equilibrium real rate of interest, but merely that it need not be satisfied. The point is that there are no intrinsic mechanisms for achieving equilibrium for a particular configuration of parameter values.

In short, looking upon monetary policy as if the State, without any constraints being imposed upon its course of action, merely has to pick out, from a computer as it were, an interest rate which it then imposes on the economy in order to stabilise it, is an altogether facile view of the matter. We have so far looked at only one obvious constraint, namely that the banks, like the workers and entrepreneurs, would also insist on obtaining a certain relative share of output, a constraint which paradoxically even those who talk of money supply endogeneity have not recognised. I say paradoxically because the question should have immediately presented itself: what social factors underlie the level of the interest rate at which money supply is supposed to adjust to demand? Yet this question has scarcely been raised in recent literature notwithstanding the substantial discussion on finance capital among Marxists earlier and even Keynes's and Kalecki's distinction between entrepreneur and rentier interests.

Third, even if this constraint is recognised, the view of the matter is still highly limited. The different social classes in a capitalist society are not exclusively concerned with their relative shares alone. Even if it is the case that their claims can be reconciled so that the economy is on a steady-growth–steady-inflation path, where the rentiers and the entrepreneurs get their desired shares and the workers are reconciled to theirs, because the level of unemployment is such that their bargaining strength would not allow them any larger *ex ante* claims, the absolute level of activity in the economy is not a matter of indifference to the various classes. If the level of unutilised capacity in the equilibrium situation is inordinately high, then the capitalists in production can scarcely be reconciled to such an equilibrium simply because their profit per unit of output remains intact. If the level of unemployment is excessively high in equilibrium then the system will scarcely be able to achieve the social stability necessary for its smooth functioning. Thus even if perchance the capitalist State is able to achieve economic stability in the narrow sense with which we have so far been mainly concerned, it does not follow that this achievement would be accompanied by social stability as well. The problem of instability of a capitalist economy in its isolation still remains.

To conclude, once we take into account the constraints imposed upon the actions of the State by the interests of the banks, monetary policy as an instrument for achieving economic stability in the narrow sense appears much less potent than is usually believed, even if we ignore all the problems associated with moving towards an equilibrium through time. Moreover such economic stability does not by any means ensure social stability. Monetary policy no doubt has its uses, especially in making adjustments in a system which derives its main source of stability from elsewhere, but it cannot itself be the source of the economic and social stability of the system.

5

State Intervention through Fiscal Policy

1. 'NEW KEYNESIANISM'

The Keynesian tradition has emphasised fiscal policy as the primary instrument of State intervention. Monetary policy, as Keynesians like Mrs Robinson were wont to argue (Robinson and Eatwell 1974), does not necessarily act in an effective manner, at any rate in an expansionary direction if not in a contractionary direction, but fiscal policy which directly impinges on the expenditure flows, provides a surer means of influencing the level of activity in the economy. Keynes himself had not remained content with underscoring the benefits of monetary expansion during the slump, but had urged the State to undertake a public works policy, 'digging holes and filling them up' if necessary, financed by budget deficits; it is this advocacy in a sense which constituted the *differentia specifica* of Keynesianism in the realm of policy. The more radical of Keynes's followers, struck by the futility of 'digging holes and filling them up' and by the dangers of piling up armaments which would fulfil the same function of boosting demand, went on to argue the need for welfare expenditure, an argument which dominated the intellectual discourse in economics for a whole generation.

The faith in the efficacy of fiscal intervention however has taken several knocks in recent years. Turner *et al.* (1970) have shown how larger State expenditure, if financed by taxation, can be inflationary, not from the demand side but through a wage–tax spiral. Kaldor (1978) has underscored the intimate relationship between budget deficits and trade deficits, since the former, instead of generating eventually a corresponding excess of private savings over investment in the domestic economy, have to be financed by capital flows from abroad, as the private sector as a whole habitually spends more or less what it earns. We shall return to Kaldor's argument later, but of late in the USA a diametrically opposite view has emerged, according to which budget deficits *per se* have no expansionary effects upon the level of aggregate demand, since, in anticipation of the future tax obligations which they entail, the private sector cuts back its expenditure immediately to generate a corresponding surplus. A logical consequence of this assertion would be that the level of the budget deficit has no impact whatsoever on the trade deficit, in contrast to Kaldor's argument that it has more or less full impact on the level of the trade deficit. This view, christened the 'new-Ricardian' argument on the basis of some remarks in Ricardo, is rather obviously far-fetched.[1] In the present chapter, therefore, where we discuss the effects of State intervention through fiscal policy, we shall ignore such fancy propositions and continue working in terms of the rules of behaviour, with such modifications as may become necessary, which we have posited in our system 1 of equations (see the appendix to Chapter 3).

2. STABILISATION POSSIBILITIES THROUGH FISCAL MEANS

Let us assume that the State incurs expenditure of a magnitude G in every period t, and imposes taxes, on workers at the rate t_1 and on capitalists at the rate t_2. These taxes are direct taxes; indirect taxes are not considered because they do not add to the analysis presented below, which captures the essential points. These taxes and expenditures have two kinds of effects: one which is discussed exhaustively in the Keynesian literature is on the various expenditure flows. Taxes paid by the workers and the capitalists would lower their post-tax

---

[1] Ricardo (1951, Vol. 4, 143–200), while mentioning the possible equivalence between taxation and borrowing, went on to say explicitly that such an equivalence would not hold in the real world. See O'Driscoll 1977. The 'New Ricardians' however insist that such an equivalence holds, i.e. that tax-cuts have no effect upon consumption; see Barro 1974. But even if we grant all the other assumptions required to make the proposition valid, it collapses if households are liquidity constrained (Flavin 1985), and the existence of a liquidity constraint upon large numbers of households is a fundamental premiss of capitalism.

income flows and hence adversely affect their expenditures, while the State's own spending constitutes an additional element of expenditure flow.

The second effect arises from the fact that taxes which have to be paid out of incomes are now taken into consideration both by the workers and the capitalists in fixing their claims upon the output. When bargaining for a wage, workers would demand a larger *ex ante* share of output because they have to pay taxes out of it as well. Capitalists would try to enforce a larger pre-tax profit margin, so that after paying taxes they get the profit margin they desire. This is a generalisation of the point made by Turner *et al.* They highlighted the effect of taxation on workers in prompting them to jack up their wage claims; a similar argument can be made as far as the capitalists are concerned. The workers' and the capitalists' claims are not jacked up as soon as tax rates are raised; there are lags and thresholds giving rise to jerky adjustments. But this fact, though important in explaining specific and concrete developments, such as the world-wide wage explosion in the late 1960s, is secondary in the context of our argument.

To incorporate these effects we have to modify several of our equations in system 1. Since in this chapter we look at fiscal policy alone, we shall move back to the assumption of a fixed real rate of interest. The modified equations are given below:

$$C_t = W_t(1 - t_1) + c_2 P_t(1 - t_2) + \alpha K_t. \tag{5.1}$$

This, while retaining the assumption that workers consume what they get and capitalists have an autonomous part of their consumption (αK_t) and a part depending on their flow income, now states that these flow incomes are all post-tax.

$$O_t = C_t + i_t + dK_t + G_t \tag{5.2}$$

This is a revision of the identity for the case where the State is a spender.

$$P_t = i_t + dK_t + \alpha K_t + c_2 P_t(1 - t_2) + G_t - T_t \tag{5.3}$$

This also is a revision of the identity: pre-tax gross profits now equal gross investment, capitalists' consumption and the budget deficit.

$$\overline{w}_t l_t = (q - rv_t) / (1 - t_1) \tag{5.4}$$

This states that for any given level of unemployment workers succeed through their bargaining in obtaining a certain level of post-tax real wages per efficiency unit of the work-force.

$$p_t = w_t l_t (\mu - \mu t_2) / (1 - t_2 \mu) \tag{5.5}$$

This states that capitalists enforce an actual mark-up such that after paying taxes they succeed in obtaining their desired share ($[\mu-1]/\mu$).

Finally, we introduce the additional equation which is an identity:

$$T_t = W_t t_1 + P_t t_2 \tag{5.6}$$

and continue with the old investment function (i), where e, though a function of the real rate of interest, can be taken to be a constant since the real rate of interest itself is given; likewise μ is a constant. In other words, as mentioned earlier, we ignore in this chapter any changes in monetary policy and revert back to the assumption of money supply being endogenous at a fixed real interest rate. The State finances its budget deficit by borrowing from the banks. The interest payment on these loans is included in G. (Strictly speaking the above identities presuppose that the banking sector's propensity to consume—it has no investment expenditure—out of its income is a weighted average of 1 and c_2 where the weights are the shares of its interest receipts from the State and the entrepreneurs to its total interest receipts). Finally, since the budget deficit adds to money supply, there being no other financial assets with the 'public', for the model to be meaningful it must be the case that the cumulated budget deficit must be less than the demand for money from the public; we assume this boundary condition to be satisfied.

Now, taking the modified equation system 1, where equations (ii), (iii), (v), (viii) and (xiii) have been replaced respectively by equations (5.1) to (5.5), together with (5.6), we have sixteen equations. There are twenty-five variables, the twenty-one listed earlier with t_1, t_2, G_t, and T_t added now. Of these t_1, t_2, and G_t are fixed by the State, which leaves us six variables to be specified, the same 6 whose specification was necessary earlier for determining the single period state. We therefore have a complete determination of the single period state in the new situation. Can this system settle in an equilibrium state of steady growth-cum-steady inflation?

It is obvious that the State now has three different instruments to play around with, the two tax-rates t_1 and t_2, as well as the level of government expenditure (relative to capital stock), or G/K. For given tax rates the State can always fix its expenditure at such a level that a steady-growth–steady-inflation equilibrium can be achieved. Likewise, for a given level of G/K, it can move either one or both the tax rates in such a manner that the economy is stabilised with steady growth and steady inflation. To be sure, changes in the tax-rates, whether only one or both, would affect not only the degree of capacity utilisation (for given G/K) and hence investment behaviour through this particular channel, but also the inflationary potential of the economy through tax-push effects on wages and profits. It follows then that in a situation of accelerating inflation the correct policy would not always necessarily be a rise in tax rates (given G/K); it could well consist in a lowering of tax rates. But as long as the State is willing to learn from experience, it can in principle gather sufficient knowledge about the economy to be able to stabilise it on a steady-growth-steady-inflation path.

The State appears to possess a sufficient number of weapons in its armoury for stabilising the economy, namely changing the overall level of expenditure for given tax rates, moving the tax rates up or down in tandem for a given level of expenditure, changing the relative tax rates, and so on. Why then all the fuss about instability? Let us turn to the constraints that exist in any real economy upon the actions of the State in the fiscal sphere.

3. RATCHET EFFECTS

The previous section is a purely formal exercise, introducing into the argument some additional variables which affect the functioning of the system and over which the State allegedly has absolute control, and deducing from it that the State can stabilise the economy by picking the right values for these variables. This amounts to treating the State as a mere *deus ex machina* for introducing stability. Even at this level of the argument, however, it remains the case that while the State can introduce stability into the system, in the realms of both output and prices, it cannot control the rate of growth and the rate of unemployment in the economy. It can ensure, even as a *deus ex machina*, that only that particular rate of unemployment prevails, and hence only that particular level of the growth rate, at which the system can experience steady output and price growth, but it cannot determine what that particular level of unemployment rate, and growth rate, should be. A Fascist State, which can smash trade unions and directly influence the workers' bargaining strength, would be an exception, but if the State had been of such a nature capitalism would not have been so durable a system.

Even in its ability to stabilise the system the State is far more constrained than our purely formal discussion suggests. It cannot for instance simply arbitrarily select whatever ratio it likes between t_1 and t_2: the necessity for legitimising itself as a seemingly supra-class entity dictates that the State should appear to have a degree of 'fairness' in the distribution of the tax burden. While in our economic model we have simply taken the workers to be exclusively concerned about t_1 and to jack up wage claims accordingly, and the capitalists to be exclusively concerned about t_2 and to jack up profit margins accordingly, in real life the workers would get restive if the ratio between t_1 and t_2 rises significantly, and the capitalists in the opposite case. The economic model is thus itself predicated upon a situation where such restiveness does not exist, and the workers are going about their 'normal' business of wage-bargaining.

Likewise the State cannot simply pick on whatever level of G it deems necessary for stability. Expenditure in any period has a history that bequeaths a certain size of the bureaucracy and of the armed forces, a certain amount of public facilities, a certain level of transfer payments and so on. While over somewhat protracted periods of time, this expenditure relative to the wealth of the country can be reduced, always by operating at the margin, it certainly cannot be reduced in any particular single period, or over a short sequence of periods, like water in a tap. And even long-run reductions in it are not all that easy to accomplish; they arouse strong sectional resentments which the State would normally try to keep under control.[2]

---

2 Both the above assertions can be contested by citing recent changes in some of the advanced capitalist countries. There can be little doubt that most notably in the USA during the Reagan era, but also elsewhere, relative tax-rates on the rich have come down significantly; likewise a tendency for the withdrawal of the State from certain spheres in the economic arena, designed to bring down the level of government expenditure, is unmistakable. The analysis of these specific developments belongs to a terrain of discourse altogether different from the one on which we have been arguing so far. Even so, I would like to make three comments. First, notwithstanding all the talk about the withdrawal of the State and 'privatisation', the level of government expenditure continues to be high in these countries. Second a change in relative tax rates when taxes in general are being reduced is likely to arouse less hostility than when no such general reduction is taking place. And third the very fact of the downfall of Margaret Thatcher (on the issue of the Poll Tax) in Britain and the election of Clinton in the USA is indicative of the resistance to such measures and

Raising expenditure is altogether easier since, except when it is in some sphere directly competing against the private sector, it does not *per se* tread on anybody's toes; and avenues of expenditure can always be found which do not compete with some existing private interest. But if an increase in expenditure calls for higher taxation that would arouse hostility. The idea that workers and capitalists take tax rates as given and protect themselves by incorporating them into their claims, as we have assumed, is obviously over simplistic. No doubt they do attempt to protect themselves. But the very act of imposing higher taxation arouses hostility against the State, engenders charges of incompetence and wastefulness and calls for closer scrutiny of State finances. The State therefore faces two kinds of ratchet effects: a ratchet effect on the expenditure side, whereby expenditures are easier to raise than cut; and a ratchet effect on the revenue side, where taxes are easier to cut than raise. It follows that the inevitable tendency is towards larger and larger budget deficits, once the State has got actively involved in the process of economic management.

4. THE MODUS OPERANDI OF BUDGET DEFICITS

There are, in addition, limits to the extent to which the budget deficit can be enlarged. In the case of specific countries, these limits arise most palpably from its impact upon the trade deficit. This will be discussed later; for the moment we continue with the analysis of a capitalist economy as a single integral unit with no external trade. Even in such a case there are limits to the extent of the deficit.

One of the fundamental weaknesses of Keynesianism consisted in its refusal to see any limits upon the ability of the State to undertake deficit financing. When Paul Baran (1957), himself starting from an underconsumptionist position, argued that the problem of aggregate demand could not be overcome by the simple 'budgetary trick' of deficit-financed State expenditure, he was criticised by Robinson (1966) for dragging in the Quantity Theory of Money. But one does not have to be a monetarist to believe that budget deficits can be potentially inflationary. The two are quite distinct positions as we hope to show below.

underscores the relevance of what we have been talking about (which is quite independent of whether the new governments do anything different).

Let us continue to assume that money supply is endogenous, that the 'Quantity equation is being read from the right to the left' as Mrs Robinson would like us to do. Now, any budget deficit must be matched *ex post* by a corresponding excess of private savings over private investment. It sets off a chain reaction through an increase in aggregate demand, whose ultimate result is to create the corresponding excess of savings over investment in the private sector. The 'new-Ricardians' deny any such chain-reaction (in the event of tax cuts) since in their view private savings rise instantaneously in anticipation of future taxes. But as we have seen there are good reasons not to accept their argument. If all wages are consumed, as we have been assuming, then this rise in private savings must be accomplished through a rise in profits, brought about through a rise in aggregate demand. If a part of profits is consumed, then the rise in profits would have to be some multiple (>1) of the budget deficit in the new situation, *ex post*. If additionally, capitalists' consumption also depends on their wealth, namely their net worth, position (and not just upon their capital stock as we have hitherto assumed), the rise in their profits would be still greater. And if investment also increases during this chain reaction, the rise in profits would be even greater.

No matter what intricate and complex developments occur during this chain-reaction, it can eventually come to an end only when the excess of private savings over investment matches the budget deficit. It is this excess which finances the budget deficit: if it is held in the form of State bonds, it finances the deficit directly; if it is held in the form of money or other forms of bank deposits, it does so indirectly via the intermediation of banks.

All this is obvious and elementary; the point in recapitulating it is to emphasise that the chain reaction set off by a budget deficit comes to an end not when private wealth has increased to an equivalent extent, but when private wealth held in a form which directly or indirectly finances the deficit has increased equivalently. How long the chain reaction will continue depends therefore, apart from the consumption effects which are well known, upon whether the capitalists will simply remain content adding to their wealth in a more or less liquid form (State bonds and bank-deposits), or whether they will try to alter the form of their wealth-holding when they find a larger proportion of it than before being held in a liquid form.

A larger proportion of wealth being held in a liquid form reduces the illiquidity risks associated with other forms of wealth-holding.

They will therefore make a great many adjustments in the form of their wealth-holding, before they are willing to hold the additional amount of money or State debt. These adjustments have nothing to do with whether money supply is endogenous or exogenous, whether the Quantity equation is read from the left to the right or the other way around. We have already seen earlier that endogenous money does not nullify the principle of increasing risk. One does not therefore have to be a monetarist to say that, quite apart from the consumption effects of a budget deficit which all Keynesians readily recognise, there is likely to be an additional effect through induced changes in the form of wealth-holding. What would be the consequences of this additional effect?

We are concerned here with how this additional effect will be felt on commodity as opposed to financial markets. One possible way that this effect can be felt on commodity markets is of course through investment decisions, as mentioned above; but let us ignore this and continue to assume that our investment function captures investment behaviour adequately. But quite apart from the effect on investment in this sense, productive investment which adds to capacity, there will be an effect on commodity stock-holding for speculative purposes which in an accounting sense is also investment.

To see the argument simply, let us, to start with, assume (somewhat unrealistically) that in all commodity markets it is output that adjusts to demand at given prices in terms of the wage unit until a state of full-capacity use is established. If there are large unutilised capacities in every sphere, virtually no one will expect the price in wage units to be higher in the next period than in the current period. Since the real interest rate is given and is positive, no one will have any inducement to hold speculative commodity stocks. Only as much stocks of commodities will be held as are required for the convenience of production and of sale. However, as the degree of capacity utilisation approaches unity, more and more persons in individual markets will come to expect an appreciation in the prices of particular commodities in terms of the wage unit, an appreciation on account of future shortages. Even so, not all who expect such an appreciation will necessarily hold speculative stocks, since for the latter to be worthwhile the extent of expected appreciation (relative to the wage unit) must exceed the real interest cost, carrying cost, and risk premium on stock-holding. Those who expect a large enough appreciation, however, would do so. At any given level of current 'normal' demand relative to capacity, the magnitude of commodity stocks which the bulls would like to hold for speculative purposes depends *inter alia* upon the risk premium they would have to provide for. As this risk premium diminishes, the magnitude of speculative stock-holding by the bulls would increase. And when the magnitude of addition to speculative stock-holding is large enough, together with the 'normal' demand, to create a total level of demand exceeding full capacity output in the current period we would be in a world of demand-pull inflation, a world different from what we have been studying until now.

The upshot is that if we plot the price level in wage units (price divided by the money wage per efficiency unit of the work-force) on one axis and the level of *ex ante* capacity utilisation (the level of capacity utilisation that would obtain with 'normal' demand) on the other, we get a picture for a single period rather like Figure 5.1. If u_{th} denotes the threshold level of *ex ante* capacity utilisation at which demand-pull pressures begin to operate, then the smaller the illiquidity risks the smaller (up to a point) would be u_{th}. More importantly, the smaller the illiquidity risks the steeper would be the curve after u_{th}. Since the profile of budget deficits affects the illiquidity risks which capitalists face, the three curves in the figure correspond to the three situations, of a high-deficit, a medium-deficit, and a low-deficit economy.

Two additional considerations strengthen the above argument. First, full capacity is not a fixed level and profit margins actually start

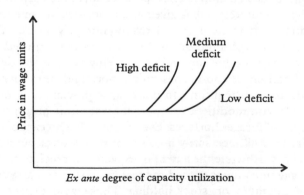

Fig. 5.1.

responding to demand long before technical limits to production have been reached. Expectations of a price appreciation in terms of the wage unit therefore would begin to arise well before so-called full capacity is reached. Second, such bullish expectations would not depend solely upon what the level of 'normal' demand relative to capacity in the next period is expected to be, but upon the level of 'normal'-cum-*speculative* demand. The possibility of speculation would be incorporated into the expectations themselves.

Not all commodities are such as would encourage the holding of speculative stocks of them, as Kaldor (1946, reprinted in 1964) had argued long ago. But this does not alter the essence of our argument here. As long as it holds for some commodities, it retains its overall validity. It also has an important implication: often a distinction is drawn between a demand constraint and a supply constraint which a particular sector, or even the economy as a whole, might be facing. Put very schematically, if full capacity output is a particular figure, and the marginal cost curve (for given money wages) has an inverted L-shape, then a situation of demand constraint is when demand, and hence output, is to the left of the kink, and a situation of supply constraint is when demand, at the supply price that would just bring forth full capacity output, exceeds the latter. In the former situation, prices are taken to be based on a mark-up, and in the latter market clearing. No doubt, a sharp L-shaped curve does not really exist, and is only meant to approximate a curve which has a more or less flat stretch, and becomes steeper and steeper. But the point is that in looking at price behaviour as demand increases, we take the transition from cost-determined to demand-determined prices as being dependent exclusively upon the conditions of production. As a matter of fact, this transition is also dependent upon the conditions of liquid wealth with the private sector, i.e. the extent of illiquidity risks which it faces.

Two objections to the above argument may be raised. First, since we have assumed the real interest rate to be fixed, the expected nominal rate must be moving up together with the expected price which should deter speculation. This however is not correct. If price in each sphere is expected to rise faster than money wages, which is considered by the speculators as a proxy for the average price increase, speculation in each sphere could be worthwhile, and hence in all spheres taken together. (This is quite apart from the fact that our assumption of a fixed real rate is itself only a simplification).

Second, it may be asked: do speculators actually gain in this case? Strictly speaking this is not relevant for our argument. Besides, if the speculators also happen to be the producers (or the normal sellers of the commodities), they can always rid themselves of speculative stocks by cutting back on output rather than off-loading them on the market at lower prices, and hence at least cut their losses substantially.

Paul Baran's position, which invited Joan Robinson's criticism, was of course milder than that stated above. Baran did not say that the State could not achieve full capacity use (or full employment) through deficit financing without precipitating an actual demand-pull inflation. His point was that if the State did so, it would succeed simultaneously in building up a large inflationary overhang which could come crashing down at some time; and the fear of this would prevent the State from using budget deficits to achieve full capacity use (or full employment).

The State's attempt to achieve full capacity use through deficit financing *would*, however, run into inflation. While different persons have different price expectations, the number of persons who would expect prices (in terms of wage units) to rise sufficiently to warrant speculative stock-holding would be greater at full capacity than below full capacity. If in addition, liquid and semi-liquid assets have been put in the hands of the private sector, so that risks of illiquidity have come down, then the number of bulls would be larger still. Now, as they start holding commodity stocks, and prices actually begin to rise, the bullish sentiment would become even more widespread and the inflationary overhang would become an actual inflation. A degree of unutilised capacity acts as an antidote against the prevalence of bullish sentiments; and how much of it would be an effective antidote depends on how much liquid wealth there is in private hands. Baran was right in his belief that the absence of this antidote, together with the build-up of private wealth in liquid form, would have great inflationary potential. He erred on the side of caution however in believing that this potential would only remain a potential as long as some chance factors or exceptional circumstances did not intervene.

5. CONSTRAINTS ON STABILISATION THROUGH FISCAL MEANS

Let us now get back to the original argument. If ratchet effects operate, in a downward direction upon government expenditure (relative to capital stock) and in an upward direction upon tax-rates, then the ability of the State to stabilise the economy through fiscal intervention is undermined. Starting from an initial situation of steady growth-cum-steady inflation, for example, with the State running a certain level of budget deficit, if there is a parametric shift in the form of a reduction in e, the State would attempt to maintain equilibrium by enlarging the budget deficit. Suppose it does succeed in this attempt. But then if at a later date e rises again, the economy would move into accelerating inflation, with the State unable to control it through fiscal intervention owing to the ratchet effects. The ratchet effects make fiscal intervention a blunt policy instrument.

The problem is only compounded by the other phenomenon mentioned above, the demand-pull consequences of budget deficits via speculative stock-holding. In the above example we assumed that when the investment drive of the private sector slackens, reflected in a fall in e, the State can maintain equilibrium by enlarging the budget deficit. But the very fact of an enlarged budget deficit sustained over a period of time could mean that the earlier equilibrium level of capacity utilisation which had entailed steady inflation via the cost-push channel, now witnesses demand-pull inflation via larger speculative stock-holding. Between the devil and the deep blue sea, between decelerating inflation and large unemployment on the one hand, and speculation-engendered accelerating inflation on the other, there may be no room for a toe-hold. The attainment of steady growth-cum-steady inflation in such a case would prove to be an elusive goal for the State.

Is the introduction of these ratchet effects a theoretical subterfuge, an attempt to get weighty conclusions through appeals to pop sociology? No. This point is deeper than appears at first sight. Our concern all along has been with the success and durability of capitalism. The existence of these ratchet effects means that this success cannot be explained by fiscal intervention by the State to stabilise the capitalist economy. If, on the other hand, these ratchet effects did not exist, then the durability of such an economy would have been threatened in a different way as the following example should make clear.

Suppose the economy which is in equilibrium gets disturbed by a parametric change, for example a rise in the degree of monopoly which increases μ, or a rise in trade union strength because of the consolidation of its organisation. The economy moves towards accelerating inflation at its old steady growth rate. The State would try to nudge the economy towards a new steady growth-steady inflation situation, and its efforts would take the form either of a cut in its expenditure (G/K), a rise in tax rates for a given expenditure, or more plausibly, a mix of the two. (We are assuming a 'normal' case where accelerating inflation is successfully combated by tax increases rather than by tax cuts.) Let us suppose that there are no ratchet effects and the State can bring about the desired stability. What would the new equilibrium look like?

The very fact of the higher tax rates which the State would use for stabilising the economy would lower the equilibrium growth rate. In addition, there would be a higher unemployment rate, and also a lower share of both pre-tax as well as post-tax wages in output. Pre-tax wages would be lower because to maintain the same post-tax profit margin as before capitalists would jack up the pre-tax profit margin (since the taxes upon them too have increased). Post-tax wage share would be lower because the workers who in any case would be earning a lower pre-tax wage share would in addition be paying higher taxes. The workers are hardly likely to acquiesce in such a denouement, where they experience both higher unemployment and a lower wage-share. If the origin of instability lay in a strengthening of trade unions, these stronger unions are bound to resist the new equilibrium. If the capitalist State had only these means of stabilising the economy, the social credibility of capitalism would have been compromised long ago. The origins of the so-called ratchet effects therefore lie in the necessity of capitalism to maintain its social credibility.

To sum up, once we get out of the purely formal discussion where a supposedly all-knowing and unconstrained State simply picks up values for certain variables in order to ensure stability in a capitalist economy, and introduce some actual history into its decisions, we can see its limitations as a stabiliser. It is bound by the past, and every parametric change involves a painful, difficult, cumbersome, and sometimes impossible process of adjustment, and that too often to new equilibria which themselves upset social stability. Capitalism as a system would not have been as successful and durable as it has been if it had to rely on the State alone, or more generally upon its own institutions, the market and the State, both for stabilising its output and price movements, and for ensuring that this stable performance was also satisfactory, with reasonably low unemployment rates and high growth rates.

6. TRADE UNIONS AND THE SHARE OF WAGES

Nothing bears this out more clearly than the proposition which followed from our discussion of the last case, namely if the workers become more militant then the share of wages falls, or at best remains constant (if the State does not alter tax rates but alters only its expenditure), while the unemployment rate certainly rises. If this is the way that a capitalist economy functions then trade union militancy appears to gain nothing for the workers. Why then do trade unions exist? And how is it that notwithstanding increasing trade union militancy in real life, we have never actually had the denouement sketched above?

Kalecki's (1971) answer to this question was ingenious but unconvincing. When trade union militancy increases, he argued, the capitalists, rather than accepting accelerating inflation, take a cut in their profit margin. Competition between capitals ensures that this happens, so that the profit margin itself becomes a function of trade union strength. In a case of many countries whose capitalists are in competition, this argument could explain why a rise in money wages in any single country was not fully passed on: when workers in any single country raised their money wages, workers in rival countries would not necessarily be doing so, and hence the capitalists of the first country would not be able to pass on the entire wage increase for fear of losing markets to their rivals (though even here the possibility of fully passing on money wage increases and simultaneously lowering the exchange rate cannot be ruled out). If however we are talking about a single integral capitalist economy (as Marx was in *Wages, Prices and Profits*) and capitalists, whether over the economy as a whole or in an entire branch of production, are all facing identical money wage increases, there is no reason why they should not implicitly collude to pass on these increases.

Rowthorn's argument states that if workers become more militant, they do succeed in obtaining a higher wage share, but only at the expense of a higher rate of unemployment. The economy moves from one NAIRU equilibrium to another involving a higher rate of unemployment. But since the profit margin itself is a function of the degree of capacity utilisation which moves together with the rate of unemployment, it is lower in the new equilibrium, and hence the wage share is higher. Even though we Rowthorn's model was criticised above, such a denouement appears on the face of it quite plausible. But if this is what actually happened, then growing trade union militancy and growing capitalist strength owing to the process of centralisation of capital over the past century should by now have led to an increasing rate of unemployment, or, alternatively, an explosively accelerating inflation. The fact that this has not happened suggests that there are other crucial elements that we have not taken into account. In other words, the purely internal institutions of a capitalist economy, as stylised above, are insufficient to explain how the system manages to sustain both output and price stability as well as high levels of activity despite the indubitable fact that it is characterised by more or less organised labour facing more or less organised capital.

7. SOCIAL PREMISES OF KEYNESIANISM

What appears surprising in retrospect is that a belief in the efficacy of State intervention in overcoming the problems of a capitalist economy should have dominated economic thinking for such a long time. To be sure, critics of State intervention were there from the beginning and have become more influential of late, but their argument by and large amounted to a denial of the problems of a capitalist economy altogether. It was conceived as a spontaneously smoothly working system where intervention by the State could only disrupt this smoothness. They shared with the Keynesians a general belief in the self-contained nature of capitalism, that as a system it had internal institutions perfectly capable of ensuring its smooth functioning. They emphasised the market as such an institution par excellence, while the Keynesians, sceptical of the efficacy of the market in ensuring smoothness, invoked the capitalist State as the institution capable of handling the economy's contradictions.

To say that this was because the Keynesians had a particular theory of the State would be tautological. This theory of the State was itself an integral part of their perception of capitalism and its problems. They believed that the problems of capitalism sprang essentially from its anarchy. The economy was capable of settling down at several different possible states of rest. Because decisions were uncoordinated, it settled at one particular state of rest, but if an external agency (external to the market place) gave it a nudge, it could move to a different state of rest where everybody could be better off. A depression provided the archetypal example. In a depression, workers suffer because of unemployment, and capitalists suffer because of idle capacity and hence low or negative rates of profit. The economy nonetheless settles into a depression because of the anarchy of the system, because the overall state of the economy is the result of decisions made by a host of particular agents, each perhaps rational in his own context but incapable on his own of altering the overall situation. State intervention for overcoming a crisis is therefore a non-zero sum game. Since everybody stands to gain and none to suffer, there would be little opposition to it. Only an intelligent understanding of the underlying phenomena and processes is needed to make intervention effective. This explains the curious Keynesian emphasis on the role of ideas, the repeated harping on the need for 'first-class brains', which may appear at first sight to be mere boastfulness but was far from being so. It was based on a genuine belief that the main obstacle to a resolution of the problems of a capitalist economy sprang from a wrong understanding, and since such a resolution would benefit everyone, the 'wrong' understanding was not rooted in material interests but rather reflected intellectual failure.

The limitation of Keynesianism arose from the fact that it saw all economic problems in this light. Capitalism however is characterised not just by anarchy but also by antagonism. While there may be a range of problems whose resolution would make everybody better off, so that the only possible contentious issue is the distribution of these benefits, a matter of secondary importance that does not stand in the way of such resolution, not all problems are of this genre.

Take for instance inflation arising from conflicts over distributive shares. Nobody likes inflation, but a resolution of this conflict requires that any one or all of the parties to the conflict should reduce *ex ante* claims upon the output, and any such reduction by one amounts to a tacit acceptance of the other's claim which was being contested in the first place. This is not a case of the sheer anarchy of the system having landed the economy in a state from where a correct understanding would provide a way out with everybody benefiting. This is a case where State intervention, if it is not to be obviously biased in favour of one class, has to undertake 'conflict management' where correct or wrong understanding ceases to be the issue at all.

Keynesianism, in looking at this issue through its paradigm of a non-zero sum game, a paradigm derived from the depression experience, argued as follows: since nobody likes inflation, there must be some agreement possible between the conflicting parties, which, even though representing a climb down from their original claims, would still be welcomed by all for keeping inflation in check. It is this which prompted the Keynesian advocacy of an incomes policy as a way out of inflation in the 1960s, an experiment that ended in failure. The fact of the matter is that the assumption that conflict-induced crises under capitalism are no different from anarchy-induced crises, that since nobody likes the consequences of conflicts they can always be resolved by agreement, was fundamentally untenable. It was rather like arguing that since nobody likes wars, all wars could be avoided by reaching agreements among contending parties in conflicts that could lead to wars, no matter what the particular contexts and historical locations of the conflicts might be. The Keynesian belief in the efficacy of State intervention, and indeed the Keynesian theory of the State as an enlightened, benevolent entity standing above classes and arbitrating between them for the good of all, is based on a downgrading of the role of conflict in a capitalist society. And it is an appreciation of this conflict that fundamentally informs the Marxist theory not only of the State, but also of crises.

If capitalism has been remarkably successful during its history in keeping conflicts in check, as indeed it has been, then the reason lies not in the conflicts themselves being intrinsically of secondary importance (the occasional explosions of conflicts bear enough testimony to this), but in its ability to resolve its internal conflicts at the expense of 'outsiders' or the 'outlying regions'. The mechanism through which this has been done will be the subject of Part III.

III

Stability through Unequal Interdependence

6

Capital Accumulation in Conditions
of Unequal Interdependence:
A Preliminary Model

We have argued so far that a capitalist economy in which organised workers face organised capital cannot achieve both output stability in the sense of a steady rate of growth and price stability in the sense of a steady rate of inflation on the basis of its spontaneous working and that even State intervention would not be able to combine both kinds of stability owing to the social constraints on the State. Even if it does manage to do so, it could be at a level of unemployment and of growth rate which would be socially destabilising. If capitalist economies have managed over long periods of their history both to perform well as well as to achieve output and price stability, the reason for it lies elsewhere, in their being coupled to pre-capitalist and semi-capitalist economies of the outlying regions. This coupling has taken the form of an 'unequal interdependence' (a term used by Bagchi 1982) that has ensured high growth as well as economic stability for the capitalist countries, and, as a consequence, social stability and durability of the system. A stylised picture of how this coupling works is the subject matter of the present chapter and of the one that follows.

The crux of the argument, in the context of the problem discussed until now, is the following. For combining economic stability with reasonable rates of growth, it must be the case that one of the premises for our problem does not hold. That premiss is that all workers whom capital directly or indirectly employs are equally well organised. If there exists a section of workers who produce commodities required by the capitalist economy but are not strong or organised enough to enforce a given *ex ante* share in the output of the capitalist economy, then they provide a cushion against accelerating inflation. Combining output and price stability then ceases to be a problem for capitalism.

If these workers are located within the boundaries of the capitalist economy, they would threaten to disrupt the social stability of the system through sporadic outbreaks. Moreover, internal political democracy where everyone is given a vote would be incompatible with such an economic arrangement. But if these workers who provide a cushion against economic instability are located outside the geographical boundaries of the system, then within these boundaries democracy, social stability, and economic prosperity can all prevail. Even if capitalism has to use periodic force, and that too through locally recruited manpower, to suppress sporadic outbreaks in these outlying regions, that would not upset domestic tranquillity. For the most part, as we shall see, it would not need to use force. Colonialism may have been necessary historically for setting up such an arrangement in the first place, but it is by no means necessary for its continuance. Indeed one of the main purposes of this book is to show how a system of unequal interdependence, once set up on a global scale, continues to operate spontaneously without any political domination of one part of the world by another. It is this spontaneous mechanism which we outline below.

1. A BRIEF DESCRIPTION OF THE MODEL

Consider a situation where there are two sectors of production, corresponding to our two worlds. One produces manufactured goods, while the other produces primary commodities. In the next chapter we shall introduce local manufacturing in sector 2 as well; for the time being however we ignore it. Primary commodities go into manufacturing production as raw materials, and also into the personal consumption of workers in the manufactured goods sector as well as in the primary sector itself. The consumption of primary commodities by the capitalists in both sectors is assumed to be small in absolute terms and therefore we shall neglect it.

Workers in the manufacturing sector bargain for, and succeed in obtaining, in any period, a money wage per efficiency unit of labour which entails command over a certain bundle of the primary commodity at its expected price;[1] the size of this bundle is inversely related to the unemployment rate in the manufacturing sector which of course is located in the advanced economy. They do not however spend their entire money wage on the primary commodity itself: their actual consumption of this commodity is only a fraction of the amount they obtain *ex ante* command over and the excess of their money wage over what they spend on this commodity is devoted to the consumption of manufactured goods.[2]

Workers in the primary sector itself however are more unfortunately placed. Located as they are in the midst of vast labour reserves which cannot migrate *en masse* to the manufactured goods sector (migration being in accordance with the rule which we have already discussed in the earlier chapters), they are handicapped even with respect to the extent to which they can enforce *ex ante* claims in the face of falling real wages. The way we express this handicap formally (ignoring any productivity growth in this sector for the present) is as follows: the money wage claim they succeed in enforcing in any period is such as to give them command over a bundle of the primary commodity at its expected price, whose size equals the previous period's actual bundle plus some compensation for the fact that the previous period's bundle may have been too low relative to recent experience. To capture recent experience we take the average of such bundles for the previous *T* periods. The entire money wage of this sector's workers is assumed in this chapter to be spent on the primary commodity itself. Thus, their *ex ante* real wage is simply a weighted average of the previous period's real wage and the average real wage of the past *T* periods. The expected price for the current period is, as before, the previous period's price extrapolated at the previous period's rate of inflation.

The capitalists in both the sectors purchase only the manufactured good, whether for investment or for consumption. In the manufacturing sector itself their consumption and investment behaviour

---

[1] The assumption that manufacturing sector workers bargain for command over a certain bundle of the primary commodity figures in Kaldor, 'What is wrong with Economic Theory?' reprinted in Kaldor (1978). This assumption can be easily replaced by an alternative assumption that the workers' *ex ante* wage claims are fixed entirely in terms of command over the manufactured good without doing any damage to our argument.

[2] This fraction of course would keep changing over time. We take it as a constant in order to obtain steady-state solutions, so that the effects of any change in it can be analysed in terms of a transition from one steady state to another.

are the same as in Chapter 3. For the primary sector we postulate different behaviour: the capitalists consume whatever is left over from profits after investing; and their planned net investment per unit of capital stock (to be realised in the next period) exceeds or equals or falls short of its current level in proportion to whether their current rate of profit exceeds or equals or falls short of some 'acceptable' rate of profit.[3] The rate of profit is defined as the money profit per unit of capital stock *at its current replacement cost.*

The assumption that the primary sector capitalists' consumption is only a residue means that there is no borrowing or lending across sectors, that trade is strictly balanced in each period.[4] We assume that pricing behaviour in the manufactured goods sector is prime-cost-plus while in the primary goods sector it is market clearing. Finally, while there should in fact be a multiplicity of manufactured goods and primary commodities, we assume only one universal manufactured good and only one universal primary commodity: the different manufactured goods in other words have identical production conditions, as do the different primary commodities.

2. HOW THE MODEL WORKS

The equations describing the investment, output, price and money wage behaviour in each sector in such a world are set out in the appendix to this chapter. The basic structure and the mechanics of the model nonetheless can be discussed here.

In the manner of Marx's two-department schema, we can imagine our two sectors exchanging their goods against one another in the following way. The surplus of primary sector products which is offered for exchange simply equals the profits of that sector, which is the amount left over after the wages have been paid (since these wages are assumed to be consumed in the form of the primary com-

---

[3] This acceptable rate of profit could be the same as the long-run average rate of profit prevailing in the advanced economy, i.e. the manufacturing sector, without jeopardising our argument. But since we are assuming that each sector's capitalists invest only in their own sector (the legitimacy of this is discussed in later chapters) the two need not be equal.

[4] This may appear to be a rigid assumption, but has the virtue that while keeping things simple it rules out *persistent* export surpluses or deficits by either sector, which surely is realistic. Balanced trade is also the assumption made by Kaldor (1978).

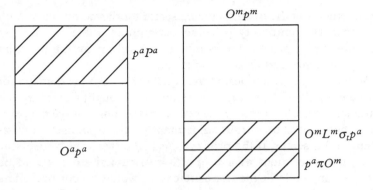

Fig. 6.1.

modity itself). On the other hand, the amount of the primary commodity demanded by the manufacturing sector is its raw material requirement and also its workers' consumption requirement. *Ex post* the two must be identical; the shaded areas in the two boxes in Figure 6.1 must be identical.

This *ex post* equality is brought about as follows. In any period, the size of the capital stock and the magnitude of investment in the manufacturing sector are given. These two between them determine the magnitude of total manufacturing profits (assuming balanced trade) and, since the share of profits is given by the mark-up margin, the total manufacturing output as well. Corresponding to this output there is a certain unemployment rate, and hence a certain level of the money wage rate of manufacturing workers and a certain per capita (and hence total) workers' consumption of the primary commodity. This together with the demand for the primary commodity as raw material, constitutes the total physical demand for the primary commodity from the manufacturing sector. In short period equilibrium the product profits in the primary sector must adjust to this physical demand.

The mode of adjustment is through variations in the primary sector's profit margin. The money wage rate in this sector is given in any period, and so is the total output, which is nothing else but the inherited capital stock multiplied by the output–capital ratio. The price of the primary commodity must be such that the total product profits, namely the physical surplus, is exactly equal to the physical requirements of the manufacturing sector for this commodity. With the primary commodity price so determined, there is a certain manufacturing price corresponding to it (given by the mark-up rule), and hence certain terms of trade.

While in a particular period the equality between the demand for and the supply of the primary commodity is brought about through variations in the level of its price relative to the money wage rate, over time there would be output adjustment via the response of investment in this sector. If the profit rate is higher than the 'acceptable rate', net investment as a proportion of capital stock would be stepped up, while in the opposite case it would be cut back. The question then arises: does a steady-growth–steady-inflation path exist for this system; does a sequence of short-period equilibria exist along which there is steady growth of output as well as of prices, with constant terms of trade and a constant ratio between the outputs?

The question of the existence, and stability of such a path is taken up in the Appendix. It is clear that such a path along which each sector is growing at the same steady rate and the rate of inflation is neither accelerating nor decelerating exists for our system. In fact there are two possible states of steady growth-cum-steady-inflation, which correspond exactly to the two steady growth solutions obtained for the system discussed in Chapter 2.

This is not surprising since in a situation of steady inflation, the investment function of the manufacturing sector in the present model is exactly the same as in eqn. (2.1″) of Chapter 2. The fact that we now have two sectors instead of one makes little difference to the argument since all that it means is that a part of manufactured goods which otherwise would have been consumed by the workers within the sector, who would be getting $1/\mu$ of the output, is now handed over to the primary sector capitalists in lieu of primary products for raw materials and workers' consumption. The share of profits in the manufacturing sector still remains $(\mu-1)/\mu$, and it is this which determines, together with the ratio of capitalists' total consumption to profits, the value of the multiplier. The primary sector's output simply adjusts over time to the requirements of the manufacturing sector in order to yield to the primary sector capitalists the 'acceptable rate of profit'. Hence paths of steady growth for the manufacturing sector are also the paths of steady growth for both sectors taken together, for the system as a whole. And these are precisely the same as in our one-sector model of Chapter 2.

Not only do steady growth-cum-steady inflation equilibria exist, but it can be shown that steady growth is incompatible with non-steady inflation. Suppose for instance the economy is growing at some steady rate g. Accelerating inflation in the manufacturing sector can occur at this growth rate only if there is also accelerating inflation in the primary sector. If there is decelerating or steady inflation in the latter, there cannot be accelerating inflation in the former. Now, for accelerating inflation to happen in the primary sector, all consumers of the primary sector's output must have downward inflexible claims upon this output. We know however that there is one set of consumers, namely the primary sector's own workers, whose claims are not downward inflexible. As a result there cannot be accelerating inflation on a continuing basis in the primary sector along a steady growth path; hence there cannot be accelerating inflation on a continuing basis in both sectors taken together along a steady growth path. Likewise, since the primary sector workers' *ex ante* claims are not upward-inflexible, there cannot be continuing decelerating inflation along a steady growth path. In short, a state of steady growth is incompatible with either accelerating or decelerating inflation: steady growth is possible only if it is combined with steady inflation, and that means that it is possible only at one of the two rates mentioned above.

We saw in Chapter 2 that the higher of the two possible steady growth rates represented an unstable trend, while the other trend which necessarily entails a lower growth rate was a stable one in the sense that if the economy departed from it there would be tendencies set at work to bring it back to that steady state. In the context of the present model which is more complex, while the instability of the higher trend rate persists, the stability of the lower steady growth solution is more problematical. All we can say is that the rate of growth cannot remain above it (and below the higher trend) for any length of time. It would move back to it (though not necessarily stabilise at it). But if the growth rate is below it, then it would not necessarily move back all the way to it, though it would not move away from it continuously: as it hits zero it would move in the direction of this trend though it may not reach it all the way. On the whole, since this lower trend is more meaningful in the sense of being a better benchmark, we shall confine our attention only to it in what follows.

3. THE MODE OF RESOLUTION OF
DISTRIBUTIVE CONFLICTS

Let us now look at the effects of some parametric changes on the steady-state configuration. Suppose within the manufacturing sector, the trade unions become stronger so that for a given level of unemployment they are able to enforce higher *ex ante* claims. This would not result either in a decline in the profit share in manufacturing, or in accelerating inflation, or in a larger level of unemployment, or in a decline in the rate of growth. While the manufacturing sector would not suffer any of these adverse consequences, the terms of trade would move against the primary sector, as is clear from the expression (see Appendix) for the terms of trade in the steady-state configuration. But since the rate of profit of the primary sector capitalists remains unchanged in steady state, it is the share of primary sector workers that would actually go down. In other words, greater trade union strength in the 'advanced' (manufacturing) sector does succeed in obtaining a larger share of wages for the workers, but at the expense of the unorganised workers of the primary sector. This does not mean that the 'advanced' sector workers 'exploit' the backward sector workers. This is the way the system works, the way it can accommodate greater working class militancy at its centre without in any way jeopardising the survival and successful functioning of the system.

In retrospect, it seems remarkable that the question whether trade unions can influence the share of wages has been discussed so extensively in the literature without the elementary point having been made that the working of the system is such that while it permits them to raise the share of wages, it passes the burden on to the shoulders of the unorganised workers. To be sure the question has always been posed within the context of a closed integral capitalist economy where the dichotomy between unorganised and organised workers does not exist. But this is not a premiss which has ever been historically realised under capitalism. To accept the reality of the working of the system does not of course mean that trade unions at the centre should voluntarily renounce wage claims for the sake of their 'poor brethren'. It means however that the working class at the centre would never make the transition from trade union to political consciousness, even when the latter is brought to it from 'outside', by being purely inward-looking.[5] The index of the maturity of its class consciousness is the extent to which it supports the formation of organisations and struggles among unorganised workers.

Richard Goodwin (1967) has attributed the success as well as the pusillanimity of social democracy to what he calls 'the iron law of the rate of profit'. Since capitalists save and invest more the larger their profits, a low wage share entails a high rate of accumulation. But since the rate of growth of the labour force is given exogenously, such a high rate of accumulation tends to raise the real wages and hence the wage share. Over time therefore the wage share, and with it the rate of profit, tends to be stable with the level of real wages growing at the same rate as the level of productivity. The basic difference between Goodwin's position and ours, which seeks to locate the success as well as the pusillanimity of social democracy in the ability of the system, in its spontaneous working and without involving any 'conspiracies', to accommodate the wage claims of the trade unions at the expense of the unorganised workers of the 'outlying regions',[6] lies in our making two fundamentally different assumptions: first, that investment behaviour is determined independently of the *ex ante* savings, and second, that the natural rate of population growth has never been a constraining factor for capital accumulation. We shall return to the theme of trade union action in the next chapter.

Now, suppose there is an increase in the profit margin, owing to an increase in what Kalecki called 'the degree of monopoly'. We have to distinguish here between two cases: one in which the rise in the profit margin is quite autonomous and unaccompanied by any increase in the accumulative urge, and the other in which together with a rise in the profit margin there is an increase in the accumulative urge. In the first case, as is clear from the discussion in the Appendix, there is a reduction in the trend growth rate. This is exactly the underconsumptionist argument (Steindl 1952; Baran and Sweezy 1966). A rise in the share of profits, if it is not accompanied by an

---

5 The argument that political class consciousness is not spontaneously developed by the workers but has to be introduced from 'outside' was advanced by Lenin (1975c).

6 Using Lenin's argument (see previous footnote) we can put the matter as follows: for the successful introduction of political class-consciousness from 'outside', the soil has to be fertile; to the extent however that trade union demands can be accommodated within the system, the soil for the introduction of political class consciousness no longer remains fertile.

increase in investment would result in a fall in aggregate demand and a lower level of capacity utilisation; and since a lower level of capacity utilisation would lower the rate of accumulation, a higher profit share would be associated with a lower rate of growth and a lower level of capacity utilisation in the new steady-state situation. If one knew the parameter values, one could work out in this case, from the other steady-state equations what would happen to the other variables. Of one thing, however, one can be sure: since the trend rate of unemployment would be larger, the share of wages in the manufacturing sector would be lower.

But in the other case where the rise in the profit margin is associated with an increase in the accumulative urge, say e, such that the trend growth rate remains the same as before, not only would the share of wages in the manufacturing sector remain unaffected, but, what is more, through an adverse shift in the terms of trade for the primary sector, it would be the primary sector workers who would experience lower wages. In the next chapter we shall return to this case which is the exact analogue of the case of increased trade union bargaining strength. In either situation, the intensity of struggle within the manufacturing sector remains muted because the primary sector workers can be squeezed.

4. A CRITIQUE OF SOCIAL HARMONISM

The idea that in a capitalist economy there is a dichotomy between 'the price-takers' and 'the price-makers' is an old one (see for instance Galbraith 1968, 1973). It has been used in recent years as an underpinning for a theory of unequal exchange.[7] We shall discuss unequal exchange in Chapter 10, but a few words are called for here on the relationship between the 'price-taker'–'price-maker' dichotomy and the model presented here. In contrast to the 'organised'–'unorganised' sector dichotomy, or the 'price-maker'–'price-taker' dichotomy, this is basically a four-class schema. The fact that the so-called unorganised sector itself is not a homogeneous entity, but has exploitation within it, is essential for our argument. Not only does it

[7] Though the unequal exchange literature is large—e.g. Emmanuel 1972, Amin 1979—the marrying of the 'price-taker'–'price-maker' dichotomy with unequal exchange is attempted in Dandekar 1981.

represent a difference in perception and emphasis, but, even more important, it allows us to explore the dynamics of the system, which is something that the dualistic theories seldom do. It enables us to answer the question: despite the fact that inflation at the core is kept in check by imposing additional burdens on the producers in the outlying regions, how is it that supplies from the latter continue to be forthcoming to meet the requirements of the core?

The difference in perception involved in the recognition of exploitation within the primary sector itself is of basic analytical significance. Kaldor (1978) for example has argued that since the manufacturing sector is characterised by cost-plus pricing and since the wages of manufacturing workers in terms of primary products are fixed in any period, and rise over time in tandem with labour productivity, the terms of trade between the two sectors are more or less fixed, so that the growth of the manufacturing sector, assuming balanced trade, depends entirely upon the extent to which its exports to the primary sector can grow, which in turn depends upon the growth of the primary sector itself. Thus it is the growth of the manufacturing sector which is tethered to the growth of the primary producing sector, and not the other way around as we have been arguing.

There is one obvious basis for our difference from Kaldor, namely that we do not take real wages in the manufacturing sector to be fixed in any period. But suppose we obliterate this difference, and conclude with Kaldor that manufacturing real wages and hence the terms of trade are fixed. It would still follow from our model, because we introduce two separate classes within the primary sector, that manufacturing output in any period can be pushed up through profit-inflation in the primary sector. In other words, while in any period, exports to the primary sector would determine the magnitude of manufacturing output, these exports themselves are not a given magnitude dependent solely upon the primary sector's output. They depend additionally on income distribution within the primary sector which determines its overall import-propensity for manufactured goods. In fact, given the primary sector's output, it is not the manufactured goods output that gets determined, but rather the income distribution within the primary sector which must adjust to accommodate a larger or smaller manufactured goods output. The manufactured goods output then has an autonomy in the single period itself. It therefore has an autonomy over a sequence of periods;

its growth rate has an autonomy. It is the primary sector's growth
rate that adjusts to the manufacturing sector's growth rate, and not
the other way around as Kaldor suggests.

In the event of diminishing returns prevailing in the primary sector, it is not the manufacturing sector's output whose growth would
slow down; there would be a secular decline in the real wages of the
primary sector workers.[8] Of course, diminishing returns are a prospect which has haunted economics since the days of Ricardo but
which are yet to materialise as a secular constraint upon growth. But
the issue here is theoretical, and does not concern the empirical
validity of diminishing returns. Economists from Ricardo to Kaldor
have theorised that diminishing returns, if they prevailed, would slow
down the rate of growth of the manufacturing sector and hence of
capitalism in general. This theorising is based on a stylisation of the
world which fails to note that capitalism takes as its premiss a mass
of unorganised workers with compressible real wages. It is the existence of such a mass in the outlying regions which enables capitalism
at the centre to achieve both output and price stability by being
coupled to such regions. It is the same coupling which, as we shall see
in the next chapter, also enables it to achieve high rates of growth.

---

[8] To be sure, once we introduce growth in labour productivity in the primary
sector, what would decline is not the absolute level of real wages per worker but real
wages per efficiency unit of labour. This needless to say holds for all the cases discussed above, e.g. where the profit margin or the workers' claims in the manufacturing sector go up.

Appendix

The formal model underlying the discussion in Chapter 6 is set out in this Appendix. Using superscript m for the manufacturing sector and the superscript a for the primary sector, we can write out the basic equations of the system as follows:

$$i_{t+1}^m = [K_{t+1}^m / K_t^m][i_t^m + b(u_t - u_0)i_t^m - \varepsilon i_t^m(p_t^m / p_{t-1}^m \bullet p_{t-2}^m / p_{t-1}^m - 1)^2]$$
$$+ eK_{t+1}^m, \tag{i}$$

which is the same as before.

$$p_t^m = (w_t^m l_t^m + \pi p_t^a)\mu, \tag{ii}$$

where π represents the physical amount of primary commodities required per unit of manufacture.

$$w_t^m = \varpi_t^m p_t^{ae}, \tag{iii}$$

where ϖ_t^m is the amount of primary commodity which the money wage obtained by the workers is supposed to give them command over at the expected price p_t^{ae}.

$$p_t^{ae} = p_{t-1}^a p_{t-1}^a / p_{t-2}^a, \tag{iv}$$

which is in line with what we have assumed till now.

$$\varpi_t^m l_t^m = q - rv_t, \tag{v}$$

as before, and

$$v_t = 1 - O_t^m l_t^m / L_t^m \tag{vi}$$

$$L_{t+1}^m = L_t^m(1 + m - nv_t) \tag{vii}$$

$$l_{t+1}^m = l_t^m / (1 + g_{pt}) \tag{viii}$$

$$g_t^p = (1 + i_t^m / K_t^m)/(1 + \gamma_t^m / K_t^m) - 1, \qquad 0 < \gamma < 1. \tag{ix}$$

The output of the manufacturing sector must equal

$$O_t^m = i_t^m + c_2 P_t^m + P_t^a p_t^a / p_t^m + \alpha K_t^m + dK_t^m + (W_t^m - \sigma\varpi_t^m O_t^m l_t^m p_t^a) / p_t^m$$
$$\tag{x}$$

i.e. gross investment, capitalist consumption in the manufacturing sector, the part of workers' consumption which is devoted to manufactured goods, and the entire profits of the primary sector capitalists, which whether devoted to consumption or investment must be spent on manufactured goods by assumption.

W_t^m it should be noted is the money wage bill in the manufacturing sector, so that

$$W_t^m = O_t^m l_t^m w_t^m. \qquad (xi)$$

Since the profits of the manufacturing sector equal investment and consumption by the capitalists of this sector (we are assuming here that capitalists in any sector invest in their own sector), we have

$$P_t^m = i_t^m + c_2 P_t^m + \alpha K_t^m + d K_t^m. \qquad (xii)$$

Finally, we have two definitional equations for the manufacturing sector

$$u_t = O_t^m / K_t^m \bullet \beta^m \text{ and} \qquad (xiii)$$

$$K_{t+1} = K_t + i_t. \qquad (xiv)$$

Now, for the primary producing sector, the following equations must hold. Since prices in this sector are supposed to be market clearing, the output simply equals

$$O_t^a = K_t^a \beta^a. \qquad (xv)$$

The profits in product terms are exactly equal to the physical amount of this sector's goods which are demanded by the manufacturing sector, so that we have

$$P_t^a = \pi O_t^m + \varpi_t^m l_t^m O_t^m \sigma. \qquad (xvi)$$

The price of the primary commodity being the sum of the unit labour cost and the unit profit, we have

$$p_t^a = w_t^a l_t^a + P_t^a \bullet p_t^a / O_t^a. \qquad (xvii)$$

The amount of investment undertaken in any period depends upon the rate of profit prevailing in the previous period, and in particular whether this rate of profit is higher or lower than some acceptable rate of profit. If higher, then the current period's rate of accumulation is higher than the previous period's rate of accumulation; if lower, then the current period's accumulation rate is lower than the previous period's, i.e.

$$i_{t+1}^a / K_{t+1}^a = i_t^a / K_t^a + z(h_t - h^*), \qquad (xviii)$$

where z is a constant and h^* denotes the acceptable rate of profit and h denotes the actual rate of profit which is defined as total money profits per unit of capital stock at its current replacement cost:

$$h_t = P_t^a p_t^a / \bar{p}_t^m \bullet K_t^a \qquad (xix)$$

The investment function relates to net investment, so that

$$K_{t+1}^a = K_t^a + i_t^a. \qquad (xx)$$

Now we come to the crucial relationship which refers to the determination of money wages in this sector. The basic proposition we have is that workers in this sector, located in the midst of vast labour reserves which cannot migrate at will to the manufacturing sector (migration being supposed to be in accordance with eqn. (vii) on which more later), are handicapped with respect to the extent to which they can enforce *ex ante* wage claims in the face of falling real wages. The way we express this handicap formally is as follows. The real wage claims which the workers succeed in enforcing at the expected price of the primary product is the previous period's real wage plus some compensation for the fact that the previous period's real wage may have been too low relative to recent experience. To capture recent experience we take the average of the real wages which have prevailed during the previous T periods, i.e.

$$w_t^a = p_t^{ae}[\varpi_{t-1}^a + y(\hat{w}_t^a - \varpi_{t-1}^a), \qquad (xxi)$$

where $y<1$ is a constant, $\hat{w}_t^a$ denotes the average real wage for the previous T periods and the real wage is defined simply as:

$$\varpi_{t-1}^a = w_{t-1}^a / p_{t-1}^a, \text{ etc.} \qquad (xxii)$$

No reference has been made in eqn. (xxi) to the rate of population growth and the change in unemployment rate which a divergence between output and population growth entails. The reasons for this are as follows. On the one hand, the backward economy is characterised by large labour reserves which make organised struggles by the workers especially in the primary sector for higher wages extremely difficult. On the other hand, the employed and the unemployed are not necessarily distinct social or even individual entities. Unemployment in agriculture for instance often takes the form of not getting work for a certain number of days in the year by the same workers who are employed on other days. Under the circumstances the sensitivity of real wage claims to changes in the unemployment rate, unless the latter falls significantly, is rather limited. It is customary in the literature to assume wage payment at a subsistence level in this situation. But subsistence is not a fixed entity; it seems more appropriate therefore to treat real wages as being capable of variation, and primary sector workers essentially as price-takers, as we have done. Eqn. (xxi) would become inappropriate if the configuration of output and employment growth was such that the unemployment rate kept falling over time to levels where the workers could become effectively organised, as in the advanced sector. But for reasons which we shall discuss later, this does not happen. And in any case, once we introduce productivity growth, as we shall do later, it is not the absolute level of the wage rate that would constitute a residue, but the wage rate relative to the productivity in this sector.

Now in this system of equations, system 2, we have twenty-two equations and thirty-two variables, which are i_t^m, i_{t+1}^m, K_t^m, K_{t+1}^m, u_t, p_t^m, w_t^m, l_t^m, p_t^a, p_{t-1}^a, p_{t-2}^a, ϖ_t^m, p_t^{ae}, v_t, O_t^m, L_t^m, L_{t+1}^m, l_{t+1}^m, g_t^p, W_t^m, P_t^a, P_t^m, O_t^a, K_t^a, w_t^a, K_{t+1}^a, i_t^a, i_{t+1}^a, h_t, ϖ_{t-1}^a, $\hat{w}_t^a$, and w_{t-1}^a. Of these in any particular period ten are known: K_t^m, i_t^m, l_t^m, L_t^m, i_t^a, p_{t-1}^a, p_{t-2}^a, w_{t-1}^a, K_t^a, and $\hat{w}_t^a$. The twenty-two equations therefore determine the remaining twenty-two variables, and bequeath to the next period the ten known variables, and so on. We thus have a complete system for the determination of the single period situation, and the sequence of single period situations which follow. The question is: can the two sectors coupled together reach a state of steady growth-cum-steady inflation?

A state of steady growth-cum-steady inflation, such that each sector is growing at the same rate and the rate of inflation is neither accelerating nor decelerating, clearly exists for system 2. In fact there are two possible states of steady growth-cum-steady inflation, where the rates of growth are g_1 and g_2 respectively, given by the roots of the following quadratic equation, which are both positive:

$$b\{(g+d+\alpha)\mu / [\beta^m(1-c_2)(\mu-1)] - u_0\}g + e = 0, \tag{A4}$$

or,

$$\mu g^2 b / \beta^m(1-c_2)(\mu-1) + g[\mu b(d+\alpha) / (1-c_2)(\mu-1) - bu_0] + e = 0.$$

(A4) is exactly the equation one gets from the system which we studied in Chapter 2 above and which yielded two possible steady-state values since the middle term is negative. The fact of the two systems having identical solutions is by no means surprising since in a situation of steady inflation, the investment function of the manufacturing sector which must eventually yield the steady growth rate for the economy as a whole is nothing else but equation (2.1″) of Chapter 2.

We saw in Chapter 2 that of the two possible steady-state growth rates only one, the smaller one, was stable in the sense that if the economy departed from it there were tendencies set at work to bring it back to that steady state, while the other was an unstable trend. Let us confine our attention therefore to the stable trend g_1, on whose stability more later, and see what the configuration of other variables will be for this trend. At g_1,

$$v = m/n - \gamma g_1 / n = v^* \tag{1}$$

$$\varpi^m l^m = q - r[m/n - \gamma g_1 / n] = (\varpi^m l^m)^* \tag{2}$$

$$u = u_0 - e/b \bullet g_1 = u^* \tag{3}$$

$$h = h^* \tag{4}$$

$$p^m / p^a = [q - r(m - \gamma g_1) / n]\mu + \pi\mu = (p^m / p^a)^* \tag{5}$$

$$\varpi^a = 1/l^a - h^*(p^m / p^a)^* / \beta^a \bullet l^a = \varpi^{a^*} \tag{6}$$

$$O^m / O^a = [1 - (\varpi^a l^a)^*] / [\pi + \sigma(\varpi^m l^m)^*] = (O^m / O^a)^* \tag{7}$$

$$K^m / K^a = \beta^a (O^m / O^a)^* / \beta^m u^* \tag{8}$$

$$p^m / p^m_{t-1} = p^a_t / p^a_{t-1} = \text{ some constant} \tag{9}$$

The corresponding values for g_2 can be found simply by substituting g_2 for g^1, wherever the latter occurs in any expression. To see the existence of a steady growth-steady inflation path, suppose the ten known variables at the start of any period are given as follows:

$$K^m_t = \text{ some } K^m_t \tag{1}$$

$$i^m_t = K^m_t g_1 \tag{2}$$

$$l^m_t = \text{ some } l^m_t \tag{3}$$

$$L^m_t = K^m_t \beta^m u^* l^m_t / (1 - v^*) \tag{4}$$

$$K^a_t = K^m_t \beta^m u^* / \beta^a \bullet (O^m / O^a)^* \tag{5}$$

$$i^a_t = K^a_t g_1 \tag{6}$$

$$\hat{w}^a_t = (\varpi^a)^* \tag{7}$$

$$p^a_{t-1} = \text{ some } p^a_{t-1} \tag{8}$$

$$p^a_{t-2} = \text{ some } p^a_{t-2}, \text{ and} \tag{9}$$

$$w^a_t = p^a_{t-1}(\varpi^a)^* p^a_{t-1} / p^a_{t-2} \tag{10}$$

Then the remaining twenty-two variables will take on such values that all outputs in the succeeding period will be $(1+g_1)$ times the output of the current period, all prices in the succeeding period will be (p^a_{t-1}/p^a_{t-2}) times the current period's price, the real wages of the primary workers will remain constant, and of manufacturing workers grow at the rate g^p.

Since the above is only a preliminary model, we discuss the stability question only cursorily. Because of the time lags which we have introduced into the equations in system 2, we cannot show that starting from g_1, if the economy, consisting of both sectors, moves away in any direction, the self-correcting mechanism implicit in the system will bring it back to g_1; there are likely to be oscillations preventing the settling down of the economy at

g_1 again. But it is clear that starting from g_1, if there is a disturbance the economy cannot keep moving away from g_1. Suppose the rate of accumulation suddenly increases above g_1. The unemployment rate will fall immediately and the rate of capacity utilisation will improve in the manufacturing sector. The fall in the unemployment rate will result in larger *ex ante* claims by the manufacturing workers and hence an increase in the rate of inflation. This in the next period will have an adverse effect on the rate of accumulation. The rise in the rate of capacity utilisation too would be insufficient to sustain the higher rate of accumulation of the current period into the next period. For both these reasons, the rise in the rate of accumulation would be unsustainable and the rate of accumulation would slide back towards g_1. Likewise, if the rate of accumulation happens to fall below g_1, inflation would decelerate exerting an adverse effect upon the rate of accumulation in the next period, while the fall in capacity utilisation would be insufficient to sustain the lower rate of accumulation into the next period. We would have two contradictory effects, but even assuming that the fall in the rate of accumulation continues, since it cannot become negative, the economy would eventually have to come back in the direction of g_1.

The rate of accumulation thus cannot remain above g_1, but less than g_2, for an indefinite period of time. Likewise the rate of accumulation cannot remain below g_1 for an indefinite length of time without in certain periods moving in the direction of g_1. From the investment function, it follows that no matter whether inflation is steady or non-steady, it always exerts a nonpositive influence upon the rate of accumulation. Whenever this rate exceeds g_1, other investment-influencing factors also have an adverse influence, and hence it tends to fall towards g_1. In the opposite case, whenever the rate of accumulation is below g_1, we do not have a symmetrical result; all we can say is that from time to time, and not monotonically, the economy would tend to move in the direction of g_1.

The same however cannot be said of g_2. Here, even if the economy had stabilised for a long period of time, a chance decline in the rate of accumulation would take it towards g_1 rather than bringing it back towards g_2. For the manufacturing sector then we cannot show local or global stability of g_1 in the strict sense. If it is to the right of g_1, there is a tendency for it to move monotonically towards g_1; but if it is to the left of g_1, it does not show any such monotonic movement. Nonetheless it would show sporadic movements in the direction of g_1. This being the case we take g_1 as the benchmark for our analysis.

7

Accumulation and Unequal
Interdependence: *A Fuller
Discussion*

In the previous chapter we assumed that the backward economy was
producing only the primary commodity. The advanced economy's
interest lay entirely in its role as a supplier of that commodity. But of
course the backward economy also produces some manufactured
goods which are consumed within it or even outside. This gives the
capitalists in the advanced economy a second kind of interest in the
backward economy, as a potential market: to the extent that the
manufactured goods produced by them can supplant those produced within the backward economy, they can enjoy a larger market
than would have been possible otherwise. In the current chapter we
incorporate this aspect of their relationship, which is logically quite
distinct from the other aspect we had looked at earlier.

1. A MORE ELABORATE MODEL

We now have two sectors in the backward economy, one producing
the primary commodity, and the other producing a manufactured
good. Both sectors produce under capitalist conditions, an assumption that may appear odd at first sight in view of our repeated
references in earlier chapters to the 'pre-capitalist and semi-capitalist
economies of the outlying regions'; but since one of our objectives is
to underline the difficulties of successful capitalist transformation in

the backward economy in conditions of unequal interdependence, the assumption that capitalist production has already taken root is a useful one for us. The capitalists in both sectors prefer to buy imported goods, but fall back upon domestic manufactures only to the extent that they are unable to do so; workers in both sectors on the other hand buy the domestic manufactured good, apart from food (the food demand of the capitalists is ignored here). This in our view is an important sociological phenomenon, namely the desire for foreign goods among the rich in the periphery, which has profound implications for the prospects of successful capitalist transformation, and we capture it by this assumption.

Two obvious theoretical objections can be raised against the above stylisation. First, it would be argued that in such situations the relative prices of the two manufactured goods would be so adjusted as to make people indifferent between the two (or to locate a marginal consumer lying between those who exclusively buy one and those who exclusively buy the other, who buys both and reaches an interior equilibrium). This however is not a realistic description: preferences are so strongly conditioned by cultural factors that for a whole range of relative prices different social groups have clear and overriding preferences for particular commodities; the capitalists especially have a clear preference for the imported good. They are however rationed, and therefore turn to the home-produced good. The implicit assumption we make for the present is that the actual relative price between the two manufactured goods lies within this range (see Chapter 12 for a fuller discussion).

The second objection would be that, even if there is no concept of a margin, rationing cannot persist if the price of the imported manufactured good is flexible upwards. Our justification for the above assumption is two-fold. First, to suppose that the price of the imported manufactured good rises to eliminate the excess demand for it is tantamount to supposing that the foreign exchange market is equilibrated through a decline in the exchange rate. For the backward economy to allow the foreign exchange market to be equilibrated through a fall in the exchange rate is, as we shall see later, a singularly silly thing to do in the context we are discussing, which we assume it refrains from doing. Instead it resorts to foreign exchange rationing, which is equivalent to a rationing of the imported good. Second, of course, the rationing of imported goods *has* been the norm in the backward economies for over half a century now owing .to the prevalence of exchange controls, so that our assumption does capture a stylised fact.[1]

If there always exists a reservoir of demand for its manufactured good in the backward economy, then the advanced economy can clearly sell as much of its manufactured good as it wishes to in this market.[2] Its actual level of capacity utilisation in such a situation then can never fall below the desired level. If it ever so fell, the advanced country capitalists could always make up the shortfall by exporting to the backward country a sufficient quantity of their manufactured good, financed by appropriate credit. It cannot also exceed the desired level of capacity utilisation, because capitalists can always cut down on exports to maintain the desired level of utilisation. Exports in other words are always such that together with investment they create a level of autonomous demand that is just sufficient to maintain manufactured goods output at the level appropriate for the desired degree of capacity utilisation.

Once we accept that the degree of capacity utilisation would always be at the desired level, the investment function for the advanced economy would have to be re-cast. There is no reason why the capitalists would ever plan to invest (in the next period) anything less than the total expected savings, as long as the inflation rate is steady and as long as capital exports for financing an export surplus fetches a rate of return net of risk which is lower than the corresponding rate of return on investment. Likewise their planned investment would

---

[1] Taylor (1983) in the context of a north-south model has assumed that the capitalists of the south spend their entire profits on imports from the north. While this corresponds to our description of preferences, it differs from our model insofaras we incorporate rationing of imported goods, i.e. an element of perpetually unsatisfied demand for such goods.

[2] It may be asked: why does the existence of manufacturing in the backward economy *per se* entail such a reservoir of demand? After all any actual supplanting of backward manufacturing by advanced manufacturing requires an export surplus by the advanced economy (see below); why did we not incorporate the effect of an export surplus on larger overseas sales of advanced manufacturing in the previous chapter where there was no backward manufacturing? The crucial point here is the following: even when the backward economy capitalists' *planned expenditure in every period equals their expected profits*, if this expenditure *ex hypothesi* is entirely on imports, then no further role for a credit-financed export surplus from the advanced economy remains. But even when the capitalists *do not plan to live off borrowings*, if domestic manufacturing exists and is second preference, a role for credit-financed export surplus from the advanced economy remains, since every such export surplus makes room for itself by reducing actual profits below the expected profits. It is for this reason that in the previous chapter we did not introduce credit-financed export surplus, while now we can.

not exceed the expected savings for the following reason: any excess of actual investment over savings at the desired capacity use would, if this level of capacity use is maintained, cause a balance of payments deficit and hence would be unsustainable for the economy. Even if the capitalists do not know this, their plans *ex post* would have to be tailored to equal the actual savings (which on our definition always equal the expected savings in the aggregate).[3] It follows then that apart from the influence of non-steady inflation, the capitalists' investment plans would always equal their expected savings. The exogenous term eK which we had introduced in order to capture the effect of innovation upon investment in any period t, would no longer be relevant. All investment would as a matter of course *take the form* of the latest available process, but the *amount* of investment would be determined otherwise. As long as inflation is not accelerating or decelerating, the capitalists would always end up investing in the next period an amount that in the aggregate simply equals the next period's expected savings, which can be taken to bear the same ratio to current savings that the next period's capital stock would bear to the current period's.

To say that eK does not appear separately in the investment function does not mean that competition between capitals which underlay this term disappears. All that it means is that competition between capitals does not take the form of each capitalist *borrowing* over and above his expected savings at desired capacity use in order to make some additional investment to be the first with an innovation. It takes other forms which we shall discuss in the next chapter.

There are two aspects of this investment behaviour that deserve notice. First, since the system is not demand constrained, owing to the existence of a reservoir of demand in the backward economy, the postulated investment behaviour reflects this fact. The investment plans made in any period (for realisation in the next) simply amount to investing the expected savings of the next period. A number of writers, such as Goodwin (1967), have postulated that capitalists invest their entire savings. Our formulation, apart from being slightly different in that planned investment equals expected savings (if inflation is steady), attributes the systematic absence of a demand constraint to the availability of backward economy markets.

The second aspect of our postulated investment behaviour is

3 See below and also the precise investment function given in the Appendix.

that capitalists prefer to invest domestically rather than run credit-financed export surpluses to backward economies. True, in the face of a domestic recession, they may run a temporary export surplus of this kind; but this is not a systematic phenomenon, as is implicitly recognised by us in postulating that the entire expected savings are planned to be *invested*. This assumption, as we shall see, does justice to historical reality.

Our complete model for the case where the backward economy also has manufacturing is set out in the appendix to this chapter. But some of the main elements of the model, especially those which do not figure in the previous chapter's, can be briefly stated here.

For all three categories of workers—those in the advanced economy and those in the two sectors of the backward economy—the money wage rate and per capita primary commodity consumption are given (though not identical) in any period. The money wage rate of the advanced economy workers is fixed, as before, at a level that gives them, at the expected primary commodity price (which is an extrapolation of the previous period's price at the previous period's rate of inflation), command over a certain bundle of primary commodities whose magnitude per efficiency unit of labour varies inversely with the unemployment rate. In the backward economy the mode of money wage determination is formally identical, in that it is fixed so as to give command over bundles of primary commodities at their expected price, but the determinants of these bundles are different. Since large labour reserves exist in this economy, and we ignore all productivity growth for the time being, the bundle for primary commodity workers is simply some average of past experience (which is the same assumption as in the last chapter); the bundle for the backward manufacturing workers is taken to be a fixed one.

A fixed proportion (which differs between the advanced and the backward economy workers) of this *ex ante* bundle in each period is assumed to be actually consumed in the form of primary commodities and the remainder is spent on manufactured goods, on advanced manufactures by the advanced workers and on backward manufacture by the backward economy workers.

Primary commodity prices are market clearing, with the output given in any period, while manufacturing prices are prime cost-plus. Manufacturing output in the advanced economy, as we saw earlier, is given by the desired level of capacity utilisation which is actually realised; in the backward economy it is demand-determined.

Regarding backward economy capitalists' expenditure, we make the following assumption out of a range of possible ones. In any period, the backward economy capitalists in the aggregate make nominal expenditure plans for the next period which are actually carried out. These plans depend upon two factors: the expected nominal profits which are but the expected real profits, based on assuming the current period's rate of profit to continue into the next, evaluated at the next period's expected prices. The second factor is the tightness of import availability, relative to some 'norm', experienced in the current period. While the first factor obviously has a positive influence on planned expenditure, the second has a negative influence. (Since we are not taking the expenditures of the two groups of capitalists in the backward economy separately we obviously allow for internal borrowings among them, but these are not explicitly considered.)

Within expenditure however we assume that investment expenditure plans occupy a special position, in that they are invariably carried out in real terms irrespective of import availability and price movements. And the investment behaviour is as follows. In the primary sector the rate of growth of capital stock in the next period compared to the current period depends upon the current rate of profit relative to some 'norm' or acceptable rate (which is the same assumption as in the last chapter); in the backward manufacturing sector the argument of the function is not the rate of profit but the degree of capacity utilisation.

2. SINGLE PERIOD EQUILIBRIUM

Let us now look at the single period situation in the context of such a model, assuming first that trade between the two economies is balanced. Since the outputs of the primary sector and of the advanced manufacturing sector are given in any period (the latter at a level which ensures that the desired degree of capacity use is realised), and so are the per capita primary commodity consumption levels of the workers, there is only one level of the backward manufacturing sector's output that is compatible with equilibrium. This output level must prevail; the demand for this sector's output therefore has to be such that it brings forth this output.

Now, in this single period, since other things are given as data, this demand depends exclusively on the primary commodity's price, and is inversely related to it. The lower the primary commodity price, the worse is this sector's terms of trade, though the lower *in absolute terms* are the manufactured goods prices. A given amount of nominal expenditure by backward economy capitalists (decided upon beforehand) gives rise therefore to a larger volume of real demand, and hence import demand (since imports are first preference). On the other hand in the advanced economy, the *absolute amount* of primary commodity requirement is given, since the level of this economy's output is given together with its raw material requirement and the per capita workers' consumption of the primary commodity. The worse the terms of trade for the primary sector, the less can the imports of advanced manufactured goods be if trade is to be balanced. Hence, the lower the primary commodity price, the greater is the spill-over demand of backward economy capitalists for the domestic manufactures of this economy itself. And of course the greater is also the demand of the domestic workers for the local manufactures, since the money wages are given and the excess of workers' income over primary commodity consumption is devoted to buying manufactures.

It follows then that there is a unique level of the primary commodity price that would ensure single-period equilibrium with balanced trade. Putting the matter differently, the demand for the primary commodity is inversely related to the price (through the functioning of the entire system, not in any partial equilibrium sense). Since the output of this sector is given, only a unique price for it would ensure equilibrium, and such a price would be attained. With it therefore all prices and the terms of trade will be determined.

Now suppose trade between the two economies is not balanced, and that the advanced economy runs an export surplus, on account of a sudden fall in its domestic investment, which is financed by credit. To accommodate the larger amount of imported manufactures, it may be thought at first sight that the domestic manufacturing sector has to shrink. This however is not the case. Since the domestic manufacturing sector has to be of a given size if equilibrium is to be established, it follows that imports cannot alter this size. Larger imports, financed by credit, would simply mean that the primary commodity price has to fall until the workers' real wages have improved to a point where they purchase the local manufactures that are abandoned by the capitalists in favour of imports. Thus under our assumptions an export surplus from the advanced economy does not adversely affect domestic employment in the backward economy; it favourably affects the level of real wages. If however we abandon the extreme assumption that an improvement in workers' real wages is spent entirely upon local manufactures, and allow for the more realistic possibility that some of this improvement is spent on increasing their primary commodity consumption as well, then an export surplus from the advanced economy would both improve real wages and cause domestic deindustrialisation in the backward economy.

Thus an export surplus undertaken in certain periods, confers on the advanced economy several distinct advantages. First of all, it prevents a domestic recession and keeps the level of aggregate demand high. Second, it simultaneously improves the terms of trade in favour of the advanced economy. Third, it sets up a claim upon the backward economy for future payments of interest as well as capital. And finally, it does all this at no cost whatsoever to the advanced economy itself, since in the absence of the export surplus its output would have shrunk anyway, causing if anything social unrest owing to unemployment.

While the effect of an export surplus in generating unemployment in the recipient country is well-known and attracted much attention years ago in discussions of 'beggar-my-neighbour' policies as remedies for depression,[4] the fact that an export surplus simultaneously worsens the terms of trade for the recipient country is of significance but less well appreciated. The usual discussion of 'beggar-my-neighbour' policies has taken place in the context of more-or-less similarly placed manufacturing economies. In trade among them, since one country can steal a march over another only by offering its goods more cheaply, the typical instrument for which is an exchange-rate depreciation, the terms of trade would, if anything, move against the exporting country. But when we are talking about trade between an integrated capitalist economy and a primary commodity producing backward economy, where at the prevailing prices the local capitalists prefer imported goods over home-produced ones, matters are entirely different. Larger exports from the advanced

---

4 The classic discussions are 'On Foreign Trade and Domestic Exports' in Kalecki 1971 and 'Beggar-My-Neighbour Remedies for Unemployment' in Robinson 1973.

country can be absorbed within the backward economy without any lowering of the price received by the producers in the advanced country. On the other hand, since such additional exports financed by credit can be absorbed within the backward economy only through a combination of some local 'deindustrialisation' and some expansion of the home market via a lowering of primary commodity prices relative to the money wages, the terms of trade move against the backward economy.

Export surpluses however are a temporary phenomenon. The backward economies, as distinct from the temperate colonies of white settlement, where such surpluses had an entirely different impact (on which more later), were never at the receiving end of any substantial and steady stream of export surpluses from the metropolis. But the very fact of easy availability of backward economies' markets, especially at critical times when domestic demand sags in the metropolis, can play, and has played, *inter alia*, the role of keeping up the inducement to invest in the metropolis, and hence making actual export surpluses unnecessary, a point made in Chapter 2 in defence of Rosa Luxemburg's argument. Let us revert back therefore to an analysis of long-run growth in conditions of balanced trade.

3. THE STEADY-GROWTH– STEADY-INFLATION PATH

It can be easily seen that the system of equations describing this model is capable of yielding a steady-growth–steady-inflation solution (see Appendix). There are certain properties of this steady-growth–steady-inflation path which can be established. First of all, it is unique. This is obvious from the fact that since along such a path, the rate of accumulation must be constant, there can be neither export surplus nor a trade deficit for the advanced country's manufacturing sector, in which case its investment must exactly equal its savings. Given the fact that this sector is always experiencing capacity utilisation at u_0, it would have to have a unique growth rate, which is nothing else but the level of net savings at the 'desired' rate of capacity utilisation divided by the capital stock.

Looking at it more closely, this is nothing else but the 'warranted growth rate' of Harrod which we had discussed in Chapter 2. The warranted growth rate which is unsustainable as long as markets external to the capitalist sector are not available, becomes perfectly sustainable once access to such markets is assured since the economy can now be pegged at the desired level of capacity utilisation. In other words, while earlier, for the economy to maintain growth at the warranted rate, it was necessary that investment itself had to be of a certain order of magnitude and there was no economic rationale for believing that this would happen, now the availability of the external market ensures that just this much investment actually takes place.

Not only do markets outside the capitalist economy permit the warranted rate of growth to become realised, but they simultaneously ensure that at this growth rate, there is neither accelerating nor decelerating inflation. The second kind of instability that we drew attention to in Chapter 3, and which we argued would not necessarily get removed by State intervention, now disappears because in the backward economy, to which the capitalist economy is coupled, the workers are not in a position to enforce their *ex ante* real wage claims. They provide therefore a cushion against accelerating or decelerating inflation. And lastly, even as the capitalist economy derives both these kinds of advantages from being coupled to the backward economy, it does not have to run a perpetual export surplus *vis-à-vis* the backward economy. Trade remains balanced but the coupling still has all the advantages for the capitalist economy.

The crucial question that now arises is whether the steady-growth–steady-inflation path is a stable one. We shall look at this question in the Appendix, but the following remarks can be made here. With the lags that we have in our various equations, including the large one involved in capturing 'past experience' in the matter of real wages of primary sector workers, we cannot of course have stability in the sense of a uniform convergence to the steady-growth–steady-inflation path starting from any arbitrary initial state, or after a local perturbation. But this path acts as a centre of gravity in the case of the advanced economy: no matter where the economy may happen to be, there would always be a tendency for the rate of growth to bounce back to g though it may not stay there. Putting the matter differently, the economy can neither have a growth rate permanently above or below the warranted rate, nor can it have a rate of inflation that keeps permanently accelerating or decelerating. In short, being coupled with the backward economy helps the advanced economy to overcome secularly perverse price movements even while maintaining a secularly high rate of growth.

4. EXCHANGE RATE AND OTHER CONSIDERATIONS

Before going on to a discussion of how parametric adjustments affect
the steady-state configuration, I should mention two particular
points. The first concerns the exchange rate. I have so far implicitly
assumed a fixed exchange rate and the question naturally arises: how
justified is this assumption?

Since the demand for the primary product in the advanced economy is assumed to be insensitive to its price, and the domestic
capitalists' absolute preference for imported manufactures is also
assumed to be insensitive to its price relative to that of the domestic
manufactured good (at least over a certain range within which all
changes are supposed to occur), an exchange rate depreciation by
the backward economy is a singularly counterproductive exercise: if
foreign trade remains balanced both before and after the depreciation, then a depreciation merely entails a loss to the economy via an
adverse terms-of-trade effect (since money wages in the advanced
economy are given in the short-run and pricing there is prime cost-
plus). The short-run effect of an exchange rate depreciation by the
backward economy in other words, if it at all lowers the export price,
is a redistribution of command over goods from the backward economy capitalists to the advanced economy workers via a terms-of-
trade shift. (The fact that the transfer is from the capitalists in the
backward economy and not the workers is entirely because of our
assumption that the capitalists' autonomous demand is fixed in the
short-run in money rather than in real terms.)

But then since the opposite happens with an exchange rate appreciation, it would appear that each of the two segments of the
world economy would have an interest in appreciating its exchange
rate *vis-à-vis* the other. How then do we have stable exchange rates?
The answer lies in a fact which has not explicitly entered our model,
namely the existence of rival national economies within each segment. An exchange rate appreciation by a single backward economy
would lose it markets as its rivals would not follow suit; a depreciation on the other hand would invite retaliation by rivals and involve
a collective loss which is why it would not be resorted to (though the
IMF, as we shall see later, imposes such collective depreciations on
backward economies). The exchange rate between the two segments
therefore would tend to be stable.

If it is stable, then no matter what its specific value is, it has no effect upon the terms of trade or upon any of the real magnitudes associated with steady state, all of which depend exclusively on the parameters highlighted in our model. Putting it differently, any change in the exchange rate has only transitional effects which vanish in the steady state if the exchange rate remains stable after the change. Since there are in addition independent reasons to presume such stability, we have not considered the exchange rate explicitly.

My second point is the following. It may be thought that the stylisation underlying our model is both rigid and internally inconsistent. For instance the most fundamental assumption of the model is that each economy's capitalists invest only in their own economies and also in lines of production embedded within their respective economies. Against this assumption, two separate questions can be raised. First, why don't the backward economy capitalists invest in the production of manufactured goods, technologically comparable to those imported, in the backward economy itself? Second, why don't the advanced economy capitalists produce the same manufactured goods, which they have been doing in their own country, in the backward economy where the wages are lower?

These are questions which go to the very root of the phenomenon of backwardness and we shall discuss them in detail in the chapters that follow.[5] But until now we have been interested in characterising unequal interdependence and its effect in terms of stabilising capitalism at the core. We take the country- and sector-specificity of investment by different capitalists as a stylised fact for the moment. Underlying this is the view that the world is not an aggregation of interior choices, so that an alteration of prices, through exchange rate adjustments for instance, makes little difference to the basic structural characteristics.

5. DISTRIBUTIONAL CONFLICTS AND UNDERCONSUMPTION

Let us now look at the effects of some parametric shifts on the steady-growth-steady-inflation configuration. Suppose there is an increase in the bargaining strength of the workers in the advanced

---

5 In addition we have assumed that the backward economy's manufactured good is not exportable. The legitimacy of this assumption will be discussed in a later chapter.

economy. Since the share of capitalists in gross manufacturing output (output inclusive of raw material value) is exclusively dependent upon the mark-up, this would not change. Likewise since the rate of growth is simply the net savings per unit capital stock at the desired level of capacity use, namely $\{[\beta^m u_0(\mu-1)(1-c_2)/\mu]-d-\alpha\}$, and none of these parameters changes when the workers' bargaining strength increases, it follows that the rate of growth too remains unchanged. Thus, an increase in the bargaining strength of the workers in the advanced economy, while it does increase their real wages, lowers neither the capitalists' share nor the growth rate, nor (it follows) the employment rate. The rise in the real wage is accommodated through a shift in the terms of trade against the primary commodities. This shift in turn does not result in a decline in the rate of profit of the primary sector capitalists. Their share in the primary sector's output goes up so that they are compensated for the adverse terms-of-trade shift and continue to earn the same rate of profit as before. A rise in the workers' bargaining strength in the advanced economy therefore is 'passed on' in the form of lower wages for workers in the backward economy. This cannot be called 'exploitation' and should not lead one to conclude that advanced country workers should refrain from organising themselves for higher wages. But this is the way that the system works and manages to ensure for itself both economic as well as social stability.

Now suppose there is a rise in the 'degree of monopoly' reflected in a higher μ. When we discussed this case in the previous chapter we drew a distinction between two cases, one where the rise in the degree of monopoly was simultaneously accompanied by an increase in the accumulative urge, and the other where this was not the case. This second case leads to the underconsumptionist argument.[6] But now that we are assuming that there is always an unsatisfied demand for advanced country manufactures in the backward economy, the underconsumptionist argument loses its sting and the need for drawing a distinction between the two cases disappears. In the short

---

[6] The underconsumptionist argument, as stated by Baran and Sweezy, refers not to a rise in the share of profits, but to a *rising* share of profits (or surplus). And the reason given for this is not a continuous upward revision in μ, but the fact that the real wages in the advanced economy grow more slowly than productivity, i.e. μ, instead of being an independent parameter, simply 'comes out of the wash', while it is the workers who, even at a given rate of unemployment, cannot maintain their claimed or *ex ante* share in output. But why the workers, if they are organised, should not be able to maintain their *ex ante* share is never made clear in the book.

run the rise in the degree of monopoly would no doubt generate a realisation crisis, but this can be warded off by appropriate export surpluses. Over a period of time, investment would rise to wipe out the export surpluses, and the growth rate would in fact be higher than before. Indeed from our steady-state comparisons it follows that with a rise in the degree of monopoly, the rate of growth would be higher in the new steady state; so would be the employment rate and the rate of growth of productivity. Workers in the advanced country thus, far from losing out in the long run from a rise in the degree of monopoly, would gain in two ways. Their real wages would be higher even for a given rate of productivity growth in the advanced economy because of the higher employment rate. And, insofar as productivity grows faster, the rate of growth of real wages would be faster too.

Once again, if the degree of monopoly rises, the terms of trade in the new steady state would be adverse for the primary sector, compared to the original steady state, and the entire brunt of the rise in the advanced sector capitalists' profit margin would be borne by the primary sector workers. The rate of growth of output and employment in the backward economy would *ceteris paribus* be higher, since this must be the same as in the advanced economy, but the primary sector workers would be worse off in the sense of having a lower profile of real wages than would have been the case otherwise.

Does this mean then that underconsumption is of no consequence even in an economy where there is no State intervention? From our argument it follows that as long as external markets are available, underconsumption can at best play a transitional role. Of course in real life this transitional role can be more or less prolonged. If the lag between an investment downturn and capital exports is long, then the downturn would become a crisis. If the lag between capital exports picking up and the subsequent revival of investment on account of the higher capacity utilisation brought about by capital exports is long, then capital exports would have to be sustained for a much longer period of time, and if this becomes difficult, then again there may be a crisis, and so on. Crises are after all a real phenomenon under capitalism; in drawing attention to the role of external markets, our intention is not to underplay this phenomenon (even though in our formal model it does not figure for reasons of simplicity), but rather to suggest that the availability of such markets enables capitalism to perform at a high level of activity through the crises.

The Great Depression, the classic case of a crisis induced by insufficient demand but far more profound than any 'normal' cyclical downturn, occurred, it must be remembered, in the midst of a world in which capital exports had virtually dried up. This also suggests that in looking at the possibility of capital exports as an offset to domestic deficiency of demand, one has to look at the contradictions between the advanced capitalist countries, something which we have not done yet. But the important point is that the availability of external markets not only can act as such an offset to domestic deficiency of demand, but, what is more, can play a role which is far more critical than a mere cursory look at statistics would suggest. By arresting downward slides in the economy and contributing generally to the maintenance of a high inducement to invest, it can lift the performance of a capitalist economy, even when over a period of time the relative magnitude of exports to external markets, or of export surpluses, appears small.[7]

In the last chapter we looked briefly at Kaldor's arguments. We return to them once again here. When Kaldor says that because savings are habitually invested by the capitalists, and because terms of trade between primary commodities and manufactures are more or less unchanged over long periods of time (an empirically questionable proposition which we discuss later), the only objection to the prognostications of 'mainstream' economic theory arises from the fact of diminishing returns, he can be criticised on two separate counts. First, the habitual investment of savings is itself predicated on the fact of availability of external markets, and cannot be taken as intrinsic capitalist behaviour. Second, the observed stability of the terms of trade (if it is conceded for argument's sake that they are stable), and of prices generally, is a feature of a world in which the wage claims of the workers in one segment are compressible. Otherwise any parametric shift, such as a rise in the degree of monopoly, instead of getting absorbed by the system, and being followed by

---

[7] Goodwin (1991) has produced a model of economic dynamics combining Keynesian and Schumpeterian elements. While he incorporates a Schumpeterian swarm of innovations, unlike Schumpeter he does not assume any tendency towards full employment. But why should output increase at the end of the swarm of innovations instead of employment declining? The answer given by him is State intervention which acts as a 'chaotic attractor'. Our argument is that sales to pre-capitalist markets have played a far more significant role as a chaotic attractor (if one talks in terms of the Goodwin model) in the history of capitalism. See also P. Patnaik 1972 and Ch. 11 below.

more or less prolonged periods of stability (after initial adjustments and an improvement in the terms of trade which even Kaldor would concede), would have thrown the system into turmoil and inflationary upheavals. The problem with 'mainstream' economics arises therefore not from the fact of diminishing returns but from an altogether different source, namely its utter inability to comprehend the functioning of the system in its totality, taking its developed and underdeveloped parts together.

In our model if the primary sector capitalists raise their share, through a parametric increase in h^* for instance, there is no effect either on the growth rate, or on the profit margins of the advanced country capitalists, or on the share of the workers in the advanced economy, or on the rate of employment in the advanced economy, or even on the terms of trade between the primary commodity and the advanced manufactured good, when we compare the two sets of steady-state values of these variables. The only effects are on the real wages of the primary sector workers, and on the relative size of the primary sector compared to the advanced manufacturing sector. Thus none of these parametric shifts that we have discussed is potentially destabilising to the system. It is only if the workers engaged in primary production in the backward economy get organised (not just one segment of them but all of them), so that they can enforce *ex ante* real wage claims; it is only if they become indistinguishable from the workers in the capitalist economy proper (not necessarily in their absolute wage levels but in their capacity to resist), that we shall be back with all the problems of instability that we discussed in chapters 2 and 3. And for this to happen, it is essential that a significant extent of the vast labour reserves that exist in the backward economy is used up.

Appendix

The system of equations constituting the model of Chapter 7 is presented below. We have already seen that since the level of capacity use in the advanced economy is always what is desired, the real net investment planned in any period for realisation in the next one is simply the expected real net savings of the next period (if inflation is steady). In other words,

$$i_{t+1}^m / K_{t+1}^m = i_t^m / K_t^m - \varepsilon(p_t^m / p_{t-1}^m \bullet p_{t-2}^m / p_{t-1}^m - 1)^2 i_t^m / K_t^m$$
$$+ (X_t - M_t p_t^a / p_t^m) / K_t^m, \tag{i}$$

where we have already substituted net investment plus 'real' export surplus for net savings in the investment function. The term involving $(u_t - u_0)$ is dropped here because it is always equal to zero.

Now we can write down the other equations involving the advanced country as follows:

$$p_t^m = \mu(w_t^m l_t^m + \pi p_t^a), \tag{ii}$$

where π denotes the physical primary commodity input per unit of manufactured good output in the advanced economy.

$$w_t^m = \varpi_t^m p_t^{ae}, \tag{iii}$$

where, as before, workers are assumed to bargain for wages in terms of a certain amount of primary commodity commanded. The money wages they succeed in obtaining is such as to give them command over ϖ_t^m amount of primary commodity at its expected price.

$$p_{tm}^{ae} = p_{t-1}^a \bullet p_{t-1}^a / p_{t-2}^a \tag{iv}$$

$$\varpi_t^m l_t^m = q - r v_t \tag{v}$$

$$v_t = 1 - O_t^m l_t^m / L_t^m \tag{vi}$$

$$L_{t+1}^m = L_t^m (1 + m - n v_t) \tag{vii}$$

$$l_{t+1}^m = l_t^m / (1 + g_t^p) \tag{viii}$$

$$g_t^p = (1 + i_t^m / K_t^m) / (1 + \gamma i_t^m / K_t^m) - 1, \qquad 0 < \gamma < 1 \tag{ix}$$

All these are exactly the same as before. Now however we have a slightly different output identity. The workers again are assumed to consume an amount of the primary commodity which is a certain constant fraction of their *ex ante* command over it:

$$\sigma_t = \sigma \varpi_t^m \qquad (x)$$

and spend whatever is left of the money wage after buying σ_t on the manufactured good. The total manufactured good output is the sum of capitalists' consumption and investment, workers' manufactured good consumption and exports to the backward economy:

$$O_t^m = i_t^m + c_2 P_t^m + \alpha K_t^m + dK_t^m + O_t^m l_t^m (w_t^m - \sigma_t p_t^a) / p_t^m + X_t. \qquad (xi)$$

These exports are not necessarily identical with the imports from the backward economy, because the possibility now exists for running an export surplus to supplant local manufacturing in the backward economy.

We assume that capitalists in both the sectors in the backward economy plan in any period to spend a nominal amount which depends upon two factors. The first is their total expected nominal profits; and the second is the tightness of import availability in the previous period. This second factor is meant to take account of the fact that imported manufactures constitute their 'first preference' goods. Our specific assumption is that there is some 'standard' level of import availability such that if the actual level in the previous period was equal to this 'standard' then they plan to spend their entire expected profits in the current period; if it was higher or lower than this 'standard' then they plan to spend more or less than their expected profits in the current period.

They stick to their plans even if their actual profits turn out to be different from what they expected, and no matter what the actual import availability is in the current period; these affect the expenditure plan for the next period, rather than of the current period. The excess of their current period's expenditure over the current period's import availability is spent by them on the domestically manufactured goods which are their 'second preference'. We thus have:

$$X_t p_t^m = \xi_t [(\xi_{t-1} / \xi^*)(p_t^{ae} P_{t-1}^a K_t^a / K_{t-1}^a + p_t^{re} P_{t-1}^r K_t^r / K_{t-1}^r)]. \qquad (xii)$$

This equation can be interpreted as follows. The two terms within the inside brackets represent respectively the expected money profits of the primary sector and the manufacturing sector (for which the superscript r is used) in the backward economy. These expected money profits are based on an extrapolation of the previous period's product profits on the basis of price expectations and the growth of capital stock. ξ represents the tightness of import availability (ξ^* being its 'standard level') and is defined by the equation itself. The equation therefore should literally be read from the left to right: it is not ξ_t that determines X_t in the current period, but rather it is X_t which determines what the intensity of rationing in the current period would be. The excess of the capitalists' demand for imported goods over what is actually available, i.e. $(1 - \xi_t)$ times the term in round brackets gets spent by them on domestic manufactures.

The 'product profits' in the advanced economy are:

$$P_t^m = i_t^m + c_2 P_t^m + \alpha K_t^m + d K_t^m + X_t - M_t p_t^a / p_t^m, \qquad (xiii)$$

which now incorporates the real export surplus.

The imports into the advanced economy are given by:

$$M_t = O_t^m (\pi + l_t^m \sigma_t). \qquad (xiv)$$

And finally for reasons already given we have

$$O_t^m - K_t^m \beta^m u_0, \qquad (xv)$$

where β^m is the output–capital ratio in the advanced economy, and the definitional equation:

$$K_{t+1}^m = K_t^m + i_t^m. \qquad (xvi)$$

Turning now to the backward economy we have the primary sector output given by

$$O_t^a = K_t^a \beta^a, \qquad (xvii)$$

which must equal the demand for it *ex post*.

Let us assume that each worker in the backward economy consumes a fixed amount ϕ of the primary commodity. (Since productivity growth within the backward economy is not being considered in the present chapter, taking ϕ as a constant amount does no harm at present). This amount could be taken to be different for workers with different wage levels, but since it does not matter for our analysis we shall take it to be the same for all. The demand for the primary commodity then would be:

$$O_t^a = M_t + (O_t^a l^a \phi + O_t^r l^r \phi) + \eta O_t^r, \qquad (xviii)$$

where η is the primary commodity requirement per unit of the local manufactured good.

The price of the primary commodity 'comes out of the wash' and there is no separate equation for it. The price of the locally manufactured good however is given by

$$p_t^r = (w_t^r l^r + \eta p_t^a) \mu^r, \qquad (xix)$$

where μ^r is a mark-up factor, so that

$$P_t^r = O_t^r (\mu^r - 1) / \mu^r. \qquad (xx)$$

Now the output of the manufactured good in the backward economy, as suggested above, is demand-determined, i.e. it equals the excess of the capitalists' real expenditure over the amount of imported manufactured good available, together with the excess in real terms of what is left over from the workers' wage bill after they have met their fixed per capita food requirement.

$$p_t^r O_t^r = (w_t^a - \phi p_t^a) O_t^a l^a + (w_t^r - \phi p_t^a) O_t^r l^r + (1 - \xi_t) p_t^m X_t / \xi_t \qquad (xxi)$$

To discuss the investment behaviour in the backward economy, we have to make some assumption about how the tightness of import availability affects planned investment. On the whole we shall err on the right side if we assume that no matter what the import availability is and no matter how squeezed total real expenditure of the capitalists may be because of unforeseen price movements, they carry out their real investment plans. It is their consumption which adjusts to both these contingencies.

We thus have the same real net investment function for primary sector capitalists as before:

$$i_{t+1}^a / K_{t+1}^a = [i_t^a / K_t^a + z(h_t - h^*)], \qquad (xxii)$$

where, once again, the rate of profit h_t is given by

$$h_t = P_t^a p_t^a / K_t^a p_t^m. \qquad (xxiii)$$

For the backward economy's manufacturing sector, we can postulate a simple investment function of the familiar kind:

$$i_{t+1}^r / K_{t+1}^r = (i_t^r / K_t^r)[1 + a(u_t^r - u_0^r)], \qquad (xxiv)$$

defining u_t^r as:

$$u_t^r = O_t^r / \beta^r \bullet K_t^r. \qquad (xxv)$$

There are two more definitions to be specified:

$$i_t^a = K_{t+1}^a - K_t^a, \text{ and} \qquad (xxvi)$$

$$i_t^r = K_{t+1}^r - K_t^r. \qquad (xxvii)$$

We come now to the determination of money wages in the two sectors of the backward economy. For the primary commodity sector where the labour reserves are concentrated, we assume as before that the money wages are such as to give at the expected primary commodity price a weighted average of the previous period's real wage (in terms of primary commodity commanded) and the average real wage of the past T periods;

$$w_t^a = p_t^{ae}[\varpi_{t-1}^a + y(\hat{w}_t - \varpi_{t-1}^a)], \text{ where} \qquad (xxviii)$$

$$\varpi_{t-1}^a = w_{t-1}^a / p_{t-1}^a, \text{ and} \qquad (xxix)$$

$\hat{w}_t$ is the average real wage of the T periods prior to t; y is a constant which is less than 1.

For the manufacturing workers, we simply assume that they obtain money wages adequate for a fixed real wage (again in terms of primary commodity commanded) at the expected primary commodity price, i.e.

$$w_t^r = \varpi^r p_t^{ae}. \qquad (xxx)$$

The expected price of the local manufacture is:

$$p_t^{re} = p_{t-1}^r \bullet p_{t-1}^r / p_{t-2}^r. \qquad (xxxi)$$

Finally, the trade deficit of the backward economy must equal the trade surplus of the advanced economy, and must represent the excess of domestic expenditure over domestic output, so that expressing everything in current price terms:

$$(P_t^a p_t^a + P_t^r p_t^r) - p_t^m X_t / \xi_t = p_t^a M_t - p_t^m X_t. \qquad (xxxii)$$

Equations (i)–(xxxii), which we shall designate as system 3 of equations, capture in a simple form the totality of interactions between the advanced and the backward economies. Many of the assumptions no doubt can be objected to; and many of the equations could no doubt have been formulated differently. Nonetheless, the system represents one particular way of capturing the essential features of this interaction.

There are altogether fifty-three variables in system 3, namely, i_t^m, i_{t+1}^m, K_t^m, $K_{t+1}^m, p_t^m, p_t^a, p_{t-1}^a, w_t^m, l_t^m, p_{t-2}^a, p_t^{ae}, p_{t-1}^r, \varpi_t^m, p_{t-2}^m, v_b, O_t^m, L_t^m, L_{t+1}^m, l_{t+1}^m, g_t^p, P_t^a$, $P_t^m, O_t^a, K_t^a, K_{t-1}^a, w_t^a, K_{t+1}^a, i_t^a, i_{t+1}^a, h_b, \varpi_{t-1}^a, \hat{w}_t^a, w_{t-1}^a, w_t^r, X_b, \xi_b, \xi_{t-1}, \sigma_b, P_{t-1}^a$, $M_b, O_t^r, p_t^r, u_t^r, P_t^r, i_{t+1}^r, K_{t+1}^r, K_t^r, i_t^r, P_{t-1}^r, p_{t-1}^r, p_{t-2}^r, K_{t-1}^r$, and p_t^{re}. Of these, twenty-one variables are already known in any period, namely, K_t^m, i_t^m, p_{t-1}^m, $p_{t-2}^a, P_{t-1}^a, P_{t-1}^r, l_t^m, L_t^m, i_t^a, p_{t-1}^a, p_{t-2}^a, \hat{w}_t^a, K_t^a, w_{t-1}^a, K_{t-1}^a, K_t^r, i_t^r, p_{t-1}^r, K_{t-1}^r, \xi_{t-1}$, and p_{t-2}^r. The remaining thirty-two are determined by our thirty-two equations to define the single-period situation. This in turn bequeaths to the next period another twenty-one known variables, and so on. We thus have a complete determination of a sequence of single-period situations.

The equations constituting our system 3 are obviously capable of describing a steady-growth-cum-steady-inflation path, along which the variables would have the following values:

$$g = g^* = \beta^m u_0 (\mu - 1)(1 - c_2) / \mu - d - \alpha \qquad (1)$$

$$v = v^* = m / n - \gamma g^* / n \qquad (2)$$

$$\varpi^m l^m = q - rv^* = q - r(m / n - \gamma g^* / n) = (\varpi^m l^m)^* \qquad (3)$$

$$p^m / p^a = \mu(\pi + q - rv^*) = (p^m / p^a)^* \qquad (4)$$

$$X / K^m = \beta^m u_0 [1 - c_2(\mu - 1) / \mu - (\varpi^m l^m)^* (1 - \sigma)(p^a / p^m)^*]$$
$$- d - \alpha - g^* = M(p^a / p^m)^* / K^m \qquad (5)$$

$$\varpi^a = [1 - h^*(p^m / p^a)^* / \beta^a] / l^a = \varpi^{a^*} \tag{6}$$

$$P^a / O^a = h^*(p^m / p^a)^* / \beta^a = (P^a / O^a)^* \tag{7}$$

$$\xi_t = \xi_{t-1} = \xi^* \tag{8}$$

$$p^r / p^a = (\eta + \overline{w}^r l^r) \mu^r \tag{9}$$

$$O^r / O^a = \frac{(1 - \xi^*)(P^a / O^a)^*(p^a / p^r)^* + l^a(p^a / p^r)^*(\varpi^{a^*} - \phi)}{1 - (\varpi^r - \phi)l^r(p^a / p^r)^* - (1 - \xi^*)(\mu^r - 1) / \mu^r}$$

$$= (O^r / O^a)^* \tag{10}$$

$$O^m / O^a = \frac{1 - l^a \phi - (O^r / O^a)^*(\eta + l^r \phi)}{\pi + \sigma(\varpi^m l^m)^*} = (O^m / O^a)^* \tag{11}$$

$$K^r / K^a = (O^r / O^a)^* \bullet \beta^a / \beta^r \bullet u_0^r \tag{12}$$

$$K^m / K^a = (O^m / O^a)^* \bullet \beta^a / \beta^m \bullet u_0 \tag{13}$$

and finally,

$$p_t^r / p_{t-1}^r = p_t^m / p_{t-1}^m = p_t^a / p_{t-1}^a = \text{ some constant}[8] \tag{14}$$

The fact that such a steady-growth-cum-steady-inflation path exists can be easily checked by giving the twenty-one known variables in any period the following values:

$$\xi_{t-1} = \xi^* \tag{i}$$

$$K_t^m = \text{ some } K_t^m \tag{ii}$$

$$i_t^m = K_t^m g^* \tag{iii}$$

$$p_{t-1}^a = \text{ some } p_{t-1}^a \tag{iv}$$

$$p_{t-2}^a = \text{ some } p_{t-2}^a \tag{v}$$

$$l_t^m = \text{ some } l_t^m \tag{vi}$$

---

[8] A simulation exercise done on this model at my request by J. Subbarao, Professor of Physics at Jawaharlal Nehru University, showed that (i) a steady-growth–steady-inflation path exists; (ii) if the system is on this path it continues to be on it; (iii) if there is a small perturbation in one of the initial conditions, starting from this path, then the system still remains close to this path for a considerable period of time, after which its behaviour shows intriguing oddities.

$$L_t^m = K_t^m \beta^m u_0 l_t^m / (1 - v^*) \qquad (vii)$$

$$K_t^a = K_t^m / (K^m / K^a)^* \qquad (viii)$$

$$K_{t-1}^a = K_t^a / (1 + g^*) \qquad (ix)$$

$$i_t^a = K_t^a g^* \qquad (x)$$

$$p_{t-1}^r = p_{t-1}^a / (p^a / p^r)^* \qquad (xi)$$

$$p_{t-2}^r = p_{t-2}^a / (p^a / p^r)^* \qquad (xii)$$

$$\eta_{t-1}^a - \varpi^{a^*} p_{t-1}^a \qquad (xiii)$$

$$\hat{w}_t^a = \varpi^{a^*} \qquad (xiv)$$

$$K_t^r = K_t^a / (K^a / K^r)^* \qquad (xv)$$

$$K_{t-1}^r = K_t^r / (1 + g^*) \qquad (xvi)$$

$$i_t^r = K_t^r g^* \qquad (xvii)$$

$$P_{t-1}^a = K_{t-1}^a \beta^a (P^a / O^a)^* \qquad (xviii)$$

$$P_{t-1}^r = K_{t-1}^r \beta^a u_0^r (\mu^r - 1) / \mu^r \qquad (xix)$$

$$p_{t-1}^m = p_{t-1}^a (p^m / p^a)^* \qquad (xx)$$

$$p_{t-2}^m = p_{t-2}^a (p^m / p^a)^* \qquad (xxi)$$

Because of the lags in the various equations, including the large one involved in the moving average term, the system cannot be locally or globally stable in the sense of converging to the steady-growth-steady-inflation path. This path however acts as a centre of gravity for the system in the following sense: it can neither experience a permanently accelerating or decelerating inflation, nor experience a growth rate (or a sequence of growth rates) that is permanently above or below the steady growth rate, nor experience a combination of the two.

The reason is clear: if the system is pegged to the steady growth rate then we know that inflation will also become steady, i.e. any acceleration or deceleration will die down. On the other hand, if the rate of inflation is steady, then the system must converge to the steady growth rate. This is because whenever $i^m / K^m < g^*$, the economy must be having an export surplus, which would always tend to push i^m / K^m closer to g^*, and likewise in the converse case where $i^m / K^m > g^*$. There remains only the question of whether variations in g *together* with those in the rate of inflation cannot keep g permanently away from g^*. We consider the following four possibilities:

(i) $g>g^*$	(ii) $g>g^*$
Inflation accelerating	Inflation decelerating
(iii) $g<g^*$	(iv) $g<g^*$
Inflation accelerating	Inflation decelerating

In the first row cases, g will obviously move to g^* since the higher rate of accumulation cannot be sustained (given the nature of eqn. (i) of system 3). It is the cases in the second row which are interesting. In the first of these cases, even if inflation is accelerating to start with, the export surplus would be putting a check on acceleration by turning the terms of trade against the primary sector. The moment acceleration in inflation comes to a halt, g moves back to g^*. In the second case, even assuming that decelerating inflation carries g to zero, g would immediately bounce back from zero to g^*, again given the nature of the investment function (i).

Thus g cannot remain permanently strictly above g^* in the advanced capitalist economy, or permanently strictly below it. In this sense the model of the present chapter differs in its stability conclusions from the model of the previous chapter, where at $g=0$, the economy would bounce back in the next period to a higher g but not necessarily all the way back to g^*. Here the bouncing back is complete.

It may of course be objected that this result is only because we have assumed that all export surpluses are sought to be liquidated in the very next period, that in short our result about the path being a centre of gravity is only a trick of assumption. But the trick of assumption corresponds to something real: when external markets are freely available, the capitalists' inducement to invest is so strong that instead of 'wasting' their savings on export surpluses which would usually fetch a much lower rate of return (here we assume a zero rate of return), they would attempt to put whatever savings they can command into investment. Thus if g cannot remain permanently below g^* the reason for that is their strong inducement to invest when external markets are freely available; and if g cannot remain permanently above g^*, the reason is their unwillingness to pile up foreign debt (which in fact is more dubious an assumption than their unwillingness to pile up foreign credit).

8

Technological Progress and Uneven Development

So far we have discussed the problem of capital accumulation without introducing technological progress in any essential way. In the case of the backward economy it did not figure at all; in the case of the advanced economy it figured only in the sense that labour productivity growth was recognised, but there was no discussion of the process underlying it. The present chapter is devoted to a discussion of technological progress. Needless to say, the objective here is not to analyse the process of innovation *per se*, but rather to draw attention to a few limited aspects of it which are necessary for carrying forward the argument of the present book.

1. THE RACE FOR INNOVATION

The process of technological change has at least three distinct components: the generation of new technologies, the incorporation of new technologies into the process of production, and the replacement in the market of the products of old technology by those of the new technology. Expenditures are incurred at each of these stages, and, we can distinguish correspondingly between expenditures on innovation generation, expenditures on innovation absorption, which include not only investment expenditure, but also the expenditure incurred in training the work-force to operate the new technologies, and finally expenditure on innovation marketing. The last of these is indistinguishable from the general sales effort undertaken by the capitalists, and a larger or smaller volume of it does not *per se* entail a more or less rapid rate of technological advance. The other two categories of expenditure, however do have a bearing on the rate of technological advance. While no determinate relationship can or need be postulated between the total expenditure incurred on innovation generation and absorption and the overall rate of technological change, the latter *inter alia* does depend upon the former. For instance it may be argued that several major inventions owe their origins to individual geniuses, so that even though their timing might have been conditioned by social factors, it was not a mere matter of how much was spent on research leading up to them. But when we come to the bulk of inventions, or rather instances of technology generation, which constitute small but discrete advances over previous knowledge and practice, clearly the concept of new technology being generated through an appropriate amount of expenditure is by no means meaningless.

Yet in much growth theory the concept of expenditure on technological progress scarcely figures. In neoclassical growth-theory, of course, technological progress, be it of the 'embodied' or the 'disembodied' variety, is treated as exogenous, as if it falls like manna from heaven. The parable underlying such theory runs as follows. As time passes, newer and newer sets of blue-prints of techniques become available, each of which entails, for all possible ratios of capital stock to the labour employed in 'efficiency units', a proportionately smaller amount (the proportion remaining constant per unit of time and equal for all possible techniques) of labour in natural units.[1]

Non-neoclassical models, such as Kaldor–Mirrlees 1962, which by-pass the production function and postulate that the rate of growth of investment per capita in any period affects the rate of growth of labour productivity, do not treat technological progress as entirely exogenous but recognise the importance of one element of expenditure, namely investment expenditure, for determining the rate of technological progress. But even they do not explore the role of other types of expenditure, nor do they see the different components of technological change in their totality. They do not for instance ask the question how the stock of knowledge, the catalogue of possibilities open to an economy in any particular period of time, itself changes over time, why the 'technological progress function' has a

[1] For a discussion of technological progress in neoclassical growth models, see the section on technological progress in Hahn and Matthews 1964.

particular position (even granting its shape), and is neither higher nor lower.

In postulating, as we did above that the rate of growth of labour productivity was a specific function of the rate of growth of manufacturing output in the advanced economy, we simply carried over this tradition without asking what lies behind this function. Once we recognise the fact however that the pace of technological progress depends *inter alia* upon the magnitude of expenditure (relative say to the total output), not only investment expenditure, but also expenditure associated with the generation of new technologies and with imparting the necessary education and training for the absorption of new technologies (all of which, as distinct from investment expenditure, we shall henceforth designate broadly as innovation-promoting expenditure) which the advanced capitalist countries in the aggregate undertake over a certain period of time, it follows that a particular value of γ in our formal model can hold only for a particular value of innovation-promoting expenditure relative to total output in the metropolis. Our model then can be reinterpreted as having been hitherto based on the assumption of a certain fixed level of innovation-promoting expenditure relative to output in the metropolis.

The metropolis however does not act as a single integral unit in this matter. Indeed the mainspring behind technological progress is the competition between capitals, and especially in the modern context, competition between different national capitals within the metropolis. Technological progress is a weapon in the struggle between capitals of different countries, and not surprisingly, the State comes to play a major role in undertaking the expenditure needed for the generation of new technology.

To say that there is competition and rivalry for markets within the advanced capitalist world may at first sight appear to contradict our assumption earlier that owing to the availability of external markets, the capitalists of the metropolis as a whole are more or less assured of being able to sell their goods. But there is no contradiction between these two statements. For any particular advanced country, while a flight to the backward economies' markets is both possible as well as advantageous in the short-run for warding off domestic recession, over a prolonged period of time it is fraught with dangerous consequences. Not that particular advanced countries do not resort to such flights; indeed they do, and thereby stabilise not only their own economies but also those of the advanced capitalist world as a whole. Capitalism would have been a far less successful system, with far more bitter rivalries among leading economies, with far less investment drive, with lower growth rates than historically experienced, and hence with lower rates of growth in productivity and real wages, if this safety-valve of a 'flight' to backward economy markets did not exist, which particular capitalist countries, usually the leader among them at the time, could resort to at certain stages of their development. At the same time such 'flights' have been a prelude to the decline of the leading capitalist countries of the time that resorted to them, as we shall see in Chapter 10.

Thus both statements can be simultaneously correct and there is no necessary contradiction between them. Taking the advanced capitalist world as a whole, the fact that some countries which have fallen behind in the race for technological advance, especially for product innovations, have resorted to a flight to backward economy markets, has been a major factor behind their high rates of growth as well as stability. At the same time countries resorting to such flights have done so not out of a voluntary desire, but for a lack of alternative, because they have fallen behind in the race for product innovation. The intense competition among the advanced countries for product innovation, and thereby for capturing one another's markets, in no way therefore contradicts the proposition that the availability of external markets, by assuring them of foreign sales, has contributed to a high level of investment and growth in all of them taken together.

What are the disadvantages for any particular advanced country in falling behind in the race for innovations and in diverting sales to backward economy markets? Let us assume that there are three economies X, Y, and Z, of which two, X and Y, are advanced economies, and the third, Z, is a backward economy. All conform to our description of such economies in the previous chapter, except for one fact: the manufactured good produced in each is changing over time, but because X has fallen behind Y in product innovation, it is always the case that Y produces 'first preference' goods, X produces 'second preference' goods and Z produces 'third preference' goods. Let us assume that steady growth at a uniform rate is occurring everywhere with X and Y buying only the primary commodity from Z, but Z's manufactured good imports emanating solely from X, that trade is balanced for each country, and that exchange rates, to start with, are fixed. There are at least three respects in which a continuance of this state of affairs would make X's position more and more vulnerable in the long-run.

First, while X is producing neither a 'first preference' good nor any essential raw material, it is piling up debts to Y, which are matched by its own claims upon Z. But since Z happens to be the poorest economy, with unemployment and social instability, the risks associated with X's foreign portfolio, of assets and liabilities, are increasing over time. At some point pressure against X's currency will build up and X will be forced either to depreciate its currency which will trigger off domestic inflation, or to raise its domestic real interest rate to ward off such pressure, which will trigger off a domestic recession. Even if recession is avoided in the short-run by export surpluses to Z, this fact will only postpone the day of reckoning. Such export surpluses cannot continue for ever; and even assuming that domestic investment in X climbs back to its original path after a brief lapse of time, despite the higher interest rate, that will only bring X back to square one where speculative pressures against its currency will again rear their head after some time, pushing the interest rate still higher, and so on. In short, the continuance of the status quo is bound to be threatened.

Second, if there is a recession in X either because financial flows into it dry up, or because financial flows from it to Z dry up, or because there is a sudden decline of primary commodity prices for exogenous reasons, which is not offset in its impact by matching increases in net lending from X, in all such eventualities, while the economy of Y will remain unaffected, that of X will decline. The multiplier effects of any initial decline of demand in X will be felt exclusively by its own goods, rather than those manufactured by Y, precisely because its own goods are 'second preference' goods, while those of Y are 'first preference' goods. Thus between X and Y, X becomes far more vulnerable to fluctuations than Y by falling behind in the race for product innovations.

Third, sooner or later, Z too would begin to buy Y-goods rather than X-goods. On our assumptions so far it would appear that in such a situation X-goods will be sold in larger quantities on the X-market itself, since the pressure from Y-competition will be less on the home market of X as it increases on the foreign market. But goods are heterogeneous, and cannot be substituted for one another instantaneously. At the existing level in X there will be excess demand for the Y-goods withdrawn and excess supply of the X-goods released from the foreign market. Since excess supply can be liquidated (through output cuts) faster than excess demand, X will run into a crisis of overproduction.

The race for product innovation among the countries constituting the metropolis is a real one, notwithstanding the fact that external markets are available. This race consists not just in promoting R&D efforts to develop new products, but also in promoting the whole gamut of activities that lead to their successful marketing at the level of the world economy.

Not all the advanced capitalist countries constituting the metropolis, which are competing against one another, find it necessary to incur roughly identical amounts (in relative terms) of innovation-promoting expenditure. The USA for instance today spends a far larger amount on basic research than its rivals such as Japan, who nonetheless benefit from the results of such research.[2] But whatever be the pattern of distribution of innovation-promoting expenditure across the rival advanced capitalist countries, itself reflective of a specific conjuncture shaped historically, its aggregate amount among all of them is an important factor influencing the relationship between the rate of growth of output and the rate of growth of labour productivity in the metropolis as a whole.

2. ENTRY BARRIERS TO THE INNOVATORS' CLUB

But innovation-promoting expenditure, a flow item, is only one element. Its effectiveness in generating new products which can be absorbed into the production structure and successfully marketed at the level of the world economy depends upon the level of development of the productive forces themselves, upon a stock item for which we can take the capital stock per unit of the population of the country as a proxy. An identical relative level of flow expenditure on the promotion of innovations in two different countries would have quite different results if the already existing facilities of research and development, the levels of domestic skill development, the levels of

---

[2] The question of whether, despite the much larger expenditure on research undertaken in the USA, it could be successfully challenged by rival capitalist powers had been a much debated issue some years ago. See for instance Rowthorn 1971.

literacy and education in society, the levels of development of the financial infrastructure, and the levels of transport and communications development vary widely between them. A minimum infrastructure for product innovation destined for the world market must exist if flow expenditure on innovation promotion is to make a difference to the country's status as an innovator on the world economy.

In much of the Third World such a minimum infrastructure does not exist. Even in larger countries such as India and China where considerable skills and scientific manpower, and even a certain domestic R&D effort exists, the other conditions, such as the communications, transport, financial and marketing infrastructure are absent, so that even these countries are handicapped as product innovators for the world market. This does not mean that they cannot be successful in some (admittedly rare) particular lines as innovators, nor that they cannot carry out innovations by adapting existing commodities to their own specific requirements. But they are in no position to break into the handful of countries that set the pace in product innovations for the world market.

Furthermore, the ability to innovate in one line of production is dependent on the existence of a sophisticated production base in a number of complementary lines of production. For instance if a country is to emerge today as a successful innovator in the automobile industry, it must have a sophisticated production base in electronics, in metallurgical industries, and in precision engineering. Thus quite apart from the infrastructural requirements mentioned above, there is a minimum level of development of sophistication in the production base that a country must have in order to emerge as a successful innovator. And in this respect too, even the better placed countries like India and China face a handicap.

Many of these factors have complex cultural roots. Caste elitism in Indian society, for example, is a major cause of the low level of literacy that contributes to the absence of innovativeness. But the one broad economic index that captures these limitations is a low level of capital stock per capita. And backward economies are backward on this index, which makes it difficult for them to be successful innovators for the world market.

It may be thought at first sight that if capital accumulation exceeds the rate of population growth, since any particular level of minimum per capita capital stock is bound to be reached sooner or later, the handicap suffered by the backward economies is only a temporary one. This presumes however that this minimum remains constant through time. But the fact of innovations itself alters the preconditions for further innovations. The requirements for breaking into the world market as successful innovators themselves become more complex and sophisticated as ever newer goods appear on the scene, raising the minimum capital stock per capita that a country must have to emerge as an innovator. This point was made by Marx in his discussion of competition between capitals (Marx 1974, 262). But what Marx had to say on this holds equally well in the context of competition between capitalist countries. The sheer fact of capital accumulation therefore does not lower the barrier which the backward economies face as potential innovators for the world market.

The foregoing has important implications. The models presented in the earlier chapters had assumed unchanging production structures everywhere, and at the very least in the backward economy. This was too simplistic and did not answer the question: why can't the backward economy capitalists undertake the production of the manufactured good which is being imported? We can now look at the more complex picture.

The production structure in neither economy remains unchanged. The capitalists in the backward economy do undertake over a period of time the production of the manufactured goods currently being imported. But by the time they do so, the production structure in the advanced economy has also changed, as a result of which entirely new goods begin to get imported, so that the unfulfilled demand for imported goods continues. This would not happen if the backward economy capitalists were not just imitators but innovators of new products, if they did not just produce tomorrow what the advanced economy capitalists were producing today, but instead produced tomorrow something altogether new which could become the first preference good in the domestic market, and even perhaps internationally. Indeed given the fact that tastes and preferences within the Third World countries are shaped by the patterns of demand prevailing in the advanced countries (owing to a variety of complex reasons including in particular the long history of colonial and semi-colonial domination), for a domestically produced good to become the first preference good on the domestic market, it must have a degree of international acceptability. If the backward economy capitalists could become product innovators on the world market, then the basic contradictions highlighted in the previous chapter as facing such an economy would lose much of their force. But for reasons we have just discussed, this is not feasible. Consequently, notwithstanding changes in the production structure in both the economies, the world continues to remain one to which the model of the previous chapter provides a fair degree of approximation.[3]

From our dichotomy between the advanced and the backward economies and our emphasis on the constraints upon the latter as regards product innovation for the world market, it should not be concluded that the advanced countries constitute a homogeneous entity and are all equally successful as product innovators. They are not. Uneven development among them is one of the most fundamental facts of life under capitalism, but this is an aspect which does not concern us here. Our present interest is exclusively focused on the constraints on the backward economies. These constraints do not tell us anything about what precise degree of development the backward economies would be, or are capable of, experiencing (steady-state assumptions after all are only a device); but they do throw light on the basic dichotomy between the advanced and the backward countries.

3. A FALLING TENDENCY OF THE RATE OF PROFIT

In this section, we shall argue that there exists a tendency for a fall in the rate of profit in the advanced economies on grounds different from those which Marx had suggested. Marx based his argument on the proposition that while technological progress under capitalism tends to increase labour productivity it also raises the capital–output

---

[3] The foregoing is thus part of the justification for our assumption in the models of the last two chapters that capitalists in each economy invest only in the activities located in that economy, a location that is exclusive: the backward economy capitalists cannot invest in advanced manufacturing since for technological reasons they simply cannot break into it. They can no doubt become rentiers to the advanced economy, but if investment and consumption out of profits are sufficiently attractive relative to the returns which rentiers get, this would not be a large-scale general phenomenon (it could happen only in particular periods of crisis of confidence in the backward economy). The other part of the story, why advanced economy capitalists do not produce sophisticated manufactures in the backward economy, will be discussed in later chapters. (They do of course exist in primary production, but modifying our model to take account of it, as indeed of rentier investment by backward economy capitalists, makes little difference to our argument).

ratio. It followed from this that if the wage share in output remained unchanged the rate of profit must fall.[4] Marx's proposition about technological progress is analogous to what conventional theory (working in terms of production functions) would call 'capital-using' technological progress in Harrod's sense, where the capital–output ratio goes up for any given rate of profit. This was very different from the assumption of Harrod-neutrality which later came to characterise the description of technological progress in much of growth theory. Harrod-neutrality is compatible with a steady state, which Marx's assumption is not. But the reason for the assumption of Harrod-neutrality in the recent literature is supposed to be not just its compatibility with a steady state. It is claimed by many that there is an independent and plausible basis for it.

If the essence of technical progress, as Marx had said, consists in the substitution of dead labour for living labour, resulting in a cheapening of commodities, there is no reason why this cheapening should not also extend to machines, so that while in any particular instance the act of technological change raises the dead to living labour ratio, the net result of all such instances is that the ratio remains unchanged *ex post*. So if technological progress is happening everywhere, including in the capital goods sector, with uniform increases in labour productivity all around, then it must be of the Harrod-neutral kind. Not only is there no reason to believe the contrary, but, what is more, if the thrust of technological progress is always directed towards the laggard sectors, then, it is argued, there is some reason for believing that Harrod-neutrality may actually come to obtain. (The only rigorous demonstration which may be said in some sense to correspond to this heuristic argument, men-

---

4 Marx's specific postulates, namely that the organic composition of capital rises over time while the rate of surplus value remains unchanged, can be restated formally as entailing an increase in the capital–output ratio but a constancy in the share of wages in output; see Steindl 1952, ch. 14. We can picture the process however in two alternative ways: in a vertically integrated capitalist economy (one which produces its own raw material requirements), the rise in labour productivity through technological progress is associated with an increase in the ratio of fixed capital per unit of output; alternatively in a capitalist economy which purchases raw materials from outside, a rise in labour productivity is associated with an increase in the ratio of fixed capital to output (including the value of raw materials consumed) at given terms of trade and given physical raw material consumption per unit output. We shall use the latter concept; as in the previous chapters we shall use the term output including within it the raw material consumed and discuss the *ceteris paribus* implications of an·increase in the capital–output ratio always on the assumption that the terms of trade and the physical raw material per unit out remain unchanged.

tioned in Hahn and Matthews 1964, and which also brings out the stringent assumptions required is by Kennedy (1964).)

This belief however has no basis. In the context of the type of model we have been discussing (or Marx was for that matter) where we eschew the concept of a book of blueprints, Harrod-neutrality would require not only that labour productivity increases per unit of time be identical between the capital goods sector and the consumer goods sector, but in addition that the new capital goods (or machines) with which these labour productivity increases are obtained in the two sectors must have the same price ratios as the machines being used prior to the labour productivity increases. Now there is no reason to suppose *a priori* why this should necessarily obtain, any more than to suppose that technical progress would be capital-using or labour-using. In short, there is no theoretical basis for preferring one assumption over the others (Hahn and Matthews 1964). But since Harrod-neutrality has been widely used, and Kuznets' data have been adduced in empirical support of the fact that the capital–output ratio has remained roughly constant in a secular sense (one of the so-called 'stylised facts' about capital accumulation listed in Kaldor 1961), we have assumed throughout our discussion that all innovation whether involving processes or products has the effect of leaving the capital–output ratio unchanged and increasing the productivity of labour. Even so there would be a tendency for the rate of profit to fall for the following reason.

Each advanced country we have seen undertakes a certain amount of innovation-promoting expenditure relative to its output in order to be able to compete with its rivals. There is however no determinate limit in the long-run to what this expenditure will be for all of them taken together. The amount which each spends depends upon what the others are spending. There is no particular level therefore to which the expenditure of all of them taken together will be tethered, and the secular tendency will be for this expenditure relative to output to rise. Exactly the same can be said of the expenditure on the sales effort. What the capitalists belonging to any particular country spend on the sales effort depends upon what their rivals are doing. While this spending in the short-run would have a certain determinate limit for reasons of inertia, no such limit would exist in the long-run. The tendency in such a case would be for this expenditure relative to total output to increase secularly for all of them taken together.

Now it may be argued that a rise in the relative magnitude of innovation-promoting expenditure would, by our argument, also raise the rate of growth of productivity for a given rate of capital accumulation. But no matter what its effect upon productivity growth, it, together with the rise in the magnitude of sales expenditure relative to output, would have the effect of lowering the rate of profit as long as the share of wages is given. This is because per unit of capital stock, if the output is given (because the capital–output ratio *ex hypothesi* remains unchanged and the degree of capacity utilisation is at the desired level), and the share of wages is given (no matter what the rate of growth of productivity), then an increasing proportion of surplus value being spent on sales and innovation promotion must mean a declining rate of profit.

Such a decline would not actually manifest itself. Instead there would be accelerating inflation as the capitalists sought to protect themselves against such a decline, and the production workers, cheated *ex post* of the share they thought they were going to get, refused to yield on their *ex ante* wage claims. The falling tendency of the rate of profit, as in Marx, is not a predictive proposition, but an analytical building block.

Why then does the rate of profit not fall? Or more realistically, why does the tendency for such a fall not manifest itself in the form of accelerating inflation? Could it be that one of the postulates underlying our proposition does not hold? There are three basic postulates in our argument; let us examine each of these in turn. The first of these is that the capital–output ratio remains unchanged as labour productivity increases, a postulate which, as we have seen, is in conformity with a widely accepted 'stylised fact'. The second postulate is that there is a tendency for the proportion of output devoted to innovation and sales promotion expenditure to increase over time, on which there may be some doubt.

The evidence, however, is quite clear, though it has often been interpreted in an entirely different manner from ours. Baran and Sweezy (1966) for instance analysed the so-called 'sales effort' in detail and produced figures on the proportion of sales effort expenditure in the GNP of the United States. Though their figures showed an increase in this proportion over a long period, the increase was less pronounced than one might have expected. Our point however concerns not the proportion of such expenditure in the GNP, but its proportion in total output inclusive of raw material consumed, what

Marx had called $C+V+S$. If we do take this proportion, then since raw material costs in the gross value of output have been declining secularly (see below), the ratio of sales effort expenditure to $C+V+S$ must have been rising at a faster rate than Baran and Sweezy's figures suggest.

Innovation promoting expenditure is not easy to define. The expenditure incurred on R&D both within the State as well as within the private sector, a large part of what O'Connor (1973) calls 'social investment', and a part of defence expenditure which is devoted either directly to the development of exportable armaments, or has an indirect effect upon promoting technological progress in the non-armaments sector, would come under this rubric. The boundaries are not easy to delineate, but given the enormous increase in the share of State expenditure in the GNP of the capitalist world, and given that our concern is with the proportion of innovation-promoting expenditure in $C+V+S$, there can hardly be any doubt about the increase in the proportion of such expenditure as well. If we take innovation and sales promoting expenditure together, then our postulate that there is a secular tendency for its share to increase in total output would thus capture an important stylised fact.

It may be objected that the motive for much of the increase in State expenditure is not a narrowly commercial one, namely the need for product innovation on the world market. In the minds of those who argue for and decide upon such expenditures there are all kinds of other objectives, even though a conscious awareness of the commercial benefits comes through to a surprisingly larger extent than one would have otherwise thought. One only has to look at the panic-stricken calls within the USA to revamp the education system 'to meet the Japanese challenge', and calls by intellectuals like Lester Thurow to undertake substantial investment in technology development in certain frontier areas if the USA is to remain a major economic power in the next century, for proof that the narrowly commercial motive is never too far behind.[5] But our point has nothing to do with motives, rather with a 'minimum objective necessity' no matter how this percolates down to the level of consciousness. And the fact that expenditure strewn under several different heads, but contributing to the promotion of innovation, must rise as a

---

[5] Lester Thurow is reported to have identified seven such frontier areas, and asked for a substantial US effort under the aegis of the State.

proportion of output, constitutes for each advanced country, and hence for all of them taken together, such a minimum objective necessity.

We thus share the underconsumptionists' recognition of the significance of growing State expenditure and sales effort, but interpret them differently. The fact that State expenditure increased significantly over a certain period may not have anything to do with the need for realising surplus value. It was on the contrary necessary for the system that the State undertake growing expenditures to maintain the competitive strength of rival capitalist powers, especially in the post-war world where the scientific and technological revolution unleashed so far has had few parallels in the history of capitalism. Not all increases in State expenditure were functionally necessary; but a good part of them are likely to have been.

The third postulate is that the share of wages of the production workers in output remains unchanged. Now if it is taken merely as an *assumption*, then the falling tendency of the rate of profit clearly follows, and the negation of this assumption would constitute not a denial of this tendency, but merely a counteracting tendency. On the other hand, if we explore the *behaviour* of the wage share as an endogenised variable when the previous two postulates hold, then the falling tendency has to be established afresh, if at all, in the light of this *behaviour*. Let us see if it can be.

It can be argued that since a rise in the share of innovation promoting expenditure in output raises the rate of growth of labour productivity for any given rate of growth of output and since the rate of growth of output itself does not undergo any change as long as the profit share (determined by the mark-up) and capitalists' consumption behaviour remains unchanged, the net effect would be a lower rate of employment growth, and hence according to our argument, a larger unemployment rate. This would in the long-run lower the wage share of the production workers, so that the higher share of innovation-promoting expenditure could be accommodated in a new steady state by its own very consequences without any tendency for the rate of profit to decline and inflation to accelerate.

To get an idea of the plausible order of magnitude of this effect, whether a rise in the share of innovation-promoting expenditure can be self-accommodating in the long-run, we have to be a little more specific about the effect of a rise in this share upon the rate of productivity growth. In terms of the model we have been discussing so far this latter effect can be captured by making γ dependent on this share λ. Let us make three simple assumptions here. First, γ is inversely but linearly related to λ. Second, whatever the value of λ, the rate of growth of employment never becomes negative for any given rate of growth of output; third, whatever the value of λ, the rate of growth of productivity never becomes negative for any given rate of growth of output. Under these three fairly general assumptions it would always be the case that the spontaneous decline in the wage share of the production workers would be insufficient to accommodate the rise in the share of innovation-promoting expenditure in output that causes this decline in the long-run.[6] The latter in other words can never be self accommodating. And if so, then the falling tendency of the rate of profit stands.

The existence of a falling tendency of the rate of profit on account of our three postulates, and its manifestation in the form of accelerating inflation, is by no means a far-fetched hypothesis. If this has not materialised, the reason has to be sought in a specific counteracting tendency which again has to do with the coupling of the advanced economies with the backward ones.

4. TERMS-OF-TRADE MOVEMENT AS A COUNTERACTING TENDENCY

To see this let us first properly introduce the modifications (mentioned in footnote 6) into our model of the appendix to Chapter 7. Let the magnitude of innovation-promoting expenditure in the metropolis be denoted by E. We ignore sales-promoting expenditure,

---

[6] This can be seen as follows: if we take the effect of λ upon γ as being captured by the equation $\gamma = \delta - \theta\lambda$, with $0 \leq \lambda \leq 1$, our third assumption states that $\delta \leq 1$, and our second assumption states that $\theta \leq \delta$. Now, with λ being a cost item, it must be that for any given λ,

$$1/\mu - \lambda = p^a/p^m \left[\pi + (q - rm/n) + rg(\delta - \theta\lambda)/n \right] \qquad \text{(i)}$$

in the steady state (see the text which follows for the derivation). If λ is small (close to 0), since the l.h.s. is less than 1 (because $\mu > 1$), and since the term in square brackets is positive, it follows that $p^a/p^m(rg\delta/n) < 1$. Now, the condition for an increase in λ to be self-accommodating through a fall in the share of wages without violating our other ceteris paribus assumptions is that $p^a/p^m(rg\theta/n) \geq 1$, whose intuitive meaning is obvious: the l.h.s. which shows the sensitivity of the product wage to a unit change in λ across alternative steady states should be larger than one. But this condition can never hold because $\theta \leq \delta$ by our second assumption.

take E as a constant fraction λ of the value of output for the moment, take γ as a function of λ, and assume that this expenditure creates in physical terms a demand for the advanced country's manufactured good itself. We thus have two additional equations:

$$E_t = \lambda p_t^m O_t^m \qquad\qquad (xxxiii)$$

and

$$\gamma = f(\lambda), \qquad f' < 0, \qquad\qquad (xxxiv)$$

or, specifically,

$$\gamma = \delta - \theta\lambda,$$

with $\delta \leq 1$ and $\delta \geq \theta$ and modifications in two other equations:

$$p_t^m = \mu(w_t^m + \pi p_t^a + \lambda p_t^m), \qquad\qquad (ii')$$

which assumes for simplicity that this expenditure is a cost item.

$$O_t^m = i_t^m + c_2 P_t^m + \alpha K_t^m + dK_t^m + O_t^m l_t^m (w_t^m - \sigma_t p_t^a)/p_t^m + X_t + \lambda O_t^m$$
$$(xi')$$

Since two additional variables have been introduced, namely, E_t and γ, and two additional equations, our system of equations remains as complete as before. The steady-state configuration would now be altered in the following manner: the growth rate would remain the same, i.e.

$$g^* = \beta^m u_0(\mu - 1)(1 - c_2)/\mu - \alpha - d, \qquad\qquad (1')$$

though the unemployment rate associated with it would now depend upon λ as well, i.e.

$$v^* = m/n - (\delta - \theta\lambda)g^*/n, \qquad\qquad (2')$$

and so would the share of wages:

$$(\overline{w}^m l^m)^* = q - r[m/n - (\delta - \theta\lambda)g^*/n]. \qquad\qquad (3')$$

The ratio X/K^m would now be:

$$X/K^m = \beta^m u_0[1 - c_2(\mu - 1)/\mu - (\overline{w}^m l^m)^*(1 - \sigma)(p^a/p^m) - \lambda]$$
$$- \alpha - d - g^* \qquad\qquad (4')$$

and the terms of trade

$$(p^m/p^a)^* = \mu[\pi + (\overline{w}^m l^m)^*]/(1 - \mu\lambda). \qquad\qquad (5')$$

The sectoral output ratios O^r/O^a and O^m/O^a would now be:

$$O^r/O^a = \frac{(1-\xi^*)(P^a/O^a)^*(p^a/p^r)^* + l^a(p^a/p^r)^*(\overline{w}^{a*} - \phi)}{1 - (\overline{w}^r - \phi)l^r - (1-\xi^*)(\mu^r - 1)/\mu} \tag{10'}$$

$$O^m/O^a = \frac{1 - l^a\phi - (O^r/O^a)^*(\eta + \phi l^r)}{\pi + \sigma(\overline{w}^m l^m)^*}, \tag{11'}$$

which are formally the same as equations (10) and (11) of the last chapter except that the variables would now have somewhat different values because of the introduction of λ.

Thus, λ enters into the determination of the terms of trade. A higher level of λ would raise the ratio p^m/p^a for the following reason: while it would raise the steady-state rate of unemployment and hence lower the steady-state real wage which figures in the numerator, since this lower real wage share would be less than the rise in the share of innovation-promoting expenditure (see above), the terms of trade would move against the primary sector.

The only case where this would not happen is if the rise in the share of innovation-promoting expenditure has the effect of reducing the raw material requirement per unit of advanced country output to a sufficient extent (and not just raising labour productivity); but then of course there would be no tendency towards a falling rate of profit. Thus whenever there is a falling tendency for the rate of profit, there would be a shift in the terms of trade against the backward economy to prevent its realisation either as an actual fall in the rate of profit or as accelerating inflation. A *rising* λ likewise results neither in a *declining* rate of profit, nor in accelerating inflation following from it, but in a *declining* tendency in the terms of trade for the backward economy.

But whether the falling tendency of the rate of profit is checked by falling raw material requirement per unit output or by declining terms of trade for the primary commodity, in either case the rate of growth of the backward economy keeps slowing down, as we shall discuss later. Moreover, if the terms of trade move against the backward economy, the real wages of the primary sector workers are correspondingly squeezed. Thus, the counteracting tendency against the falling tendency of the rate of profit in the advanced economy is provided by a squeeze on the primary sector workers' real wages.

This does not of course mean that these workers become progressively worse off in absolute terms. Their real wages fall relative to their productivity. To complete our discussion let us introduce productivity growth into the backward economy.

Little can be said *a priori* about the rate of productivity growth in the primary producing sector. Though, as we shall see, the level of innovation-linked expenditure in the advanced country has a bearing upon it, suggesting any kind of a deterministic relationship between the two would clearly be unreal. As regards the backward economy's manufacturing sector, since by and large it produces commodities which have been produced earlier in the advanced economy, and using the same methods of production, its rate of growth of productivity would depend *inter alia* upon the rate of accumulation in this sector and the rate of productivity growth in the advanced economy. We shall investigate this further in Chapter 12; for the time being however we shall simply assume that in each sector of the economy the rate of productivity growth is a constant autonomous magnitude.

Likewise how exactly real wages would move when productivity increases is not easy to formulate. At one extreme is the Lewis-type assumption (1954) that real wages would remain unchanged as long as there is surplus labour. At the other extreme one can assume that the workers' wage claims keep pace with productivity increases, though at any given level of productivity these claims depend upon considerations such as we discussed in the last chapter. Though in reality we are likely to encounter a situation which lies between these two extremes, in order to keep the analysis tractable, we shall make the latter assumption on wage claims. Thus:

$$l_{t+1}^a = l_t^a / (1 + g_t^{p^a}) \qquad\qquad (xxxv)$$

for all t, and

$$l_{t+1}^r = l_t^r / (1 + g_t^{p^r}) \qquad\qquad (xxxvi)$$

for all t.

The wage claim equations would now be:

$$w_t^a l_t^a = p_t^{ae} [\overline{w}_{t-1}^a l_{t-1}^a - y(\overline{w}_{t-1}^a l_{t-1}^a - \hat{w}_t)], \qquad\qquad (xxviii')$$

where

$$\hat{w}_t = \sum_{t-1}^{T} \overline{w}_\tau^a l_\tau^a$$

and

$$w_t^r l_t^r = p_t^{ae} \overline{w}^r. \qquad\qquad\qquad (xxx')$$

Now moreover we shall take ϕ to be time-dependent:

$$\phi_t^a = \phi w_t^a / p_t^{ae} \qquad\qquad\qquad (xxxvii)$$

$$\phi_t^r = \phi w_t^r / p_t^{ae} \qquad\qquad\qquad (xxxviii)$$

as a result of which we have to have some modifications:

$$O_t^a = M_t + O_t^a l_t^a \phi_t^a + O_t^r l_t^r \phi_t^r + \eta O_t^r \qquad\qquad (xviii')$$

$$O_t^r p_t^r = O_t^a l_t^a (w_t^a - p_t^a \phi_t^a) + O_t^r l_t^r (w_t^r - p_t^a \phi_t^r) + (1 - \xi_t) p_t^m X_t / \xi_t \qquad (xxi')$$

Once again the system can be seen to be complete once $g_t^{pa}, g_t^{pr}, \hat{w}_p$ l_t^a, and l_t^r are known. That a steady-state path with constant growth and inflation rates exists can be easily checked. But the important point is that the tendency towards a falling rate of profit in the metropolis can be checked, with a given π, through shifting terms of trade against the backward economy which lowers its growth rate causing uneven development between the two segments of the world economy, and which keeps lowering the real wages relative to productivity in this segment.

5. CONCEPTUAL ISSUES RELATING TO THE TERMS OF TRADE

The fact that there has been a secular decline in the value of raw material inputs in the gross value of industrial production in the advanced economies is well-known (empirical information on this is contained in Chapter 12). In the absence of such a decline, the rise in sales and innovation-promoting expenditure would have been impossible because of the tremendous inflationary pressures it would have generated. But how was this decline in the share of raw materials in the gross value of industrial output achieved? The fact that this sharp and secular decline was not accompanied by any similar decline in the terms of trade for primary commodities, no matter what view one takes about their secular movement, may give rise to the impression that capitalism has achieved a secular decline in the technologically required raw material input per unit of output, that technological progress has indeed taken the form of a decline in π.

That this view is widely held is undeniable. It is even adduced often as an argument against any theory of the necessity of imperialism for advanced capitalist countries. If, thanks to Keynesian demand management, the need for external markets is obviated, and if, in addition, it is also the case that raw material requirements per unit of gross industrial output have been dwindling to a point where they are already quite remarkably low, then surely, so the argument runs, those who talk about an imperialist system in contemporary capitalism are barking up the wrong tree. Harry Magdoff (1969) has already criticised this view forcefully: the fact that raw material requirement per unit of gross manufacturing output has been declining does not mean that the manufacturing sector of the world, located in the advanced capitalist economies, can do away with raw materials altogether; they are still needed as essential components of manufacturing and the need for controlling the sources of raw materials continues to be a very real one.

In addition, however, implicit in this view about the dwindling significance of raw materials is a confusion between what Marx called 'use value' and 'exchange value'. All manufacturing eventually amounts to a processing of raw materials with the application of labour, supplemented by instruments of production such as machinery and equipment, for turning out products of final use. One can in the process of manufacturing replace one kind of raw material by another, but raw materials as a use value do not diminish in significance. In any given line of production using any particular raw material, the physical amount of it needed per physical unit of the manufactured product can be brought down somewhat, by eliminating waste and inefficiency. But there is a strict limit to it: one cannot manufacture steel without using iron to a certain irreducible minimum extent, nor can one manufacture copper wire of a certain length and thickness without using an irreducible minimum amount of copper. What technical progress has primarily achieved therefore is not reductions of this sort, which are strictly limited, but rather a substitution of one kind of raw material for another, new raw materials for old ones, less used raw materials for more extensively used ones, a process that goes hand in hand with the process of product innovation. The declining value of raw material per unit of gross value of manufacturing therefore entails a comparison across different kinds of raw materials, and takes us to the realm of exchange value.

Suppose $100 of copper was needed for producing a unit of a commodity, but because of technical progress only $40 of some other material becomes sufficient to produce a unit of the same commodity, or some other commodity of the same value which the consumers of the former now shift to. The raw material component in the value of the manufactured output has gone down. But this is not because there has been any physical saving of raw materials, any reduction in the consumption of raw materials seen as a use-value: if the $100 of copper used earlier represented X tonnes, while the $40 of the new material represents only X lbs., that still does not amount to any raw material saving, since one use-value cannot be directly compared to another.

Why do X lbs. of the new material not have the value of $100 which, in the form of X tonnes of copper, they are replacing? Because the amount of labour needed to produce X lbs. of the new material is less than what was needed to produce X tonnes of copper, while the wage rate of the former has not gone up *pari passu*. What has happened is that the productivity of labour in terms of the value equivalent that its product replaces has gone up while its real wages have not gone up correspondingly. It is mainly this which explains why the raw material component in the gross value of manufactured output has come down.

Formally this case is no different from the one in which the productivity of the copper workers itself goes up, without a change in their real wages, and without involving any product innovation or raw material substitution. If an increase in the productivity of copper workers, not accompanied by any increase in their wages, brings down copper prices to a level where $40 of copper are now enough to produce a unit of the final commodity (we are assuming in both cases that the final commodity price remaining unchanged, the larger 'value added' is matched by a correspondingly larger expenditure on the commodity), then too we would find a reduction in the weight of the raw material in the gross value of manufacturing output.

But while the two cases are formally identical, each involving an increase in labour productivity in the raw material sector (defined slightly differently for the two cases), without a corresponding increase in real wages, they are different in two practically significant ways. First, the advanced country is more likely to induce productivity growth in the form of product innovation in the raw material sector, in keeping with its own product innovation, than in the form of process innovation increasing the rate of productivity growth in the production of some already widely used raw material. This is partly because of its own interest in its own product innovation, of which the productivity growth in the backward economy in the first case is a mere fall-out, and partly because process innovations have got to be 'sold' to backward economy capitalists (by those in the advanced economy for whom they constitute product innovation), while the demand for new raw materials transmits itself through market signals and brings forth, almost automatically, an increase in labour productivity relative to wages.

Second, when productivity growth takes the form of product innovation in the raw material sector (or the form of expanding hitherto less important raw materials in lieu of more established ones) without an increase in real wages *pari passu*, it is unlikely to manifest itself statistically as a decline in the terms of trade for the backward economy. Suppose in other words ten raw materials are being exported in a particular period. If productivity increased in any one of them without a corresponding rise in real wages, resulting in a relative cheapening of it, this fact would get picked up immediately in an index of terms of trade based on these ten commodities. But if an altogether new raw material gets demanded and hence produced, costing much less than the equivalent amount of some other raw material it replaces, this would certainly not get picked up in any price index, and hence in any terms-of-trade index.

This is not a question of Laspeyre versus Paasche. No price index can pick up such an implicit movement in the terms of trade against the primary producing sector. This remains true even if we are not talking about an altogether new raw material. Suppose all prices and wages remain unchanged, and there are only these ten raw materials. And suppose product innovation in the advanced country is such that $400 worth of some existing final good which needed $100 worth of one of these ten raw materials, are replaced by $400 worth of some new good requiring only $40 worth of another of these ten raw materials. There is an implicit worsening of the terms of trade for the backward country, but no index will pick this up.[7]

---

[7] I literally mean *no* conventional terms of trade index. The fact that no barter terms of trade index is conceptually adequate to capture the more inclusive notion of the terms of trade we have been discussing is obvious from the example given in the text. Even the double factorial terms of trade, insofar as they are derived by using

This suggests that the concepts we have hitherto been using in economic theory, and the measures we have adopted, for analysing the relationship between advanced and backward economies, are far from adequate. The concepts and measures, both of labour productivity in the production of primary commodities, and of terms of trade, have to be far more inclusive than has been the case in order to capture this relationship in its totality.

In fact, the strongest evidence for it comes precisely from the very fact that critics use for discrediting theories of imperialism, namely the decline in the raw material component in the total gross value of manufacturing output in the advanced capitalist economies. This makes it clear that we are confronting a major conceptual hurdle. It can even be argued that compared to the usual terms-of-trade measures, the proportion of primary commodity value in the gross value of manufacturing output provides a better index of terms-of-trade movements in an inclusive sense (see fn. 7), so that what is commonly adduced as a negation of imperialism is in fact its strongest confirmation. If the primary sector workers had been organised enough to ensure that their real wages moved up with productivity in the sense of the raw material equivalent they replaced, then the secular decline in the weight of primary commodities in gross manufactured output would not have taken place, and certainly not to the same extent.

---

ratios of productivity which are calculated on the basis of given production bundles, are inadequate for our purpose. It may be thought that income terms of trade would capture any worsening of primary producers in the periphery since they measure the command over manufactured goods. But they have three obvious limitations. First, they measure absolute command over manufactured goods while what is relevant is the relative command, i.e. command over manufactured goods as a proportion of manufactured goods output. Second a lowering of π would *ceteris paribus* reduce income terms of trade for primary producers, while theoretically we have been distinguishing between a lowering of π and a worsening of the terms of trade. Third, in an exactly analogous fashion, a lowering of σ would worsen the income terms of trade, though this is not our conception of a terms of trade change (σ it should be noted does not enter eqn. 5′). Within the assumptions of our model, i.e. that primary production is exclusively undertaken in the periphery (so that the question of shifts in its location did not arise), an appropriate terms of trade index would be one which measures the primary producers' command over manufactures as a proportion of the latter's output, corrected for physical raw material saving per unit output and shifts in final consumer demand away from the primary commodities. If this physical saving in raw material is ignored as being small, a proxy for such an index would simply be the value of the primary products used in productive consumption divided by the value of manufactured good output inclusive of it.

To sum up, the rising share of sales and innovation promoting expenditure in gross output (without deducting raw materials consumed) in the advanced capitalist economies, which would otherwise have created severe inflationary pressures, has not done so because the value of primary commodities in the gross value of output has declined. This is because primary sector workers have not been able to raise their wages in keeping with their value productivity (the value of the raw materials they substitute for in the innovation process). This amounts to an implicit movement in the terms of trade against the backward economies, which the commonly used indices are intrinsically incapable of capturing.

6. THE CAUSES OF UNEVEN DEVELOPMENT

We mentioned earlier that declining weight of primary products in the gross value of the manufactured output in the advanced economy, which results from a rising λ, has the effect of slowing down the rate of growth of the backward economy for a given rate of growth of the advanced economy. Let us look at this proposition a little more closely. In what follows we shall abstract from productivity growth in the backward economy in order to be able to use the steady-state conditions (10′) and (11′) developed above; the argument however remains unaffected even if productivity growth in the backward economy is introduced.

The proposition regarding the slowing down of the growth rate in the backward economy is quite general. It is independent of whether it is π which is declining or p^a/p^m.

Consider a once-for-all increase in λ. Let us suppose π falls sufficiently to leave p^a/p^m unchanged; then it is obvious from the steady-state conditions (10′) that O^r/O^a will remain unchanged since all the terms figuring in it remain unchanged. As regards O^m/O^a, while the numerator remains unchanged, the two terms in square brackets in the denominator move in a downward direction. A larger λ, by increasing productivity growth in the advanced country, and hence requiring a lower rate of immigration, would entail a higher rate of unemployment and hence a lower share of wages, and a lower demand for the primary commodity for workers' consumption. On the other hand, *ex hypothesi* it means a lower π. It follows therefore that O^m/O^a rises, which means that for a given O^m, both O^a and O^r

will be lower along a steady-state path with a higher λ. Since the effect of a rising λ can be analysed in terms of a series of transitions from one steady-state path to another, and yet another, it follows that for a given rate of growth of the advanced economy the rate of growth of the backward economy will keep slowing down as λ keeps increasing.

Now suppose π remains unchanged as λ rises, so that the terms of trade move against the primary commodity. From (10′) O^r/O^a falls, because $\bar{w}^a$ falls; as regards O^m/O^a, again there are two mutually reinforcing effects. As before the advanced country workers' consumption of the primary commodity will be lower; in addition, there would be a reduced demand for the primary commodity arising from the decline in the backward economy's manufacturing sector. It follows then that the steady-state path associated with a higher λ will have a lower level of backward economy output, in both its sectors, for a given output of the advanced economy. A rising λ therefore will entail a slowing down of the rate of growth of the backward economy for a given growth rate of the advanced economy.

Uneven development between the advanced and the backward economies results not only from a rising λ, but for an even more powerful reason, which is widely discussed in the literature, namely the changing consumption demand away from primary commodities, as incomes increase in the advanced countries. In terms of our model this can be interpreted in terms of a decline in σ. While such a decline has no effect on the terms of trade within our assumptions, since σ does not figure in our condition (5′) above, it lowers exports from the advanced economy and imports into it; this, as condition (11′) shows, raises the ratio O^m/O^a. A declining σ therefore has the effect of slowing down the rate of growth of the backward economy for a given rate of growth of the advanced economy.

Our model thus arrives at the same conclusion as Seers (1962) and others, but through a somewhat different route.[8] In practice the switch away from primary commodities in the consumer demand of the advanced countries is not just towards manufactured goods, but also, and more importantly, towards services. But this in no way affects the basic argument. Quite apart from the fact that the advanced countries' growth rate would be higher on account of the inclusion of services, even if services are excluded from output and

---

[8] For a recent theoretical model of uneven development, see Dutt 1988.

all payments for services are simply treated as transfer payments, if taking just primary commodities and manufactures we find the share of the former coming down in total consumer demand as incomes increase, the argument stated above holds exactly in its present form.

Thus, changes in both technology as well as consumer demand in the advanced countries tend to produce over time uneven development between them and the backward economies. The question however arises: if the effect of changing technology and tastes is to reduce the weight of the primary commodity in the economy of the advanced country, then how can the cushion provided by the compressible wages of the workers producing this commodity continue to play the role of a stabiliser for the advanced economy? Doesn't the very squeeze on the primary sector workers, if secularly applied, lose its significance beyond a point? This question will be discussed in the next chapter.

9

A Critical Review of the
Argument So Far

The argument presented over the last three chapters has two distinct strands. First, in a capitalist economy where organised workers and organised capital both seek to enforce *ex ante* claims upon output which are rigidly sustained, the stability of the system at high rates of growth is achieved at the expense of the unorganised workers who also nourish capital and who lack the ability to enforce any rigid *ex ante* claims by virtue of their lack of organisation. These workers are typically located in the outlying regions so that social stability in the metropolis is not threatened. Second, any parametric shift which raises either the *ex ante* wage-share in the metropolis or the *ex ante* claims for surplus value (such as the need for higher shares of innovation and sales-promoting expenditure) gets resolved through a lowering of the real wages relative to productivity of the unorganised workers via an adverse terms-of-trade shift against the commodities which they produce. This together with shifts in consumer demand away from these commodities in the metropolis is the cause of uneven development on the global scale.

1. PRIMARY PRODUCTION AT THE CORE AND THE PERIPHERY: THE CONTEXT

Two obvious objections can be raised against this argument. The first is that primary production is far from being confined to the periphery as we have assumed in our theoretical presentation. The identification of a worsening terms of trade for primary products with a squeeze on the workers in the periphery therefore, though valid, is only part of the story. The workers in the metropolis engaged in primary production would also witness a decline in product wages relative to productivity in the event of an adverse terms-of-trade shift; how then can we talk of such an adverse shift providing a mechanism for economic and social stability under capitalism?

The answer to this is that typically the decline in product wages relative to productivity of *all* primary producing workers which occurs in the event of an adverse terms-of-trade shift, impinges in a *dissimilar* manner upon the two sets of primary producing workers: those in the metropolis and those in the periphery. For the latter it is wages which fall while the profile of productivity remains unchanged; for the former it is productivity which rises while wages *more or less* retain their relative position *vis-à-vis* those of manufacturing workers. Perhaps this is an extreme statement, but the fact remains that in the periphery the adjustment is of wages while in the metropolis the adjustment is also in productivity.

There are three mechanisms through which such productivity adjustments could come about. The first, based on Kaldor (1968), presupposes the existence of labour reserves in the advanced economy's primary sector as well, where self-employed petty producers constitute a sizeable segment. If the manufacturing workers, who are organised, demand higher wages relative to their productivity on account of an increase in their trade union strength, the capitalists in that sector would pass on the higher wages in the form of higher prices. The higher manufactured goods prices would squeeze out some of the disguised unemployed from primary production without any adverse consequences for output and thereby raise labour productivity in that sector. The labour reserves so squeezed out of the primary sector, however, get absorbed into the manufacturing sector in time, so that the final result is an overall increase in the economy's productivity with nobody made worse off in the long-run by the higher wage demands of the manufacturing workers.[1] By contrast the same increase in the manufactured goods prices has the effect of squeezing the workers in the periphery through lower wages because they have nowhere else to go.

The second mechanism assumes that the workers in the primary

---

[1] The using-up of internal labour reserves existing in the primary sector during the period of post-war growth was highlighted by Kindleberger (1967).

sector in the metropolis are also organised, and works through the diffusion of primary production to the periphery. Again taking the previous example, suppose with the rise in the manufacturing sector's wages and prices, the primary sector workers, who too are organised, demand and obtain higher wages to maintain their wage relative to that of the manufacturing workers. Since the capitalists in the primary sector cannot pass on their higher wages, as they compete with the periphery's primary sector, their profit margin will be squeezed. This would mean a closure of low-productivity units in this sector, the lay-off of workers who are absorbed in time into manufacturing, a reduction in the primary sector's output that has to be eventually made up by an appropriate expansion of the periphery's primary sector, and a rise in the average labour productivity in this sector owing to this shake-out.

That there is a tendency for such a diffusion in some cases is undeniable (see Magdoff 1969, 47 on the diffusion of mineral production away from the USA). But to insist that it necessarily occurs in the aggregate is unrealistic. The third mechanism assumes that the workers in the primary sector in the metropolis are organised and yet does not entail a steady diffusion of primary production to the periphery. If the rate of growth of labour productivity in this sector in the metropolis is inversely related to the profit rate, then in the event of the manufacturing sector's wages and prices rising and the primary sector workers demanding and obtaining higher wages to maintain parity, the primary sector capitalists introduce technological progress at a pace which eventually leaves their share of primary production and their rate of profit intact. Workers released from this sector are absorbed in time into manufacturing.[2]

2 Indeed if we assume that the capitalists in this sector invest all their savings in this sector, that the rate of growth of labour productivity relative to the rate of growth of output is higher than the corresponding ratio for the manufacturing sector whenever the rate of profit is lower than in manufacturing, and lower when the rate of profit is higher, and that the rate of growth of the work-force in the metropolitan economy is inversely related to the unemployment rate prevailing in this economy as a whole (including both sectors), then the existence of a steady-growth–steady-inflation path can be demonstrated along which the wage-relativities in the core, the distribution of primary production between the core and the periphery, and the rate of profit in the core (identical between the two sectors) remain constant. (What determines the steady-state distribution of primary output between the core and the periphery of course has to be additionally specified). An adverse shift in the terms of trade, say on account of a larger share of State expenditure, lowers the product wages relative to productivity of all primary producing workers, but in one case through a rise in productivity across steady states and in the other case through a decline in wages.

The assumption of the pace of technological progress being influenced by the profit rate is by no means a far-fetched one for at least two reasons. Large sections of primary sector workers tend to be reluctant to move out of their traditional occupations and would permit the introduction of more labour-saving technology only under the compelling circumstances of a decline in the average rate of profit which threatens jobs *en masse*. Second, the governments in the advanced economies act to preserve primary production and are likely to encourage more rapid technological change in the face of a threatened diffusion of such activities away to the periphery.

No matter what mechanism we invoke—and they may all have played their roles—it follows from the above that the existence of labour reserves in the periphery is responsible for making primary product prices play the role of a shock-absorber-cum-stabiliser for capitalism even when primary production is *not undertaken exclusively in the periphery itself*. As long as primary product prices, no matter where the production takes place, move up or down together, the existence of these labour reserves ensure that they play a stabilising role for capitalism.[3] The argument that since the underdeveloped countries produce only a part of the total primary product requirements of the capitalist world, their labour reserves are of little consequence in imparting stability to the system is therefore invalid.

2. THE DECLINING ROLE OF PRIMARY PRODUCERS: IMMIGRANT WORKERS AS A NEW PROP

A second objection could be the following. No matter how primary production is distributed between the core and the periphery, if the secular tendency is for their weight to decline relative to the value of manufactured goods output, for reasons we have discussed, then surely the stabilising role of the primary producers of the periphery gets progressively attenuated over time. The processes we have discussed earlier are surely inherently self-limiting. To believe that when the relative value of the primary products used has already dwindled considerably, it can still play the role of a stabiliser-cum-

---

[3] The existence of price-support policies for agriculture in many core countries insulates to an extent their own prices from the world price movements, but the insulation is never complete. See Beckerman and Jenkinson 1986.

shock-absorber is like believing that the tail can stabilise the dog. How does this affect the argument put forward so far?

The scope of this criticism should not be misunderstood. It does not rob the argument either of logical validity or of historical relevance;[4] indeed the self-limiting nature of our argument is implicit in the argument itself: its very validity reduces its scope over time. So this criticism is really not a criticism. What it points to is the need to examine what *new props capitalism can find for stabilising itself*. And some of these are examined in the rest of the present chapter.

The first of these is the creation of a dichotomy within the workforce directly employed by capital in the metropolis. This is but an extension of the dichotomy between the workers in the metropolis and those in the outlying regions that we have been discussing. This latter division begins to be imported into the metropolis itself. Output-cum-price stability is achieved at the expense not only of the workers in the outlying regions but also a section of the domestic workers. Increases in the *ex ante* claims for surplus value are accommodated through a squeeze on the wage rate per efficiency unit not only of the workers employed in the outlying regions to subserve the needs of metropolitan capital but also of the workers directly employed by it within the metropolis itself.

The creation of this dichotomy on the home front presupposes the existence of large labour reserves which is essential for keeping this section of domestic workers unorganised, but these labour reserves do not have to be located within the metropolis itself. In effect if at least some of the same workers who nourished capital when located in the outlying regions and who had the disadvantage of being surrounded by large labour reserves are physically shifted to the metropolis to serve the needs of capital directly there, then they would continue to fulfil the same function within the metropolis as their fellow workers in the periphery. The classic case of producing this internal dichotomy is through the employment of immigrant workers not on a par with domestic nationals but as a sub-proletariat.

In our theoretical discussion so far while have recognised that labour supply under capitalism adjusts to demand through migration

---

4 The fact that adverse terms of trade shifts against the primary producers were a major factor underlying the price-stability achieved at the capitalist core in the latter part of the nineteenth century is noted by Bagchi (1979); even as late as the 1980s the scope for this mode of price-stabilisation had not been exhausted according to Beckerman and Jenkinson (1986).

of various kinds, we have always assumed that within the metropolis there is no segmentation among workers. All workers, no matter what their origins, stand on a par *vis-à-vis* capital and have pay differentials which are only such as to compensate for skill differentials. It is this assumption which becomes progressively untenable as capitalism develops a new prop for stabilising itself through the recruitment of a segment of underpaid workers.

Three caveats are in order here. First, it is no part of our argument that these underpaid workers obtain real wages which are identical with, or not much higher than, the real wages of the workers in the backward economies from where they are recruited. On the contrary, their wages may be considerably higher than those prevailing in the places of their origin, and usually are. But this fact still does not prevent their acting as a cushion against the instability of capitalism.

Second, the fact of their being underpaid does not necessarily mean that they get less *for the same work* than the native workers of the metropolis. They move into underpaid jobs as the previously employed native workers in these jobs move up into better-paid occupations. But they are underpaid in the sense that if the previously employed native workers in these jobs, who are of a comparable level of skill or the lack of it, had not moved into better-paid occupations but had continued in these very occupations, then they would have demanded and obtained higher wages than the immigrants. So the underpayment does not necessarily constitute an example of visible discrimination.

Third, it is also not essential to our argument that the proportionate gap between the average wage of the native workers and that of any particular group of immigrant workers should increase over time, assuming identical productivity growth everywhere. Even if every particular group of employed workers witnesses real wage increases in tandem with productivity growth over time, but the 'floor' wages at which fresh immigrants are recruited (into the lowest-rung jobs) do not increase *pari passu* with the average productivity growth in the economy, the rate of surplus value will still increase and this may be quite enough to accommodate the increasing *ex ante* claims for surplus value.

Such a state of affairs is sustainable only if the jobs into which the fresh immigrants come are not within the ambit of unionisation which enforces floor real wages that move up with productivity over time. With time and experience they may move into better-paid jobs and become part of the unionised work-force, obtaining wage increases in tandem with productivity increases (in which case there would be a dichotomy within the immigrants). But the workers in low-rung jobs remain unorganised or insufficiently organised. It is not even necessary that there should be a particularly high incidence of unemployment within the metropolis itself among the workers vying for such jobs. There are for a start important cultural barriers to any attempts by the existing unions to organise fresh-immigrant workers. Moreover given the existence of large labour reserves in their places of origin, these workers are easily cowed down by the possibility of deportation which remains a perpetual threat for them owing to the activities and demands of right-wing political groups.

Without invoking any conspiracy theory one can still see the connection between the politics of such groups (as long as it remains a 'fringe politics' or, as Kalecki (1972) put it, 'a dog on the leash') and the stability of 'liberal capitalism'. A cushion is provided against price instability and the need for a higher share of surplus value is met without engendering accelerating inflation, even as the unemployment rate is kept within bounds, by having a section of domestic workers that is sufficiently cowed to play the same role of shock absorbers as the workers in the periphery. What is more, these workers, despite the fear of attacks from right-wing groups and despite receiving low or declining real wages per efficiency unit, are far from dissatisfied with their situation which compares so favourably with what they left behind back home.

Underlying this happy state of stability, however, is the existence of large labour reserves, located of course at a respectable distance. These labour reserves underlie not only the basic dichotomy between the advanced and the backward economies, but also the internal dichotomy within the advanced economy workers. It may be argued that wage differentials between the metropolis and the periphery would have pulled immigrant workers into the former, and created an internal dichotomy within it, whether or not there are large labour reserves in the latter. But the width of the wage differentials themselves is not independent of the large labour reserves (a matter we discuss later). Besides it is not just the lure of a better wage that overcomes for the immigrant worker the pain of leaving his native land, but the complete absence of hope for a better future that becomes so endemic a part of his life back home. And this absence of hope has to do with the state of unemployment, poverty and social turmoil prevalent there.

3. CAPITAL MIGRATION AS AN ALTERNATIVE PROP

The second kind of possible new prop is in a sense the mirror image of the first. Instead of recruiting workers from the periphery to form an internal pool of unorganised workers under its direct employment, capital can move out from the metropolis to the periphery to employ workers there at real wage levels below what prevails within the metropolis. If the first case, discussed above, represents a stretching of the periphery into the metropolis, this second case represents a stretching of the metropolis into the periphery. Either kind of stretching, seen as a process, is *ipso facto* a process of increasing the share of surplus value in the total output produced under the aegis of metropolitan capital (or what we have called the 'manufacturing sector' in the models of the earlier chapters). It accommodates therefore the higher claims for surplus value in the metropolis (on account *inter alia* of the increasing share of innovation and sales promoting expenditure) without engendering accelerating inflation. And it acts in the direction of stabilising capitalism by keeping under its direct employment a pool of workers whose wage claims are not rigid either because they are not organised enough, or because metropolitan capital can always move to fresh areas where unorganised workers are available for employment.

The caveats mentioned for the earlier case apply equally to the current case. The wages of the workers of the periphery who are under the direct employment of metropolitan capital are not necessarily identical with the wages of the other workers in the periphery. On the contrary, they *are* much higher, though lower than those of workers of comparable skills in the metropolis itself. Likewise it is not necessarily the case that the proportionate gap between the wages of any such group of workers and those of comparable workers in the metropolis must widen over time. It may, but even if it does not, the fact of direct investment by metropolitan capital in the periphery can still provide the necessary cushion for stabilising capitalism. By either changing the proportion between home and foreign investment or moving to ever newer areas and recruiting fresh workers at lower wages it can always ensure that the time profile of the average wage rate it offers is below that of the average productivity of all workers employed by it, to the requisite extent.

The two cases discussed above, while similar in enough respects that they appear to be mirror images of one another, nonetheless differ significantly. In the case of an internal dichotomy within the metropolis, no matter how large the wage differential between the two categories of workers, the unions can still prevent the substitution of low-wage unorganised workers for the higher wage organised ones (of comparable skills). The relative weights of the two categories of workers is not necessarily altered by the size of the wage differential. As a result it is the size of the wage differential alone that is the stabilising mechanism. But in the second case, there are two quite distinct mechanisms. For any given wage differential the relative weights of the two categories of workers can be altered for stability. Additionally the wage differential itself may widen for given relative weights of the two categories of workers by employing fresh workers in the periphery at lower wages. So the stabilising mechanism in the first case operates through the wage differential while in the second case there is an *additional* mechanism that operates through the relative weights of the two categories of workers. The appendix to this chapter presents two models corresponding to our two cases; it focuses on this additional mechanism alone in the second case to highlight the distinction between the two cases, and also clarifies the entire argument.

The belief that capital from the metropolis would move into the lower wage periphery in quest of a higher profit rate has long been entertained in economics and has been as consistently proved to be false (except as a marginal phenomenon). This belief characterises the writings not only of neoclassical economists who postulate 'factor mobility' (at least capital mobility) and profit-maximising behaviour, but also of many Marxist economists. They see capital exports in this sense as overcoming the falling tendency of the rate of profit in the metropolis, whether this fall is due to the reasons given by Marx or due to the using up of labour reserves within the metropolis (Dobb 1940). Yet historically metropolitan direct investment in the periphery has been of limited significance. More recently this argument has been resurrected in the writings of authors as diverse as product cycle theorists like Vernon (1966) on the one hand and the Starnberg group (F. Froebel *et al.* 1980) on the other. It has now even become the official orthodoxy of agencies like the IMF and the World Bank who prescribe their particular brand of 'structural adjustment' to Third World countries on the grounds that by pursuing it they would be able to attract foreign investment on a scale that would overcome their backwardness. Capital, it is claimed, is no longer region specific in its location. It sees the whole world as its theatre of operation and can locate itself anywhere. It follows from this that the basic cause for the perpetuation of an international dichotomy between advanced and backward economies lies in the policies of the latter which, because of their hostility to foreign capital, fail to take advantage of its willingness to flow into these economies.

We shall have occasion to examine this argument later. Even at this stage however it is necessary to emphasise that this argument differs from ours in its thrust as well as its content. The thrust is different in at least two ways. First, we regard capital exports in the sense of direct investment in the periphery as a *possible* stabilising mechanism for capitalism as its traditional stabilising mechanism becomes progressively weakened. We are not making any prognostications about whether capital exports of a requisite order, let alone large-scale capital exports, would take place. Such capital exports depend on a host of other factors which we have not yet discussed. And it is by no means inevitable that capitalism would always necessarily succeed in stabilising itself. Second, even if it does succeed in stabilising itself through undertaking appropriate capital exports, the very basis of its success lies precisely in the continued existence of large labour reserves in the backward economies. To believe that capitalism in its unfettered operation would eliminate these labour reserves and yet continue to thrive is like believing that a person standing on the branch of a tree can lop it off without damage to himself.

As regards the content, it is no part of our argument that capital has ceased to be region specific. On the contrary it has a distinct 'home preference' for the core itself. This may help to explain the difference between our argument and that of many radical writers, such as the Starnberg group, who see in capital exports from the metropolis to the periphery a source of *crisis at the core, of instability, rather than of stability* as we have claimed. The main difference lies in our assumption that *ceteris paribus* capitalists at the core prefer to invest within it. This preference has to struggle against the fact of wage differences between the core and the periphery, but the outcome of this struggle need not be a steady and continuous increase in the proportion of 'outside' to 'home' investment. The proportion of 'outside' investment would increase only when some parametric shift makes the contradictions at the core irreconcilable, and the result of such an increase would be to overcome these contradictions, to act in the direction of stabilising capitalism. On the other hand, if no such 'home preference' is postulated, and capital mobility is assumed to occur in response to wage differentials *alone*, then it is not surprising that 'outside investment' may become so large as to cause a crisis of unemployment at home together with social instability. The assumption of 'home preference' however appears to be justified in the light of historical experience.

4. EFFICACY OF THE NEW PROPS

How far these new props would help to sustain the stability of capitalism remains an open question. A widening of the wage differentials within the metropolis might be socially explosive; in any case it would detract from the élan of capitalism. Right-wing racism, Kalecki's 'dog on the leash', might get out of hand, especially in conditions of rising unemployment which are bound to arise periodically, despite the basic economic stability of the system, owing to well-known processes which we have not specifically discussed in this book. And in such an event the very fact that a section of the immigrant workers is unionised and 'doing well' would be grist to the mill of the racists; the very fact of the internal dichotomy within the metropolis *not being drawn along racist lines* would be exploited by the racists. An internal dichotomy within the metropolis, though a logical way out of the problem of instability, is fraught with serious consequences, and this very fact would limit its practical relevance.

As for the other prop, investment abroad, the very fact of the extant dichotomy between the advanced and the backward economies, with the latter characterised by poverty, unemployment and social turmoil, acts as a deterrent. Capital can never be confident about the hospitability of the environment it encounters in the absence of direct political control, and perhaps not necessarily even then. There is a vicious circle here. If there was a large outmigration of capital, creating an altogether new scenario of development, and a new hope in the Third World, then the environment itself might undergo a change for the better from the point of view of capital (though the

resulting unemployment would create problems within the metropolis itself). But given its 'home preference' and the fact that any
outmigration would tend to be only at the margin, in response to
specific contradictions back home, this situation of lack of confidence in the recipient country's continuing to act as a hospitable
environment would be self-perpetuating. This prop therefore would
again be an unreliable and inadequate one.

So neither of the possible new props that we have discussed is as
effective as the one outlined in the earlier chapters. The beauty of the
latter lay in the fact that it operated behind the back, so to speak;
because it operated through complex mediations it did not necessarily entail any direct relation between metropolitan capital and
the mass of unemployed and unorganised workers. It did not even
require any kind of political control over the outlying regions (except
at the very beginning). As it declines in importance, any new mechanisms that might replace it would lack this advantage, and therein
lies their limitation.

From this fact however it would be facile to draw any conclusions
about a possible decline or collapse or protracted crisis of capitalism,
since any such conclusion attributes to the functioning of a system
inadequacies that only reflect one's own limitations in compre-
hending the range of future possibilities. True, in the interregnum
during which the old stabilising mechanisms are losing their efficacy
and new ones have not been found there would be more or less prolonged periods of high unemployment in the metropolis. This may
be one of the factors underlying their current state. But one cannot
absolutise it into a 'no exit' situation. Novelty has always played a
role in determining the historical contours of capitalist evolution
(Chakravarty 1986). To shut it out is as facile as to insist that
capitalism would *always* find a novel solution to whatever problems
it comes up against. In short the future contours of capitalist evolution would be decided in a terrain quite different from the one in
which analysis such as the current one is conducted. Meanwhile
however the stabilising mechanism discussed in the earlier chapters
has not ceased to operate; nor would it cease to operate in the future,
no matter how much its efficacy declines through time. And since
the fate of the Third World with which we are primarily concerned is
linked to its operation we shall continue to discuss it in the following
chapters without being concerned with the question of its declining
efficacy.

Appendix

For the sake of clarity we shall set out the two cases discussed in the text of this chapter in the form of simple formal models here. Since we are concerned with stabilising mechanisms other than what was discussed in earlier chapters, we shall deliberately rule out any scope for terms of trade movements by assuming that the capitalist metropolis (our 'manufacturing sector' of the earlier chapters) is vertically integrated. Other simplifying assumptions will be mentioned as we go along. The equations underlying the first case which are but modifications of those appearing in the appendix to Chapter 7 and in Chapter 8 where the symbols are explained, are as follows:

$$p_t = \mu(w_t^0 l_t^0 + w_t^u l_t^u + \lambda p_t), \qquad\qquad (i)$$

where w^0 and w^u refer respectively to the money wage rates of the organised and the unorganised workers. The former are employed in certain activities; in others the latter. The total output is the result of both sets of activities, and the labour requirements per unit of output in the two sets respectively are l^0 and l^u.

$$w_t^0 = \varpi_t p_t^e \qquad\qquad (ii)$$

$$\varpi_t l_t^0 = q - r v_t, \text{ which is the same as before} \qquad\qquad (iii)$$

$$w_t^u = p_t^e [y w_{t-1}^u l_{t-1}^u / (p_{t-1} l_t) + (1 - y) w_{t-2}^u (l_{t-1}^u / l_t^u)^2 / p_{t-2}] \qquad\qquad (iv)$$

which is just a way of formalising the price-taker position on a simplifying assumption, namely that they behave as if last year's productivity growth was the same as this year's.

$$p_t^e = p_{t-1} p_{t-1} / p_{t-2} \qquad\qquad (v)$$

$$v_t = 1 - O_t (l_t^0 + l_t^u) / L_t \qquad\qquad (vi)$$

$$L_{t+1} = L_t (1 + m - n v_t) \qquad\qquad (vii)$$

$$l_{t+1}^0 = l_t^0 / (1 + g_t^p) \qquad\qquad (viii)$$

$$l_{t+1}^u = l_t^u / (1 + g_t^p) \qquad\qquad (ix)$$

$$g_t^p = (1 + i_t / K_t) / (1 + \dot{\gamma}_t / K_t) - 1 \tag{x}$$

$$\gamma = \delta - \theta\lambda \tag{xi}$$

$$O_t = P_t + O_t(w_t^0 l_t^0 + w_t^u l_t^u + \lambda p_t) / p_t \tag{xii}$$

$$K_{t+1} = K_t + i_t \tag{xiii}$$

$$P_t = i_t + c_2 P_t + \alpha K_t + dK_t \tag{xiv}$$

$$O_t = K_t \beta u_0 \tag{xv}$$

where, for simplicity, we have continued with the assumption that capacity use is at the desired level, without explicitly introducing any export surplus term, by postulating that savings in any period are invested.

There are twenty-four variables in these equations, namely p_t, w_t^0, w_t^u, l_t^0, l_t^u, ϖ_t, p_t^e, v_t, w_{t-1}^u, w_{t-2}^u, l_{t-1}^u, p_{t-1}, p_{t-2}, L_t, L_{t+1}, l_{t+1}^0, l_{t+1}^u, g_t^p, K_t, i_t, O_t, P_t, K_{t+1}, and γ. Of these nine in any period are known, which are l_t^0, l_{t-1}^0, l_t^u, w_{t-1}^u, w_{t-2}^u, p_{t-1}, p_{t-2}, L_t, K_t. The rest are determined by the fifteen equations to give the single-period equilibrium. It can be seen both that a steady-growth–steady-inflation solution exists owing to the downward flexibility of the un-organised workers' wage rate relative to their productivity and also that any parametric changes such as in q or r or λ or μ merely take the economy to a different steady-growth-steady-inflation path without undermining its basic stability.

In case 2 the dichotomy between the two sets of workers arises not so much because of separation of activities, as because of the difference in location. We shall put down below only the modified equations and the additional ones. Thus

$$p_t = \mu(s_t w_t^h l_t + (1 - s_t) w_t^f l_t + \lambda p_t), \tag{i$'$}$$

where s and $(1-s)$ are the weights respectively of the home-invested and foreign-invested capital stock in the total.

$$w_t^h = p_t^e \varpi_t^h \tag{ii$'$}$$

$$\varpi_t^h l_t = f[v_t, (i_t^h / i_t - s_t)], \qquad f' < 0 \text{ and } f'' > 0, \tag{iii$'$}$$

where the additional term states that trade unions in the metropolis scale down their wage claims if they find capital exports rising at the margin. Here v refers exclusively to the metropolis.

$$w_t^f = p_t^e [y w_{t-1}^f l_{t-1} / (p_{t-1} l_t) + (1 - y) w_{t-2}^f (l_{t-1} / l_t)^2 / p_{t-2}], \tag{iv$'$}$$

where the only difference from (iv) is the dropping of the superscript for l.

$$v_t = 1 - O_t^h l_t / L_t, \tag{vi$'$}$$

with L_t like v referring exclusively to the metropolis.

$$l_{t+1} = l_t / (1 + g_t^p),\tag{$viii'$}$$

which differs from (viii) only in the dropping of the superscript.

$$i_t = i_t^h + i_t^f,\tag{ix'}$$

which is self-explanatory.

$$O_t = P_t \mu / (\mu - 1)\tag{xii'}$$

$$O_t^h = K_t^h \beta u_0\tag{xv'}$$

$$O_t = K_t \beta u_0\tag{xvi}$$

$$K_t = K_t^h + K_t^f\tag{$xvii$}$$

$$s_t = K_t^h / K_t\tag{$xviii$}$$

$$K_{t+1}^h = K_t^h + i_t^h\tag{xix}$$

$$K_{t+1}^f = K_t^f + i_t^f\tag{xx}$$

$$i_t^h / i_t - s_t = a v_t - b(w_t^h / w_t^f - R), \text{ where } R > 1.\tag{xxi}$$

This last equation needs an explanation. As long as the wage differential does not exceed some critical level, the greater is the availability of domestic labour (captured by the unemployment rate) the greater is the proportion of home investment. This is the essence of 'home preference'. But excessively high wage rates at home compared to abroad act in the opposite direction.

We have thirty variables, namely i_t, K_t, v_t, w_t^h, w_t^f, K_t^h, K_t^f, ϖ_t^h, O_t, O_t^h, P_t, i_t^h, l_t, g_t^p, L_t, L_{t+1}, l_{t-1}, l_{t+1}, s_t, γ, i_t^f, w_{t-2}^f, p_{t-1}, p_{t-2}, p_t^e, w_{t-1}^f, K_{t+1}, p_t, K_{t+1}^h, and K_{t+1}^f. Of these nine are known in any period, namely, K_t^h, K_t, w_{t-1}^f, w_{t-2}^f, l_t, L_t, l_{t-1}, p_{t-1}, p_{t-2}. The rest are determined by the twenty-one equations. It can be seen that a steady-growth–steady-inflation path exists for given parameter values along which s is a constant. Let us now consider the effects of parametric changes.

If the workers' bargaining strength improves, through a rise in q or a fall in r, since the steady-state growth rate remains unchanged, and with it the employment rate in the metropolis, it follows from eqn. (xxi) that the wage differential also remains unchanged in the new steady-state. If on the other hand, λ or μ increases then there is some effect on the new steady-state employment rate and hence upon the wage-differential. But in each of these cases the proportion of home capital stock in the total, i.e. s will be lower in the new steady state. This additional mechanism is the chief hallmark of the second case, as argued in the text.

IV

Imperialism and Third World Development

10

A Theory of Imperialism

1. A CHARACTERISATION OF IMPERIALISM

The argument developed over the last few chapters suggests that capitalism at its core is indeed a reasonably coherent, durable and successful system. But these characteristics arise for reasons quite different from what either the Walrasians, or neoclassical economists of other persuasions, or even the Keynesians think. They arise because of its coupling with outlying regions, with pre-capitalist or semi-capitalist economies. This confers on the system at its core certain benefits of tremendous significance.

First, by providing external markets it keeps up the level of activity at a reasonably high tempo for long stretches of time, and thereby boosts the domestic inducement to invest at the core. This results not only in impressive growth rates in output and productivity, which permit significant increases in real wages at the core, but also in a situation where resort to external markets via export surpluses do not have to be a perennial feature of the system.

Second, it keeps inflationary pressures in check at the core, because in the outlying regions, owing to the existence of vast labour reserves, the *ex ante* claims of the workers are compressible; these workers provide a cushion against accelerating inflation at the core.

Third, it can draw upon these labour reserves at will, and yet they are physically distanced from its main theatre of operations. It is as if the reserve army of labour, which, in Marx's theoretical schema, fulfilled the same role of keeping down wage claims and providing a source for potential recruitment of labour power to keep the tempo of capital accumulation going, was physically kept distant from the active army at the core of the system. This physical distancing incidentally ensures both domestic social stability at the core, since the workers there can enjoy rising real wages through successful trade union struggles and a degree of democratic rights in an atmosphere comparatively free from acute social tensions, as well as ideological hegemony. Since the system performs well at the core, it appears that this is the inherent property of the system. If in the outlying regions there is misery, unemployment and social turmoil, it appears as if all this is because of the insufficient development of capitalism there, for who would deny that at the core the system performs reasonably well? Its ideological triumph consists in the illusion that it creates, including among its victims, that its success at the core is replicable everywhere.

And this illusion is sustained by the occasional 'success stories' among Third World countries that make good. Just as the occasional worker rising to the ranks of capitalist magnates creates the illusion that there is no class division but free social mobility, just as the occasional Harijan climbing to the top echelons of the Indian bureaucracy creates the illusion that caste is no barrier to upward mobility if only one worked hard and did the right thing, likewise a few Third World countries making good within the existing international order sustains the belief among all of them that they too can make it good if only they created the right climate for capitalism to flourish. A certain geographical diffusion of the capitalist core which occurs over time creates the illusion that the distinction between the core and the outlying regions is not a necessary one for the sustenance of the system.

But the triumph is not merely ideological. The shining example of life at the core acts as a magnet for the most highly qualified, the talented people within the Third World societies. All the social resources expended upon the nurturing of such talent within the Third World country, all the potential benefit that such societies could reap from such talent, come to nought as it gets drained away to the core. The core in other words not only draws upon the labour reserves of the outlying regions at will, but picks the best talent from the outlying region and 'drains' it away.

But that is not all. Among those who are left behind and are aware of the life-style at the core, there is a hankering after this life-style, a perennial unfulfilled desire for imported goods, which, even while acting as a powerful pressure for the domestic production of such goods, continues to remain frustrated for the lack of 'first preference' imported goods. A powerful social base among the elite for consumerism and 'metropolitan life-styles' is created with important implications that we shall examine later.

Finally, with increases in sales- and innovation-promoting expenditure, the squeeze on the workers of the outlying regions can increase without its having any adverse repercussions on the economy at the core. Likewise, increases in trade union bargaining power, or increases in the degree of monopoly, in short parametric shifts in the functioning of the system at the core, which otherwise would have thrown it out of gear, are absorbed smoothly by passing the burden on to the workers of the outlying regions.

Thus a spatial dichotomy between the core and the periphery gives the system enormous flexibility and survival ability. It blunts domestic class struggle and denies a clear target to the class struggle in the periphery, diffusing its thrust and subverting its ideological coherence through the dazzle of the apparent success of capitalism at the core. It is the totality of this system of relationships, the functioning of this coupled system with its spatial dichotomy but economic unity which I call imperialism. This definition of course is wider than Lenin's (1975*b*) in the sense that according to this view one can draw a distinction between the colonial and the postcolonial phases of imperialism, but not between the imperialist and the pre-imperialist phases of capitalism.

Capitalism from the very beginning has been imperialist. The specific features which Lenin discussed as constituting imperialism *per se* can be seen as a phase of imperialism rather than a strict discontinuity. Partly perhaps the difference of this position from the classical Leninist one hinges on a question of nomenclature, but partly it stems from a belief, derived from Kalecki that the so-called 'free competition' phase of capitalism never really existed.[1] The wave of cartelisation that swept the advanced capitalist economies around the turn of the century, marked neither a permanent state of affairs, nor a sequel to a state of affairs where capitalist producers did not

---

[1] Kalecki's specific remark refers of course to 'perfect competition' and not 'free competition': 'Let me add immediately that this is a most unrealistic assumption not only for the present phase of capitalism but even for the so-called competitive capitalist economy of past centuries . . .'. But the context of his argument makes clear that he believes 'imperfect competition', 'semi-monopolistic' and 'monopolistic' factors to have been important from the very beginning of capitalism. See Kalecki 1971*a*.

implicitly collude to fix prices, or remained meekly confined to the economic terrain without directly influencing State policy. Even Adam Smith and Marx after all had talked about combinations of capitalists, Marx detailing the influence on British State policy of the Manchester 'millocracy'. So it is legitimate to talk of a rise in the 'degree of monopoly' in the late nineteenth century but not of a transition, representing a sharp discontinuity, between free competition and monopoly. If this view is accepted, then imperialism simply becomes a term encompassing the advanced and the backward parts of the system as a whole, which have always been coupled and continue to remain so.[2]

It is against the background of this coupling that State intervention in the advanced countries has to be located. Just as there is no water-tight division between free competition and monopoly capitalism, likewise there is no water-tight division between laissez-faire capitalism and State intervention. The capitalist State has always been an interventionist State. The domain of intervention, the instruments of intervention, the objects of intervention have no doubt changed according to circumstances, but State intervention certainly did not begin at some particular date in the history of capitalism, such as the turn of the century or the 1930s. Nowhere has State intervention been more manifest than in colonial policy and this policy dates back to the very origins of capitalism.

At the same time the undoubtedly larger domain over which State intervention operates in modern capitalism has neither obviated the need for the coupling of the advanced capitalist economies with the outlying backward economies, nor made the functioning of the system altogether a matter of discretion. This coupling gives the system a degree of coherence in its functioning which State intervention both helps to improve as well as seeks to buttress, by preserving its foundations, by sustaining with arms if necessary the basis on which the economic logic works itself out relentlessly. In addition, State intervention is of course central for particular national capitals in their rivalry against other capitals. But we should not get befogged by the fact of State intervention, especially in demand management in advanced capitalist countries, to lose sight of the relentless logic

---

[2] To say this does not mean that significant changes did not occur at the turn of the century which Lenin highlighted; see for instance Bagchi 1986. But an awareness of these changes should not be allowed to obliterate certain basic continuities in the functioning of capitalism.

working itself out, at least in the relationship between advanced and backward countries, in the economic terrain.

2. REPRODUCTION OF UNEQUAL INTERDEPENDENCE

The hallmark of any durable system is that through its working it reproduces in the normal course, without necessarily always at the point of a gun, the social relationships which underlie it. Marx's analysis of the accumulation process consisted of a demonstration not just of how the quantitative economic magnitudes grow through expanded reproduction, but, more importantly, of how the social relationships underlying capitalism are continually reproduced. The power and durability of the capitalist system derives however from the reproduction not just of the capital-wage labour relationship within the domestic economy but of the entire gamut of relationships of unequal interdependence in the international economy.

As product innovation occurs in the advanced countries, the production of older products shifts gradually to the backward countries. To be sure, there is a resistance to such shift (which we shall examine later), but some shift does occur. What the advanced country produces today, the backward country produces tomorrow, by which time the advanced country has gone on to produce a set of new products (some of which are variations of old products). Technological progress in the backward economy thus is conditioned by technological progress in the advanced economy. The fundamental characteristic of the latter however is to save on labour, and this characteristic gets repeated in the backward economy as well.

The rate of growth of output in the backward economy on the other hand depends upon the rate of growth of its exports. Owing to changes in the consumption pattern, and the increase in innovation-linked expenditure in the advanced economy, this entails (as we have seen earlier for the case where real wages in the backward economy were rising in tandem with productivity) a slower growth rate in the backward economy than in the advanced one, that is uneven development between the two economies. At this slower growth rate, the backward economy experiences an even slower rate of growth of demand for labour because of increases in labour productivity. In the previous chapter we took these increases as being at a constant autonomous rate. Even if we drop this assumption for the backward economy's manufacturing sector now, and make its productivity increase a function of its own growth rate (since the rate of productivity growth in the advanced economy's manufacturing sector, the other major determinant of the backward manufacturing sector's productivity growth, is given), the growth rate in the demand for labour in the backward economy must still remain below its output growth rate. And if the rate of growth of the work-force exceeds this growth in the demand for labour, or at any rate does not fall below it, labour reserves are continuously reproduced on an extended scale, certainly absolutely, and possibly also in relative terms. Unemployment grows, certainly in absolute numbers, and possibly even relative to the size of the work-force. The so-called dualism which has been noted by many as characterising the internal structure of backward societies is thus a reproduction within the economy of the dualism which exists at the international level.

This argument is only preliminary; its limitation lies in the fact that it makes the perpetuation of unequal interdependence a result almost of a set of happenstances. First of all, it assumes that wages in each sector in the backward economy rise *pari passu* with productivity. This gives the impression that if this did not happen, then the backward economy could expand its exports of manufactures, so that its rate of growth of exports could increase, and thereby raise the overall growth rate of the economy and absorb labour reserves despite increasing labour productivity. Second, even with wages rising with labour productivity, the fact that it is unable to absorb its labour reserves appears *inter alia* to result from a high rate of population, and hence work-force, growth. In other words, the fact that the relations of unequal interdependence are reproduced over time appears to be unrelated to any immanent logic of the functioning of the interlinked system, but rather to be a fortuitous occurrence thrown up by a particular combination of wage and population movements. We shall show in Chapter 12 that such is not the case, that the reproduction of the labour reserves in the backward economy, and with it the reproduction of the entire system of unequal interdependence, occurs no matter how wages in the backward manufacturing sector behave relative to productivity, and no matter what the population growth rate in the backward economy happens to be. The above argument is nonetheless useful for capturing one possible scenario of spontaneous reproduction of unequal interdependence, which is illustrative of the basic argument but does not constitute it.

This scenario would not occur if the backward economy capitalists did not have a distinct preference for imported over home-produced goods. But they do have such a preference and the reason is obvious: innovations are being undertaken in the advanced economy which the backward economy imitates only with a lag, so that at any given time there are a whole range of new goods produced abroad which are not domestically produced. If the State could coerce them into purchasing whatever is domestically produced, or, if, in case they reacted to the non-availability of imports by reducing their consumption altogether, as we assumed in Chapter 7, it could hold unwanted stocks of the domestically produced manufactured goods, financed through borrowing, then the import propensity could be brought down and the output growth rate of the backward economy could be stepped up beyond what export growth would have otherwise permitted. But this possibility, which we shall examine in Chapter 13, is conditional in any case on a certain type of State which has already decided on a degree of delinking from the imperialist system. Keeping this possibility out for the time being, we can say that as long as the economy remains within the imperialist system, since it does not have control either over the rate of growth of its exports or upon its output growth rate, or even upon the pace and pattern of technological progress domestically, it continues to reproduce its labour reserves, its poverty, and consequently its role as a shock-absorber for impulses emanating from the core.

Now, it may be asked: since the reproduction of the relationships at the international level that give rise to uneven development is not in any way consciously engineered by the advanced countries (except that a sharp break from them invites retaliation and even the use of force), and since these relationships are mediated by the preference patterns internalised by the social classes and groups in the backward economy, how can the advanced countries be blamed for the perpetuation of poverty and unemployment? To ask this question however is to misunderstand our argument. The point being made here is not a moral one; the issue is not to apportion blame.

An analogy with Marx's argument may be useful here. When Marx talked of the reproduction of the social relationships underlying capitalism, he was not making a moral point against one particular group, namely the capitalists. The capitalists too are alienated under the capitalist system; they are coerced into undertaking certain types of action by the logic of the functioning of the system itself. In Marx's view they were 'capital personified'. So his concern was with this logic, and not with moral tirades against capitalists. Likewise the question here is to look at the logic of the functioning of imperialism which is not a conspiracy but an entire system. True, this system is buttressed in the last analysis by the use of force, just as the capital-wage labour relationship is buttressed in the last analysis by the use of State power. But from this to jump to the conclusion that the essence of the system is merely the use of force by one component of it against the other would be reminiscent of the method of Duhring, and not that of Marx.[3]

No doubt in the origin of the system (as indeed in the origin of the capital–wage labour relationship which Marx studied under the rubric of 'primitive accumulation of capital') force plays the most important role. In our case the use of force is what the colonial period of imperialism is all about, but imperialism is neither identical with colonialism nor a phase apart from it. Colonialism is the early phase of imperialism where explicit use of coercion is essential to keep the system of interrelationship going. Let us turn briefly therefore to an analysis of colonialism in the context of our views on imperialism as a whole. In what follows we shall take India as our implicit prototype, though what is said about India is not without a certain general relevance.

3. A BRIEF EXCURSUS INTO COLONIALISM

The pre-colonial social structures in the countries which became colonies were considerably diverse. Some were characterised by a virtual natural economy with at best the rudiments of commodity production. Others like India which had seen centuries of centralised State power had a considerable degree of development of commodity production, though it can be argued that it was only the surplus extracted by the central authority through its local officials or allies that was in fact commoditised (Habib 1963). But no matter

---

[3] For Marx's and Engels's well-known strictures against Duhring see Engels 1954, to which Marx is believed to have contributed as well as going through the entire manuscript.

what the original pre-colonial society was, colonialism brought with it certain clear-cut changes.

First, it introduced a tax-system, which, while appropriating the bulk of the economic surplus of the colonies, also brought them into the vortex of commodity production. Where the natural economy existed earlier, having to pay taxes to the colonial government in cash destroyed the natural economy, a process discussed by Rosa Luxemburg using sources available to her at the time. Even in countries like India where a tax system and cash payment had existed earlier under pre-colonial rulers, the change in the form of taxation had a significant effect. The Mughal land revenue system had entailed a tax on produce. The British land revenue system, though it built on the Mughal one, shifted to a tax on land.[4] The magnitude of this tax was fixed. It was extracted fairly rigidly with little relaxation or discretionary concession, irrespective of the amount or the price of the produce. By insisting on the payment of this tax by a certain date, failing which the peasants lost their rights to the land, which were now adjudicable in a whole paraphernalia of law courts, it forced the peasantry to become indebted to a group of traders-cum-money lenders, or money lenders pure and simple, which brought about a process of forced commercialisation of agriculture.[5]

Second, it brought about a decline of domestic craft production, a process which has been referred to widely as 'deindustrialisation'.[6] There were two obvious contributory factors towards this. First, while the earlier rulers had used the economic surplus extracted from the peasantry for expenditures on domestically produced luxury goods and craft products, this surplus was now siphoned abroad. Its multiplier effects were now no longer felt within the domestic economy and this brought about a decline, especially of urban crafts. In addition, such crafts which were sustained by the peasants' own demand, that is by demand arising from that part of the peasants' income which was retained by them after handing over the surplus,

---

[4] For a succinct presentation of the difference between the pre-British and the British systems see Habib 1975.

[5] For a theoretical discussion of forced commercialisation, see Bhaduri 1983 and Utsa Patnaik 1975; a historical discussion is contained in Chowdhury 1964.

[6] For an attempt at estimating the magnitude of deindustrialisation in a particular region see Bagchi 1976; for a theoretical discussion of the process, the fact that it can occur even in the absence of an import surplus in certain circumstances, see Patnaik and Ghosh 1991.

now faced competition from cheap manufactured goods imported from abroad, and went into a process of decline. The working population earlier engaged in craft production now found itself deprived of its livelihood and was thrown on to the land. Since land availability or land productivity did not increase to any corresponding extent (the colonial government, apart from a few exceptions, such as the canal colonies in Punjab, did not make any significant investment on irrigation or other agricultural infrastructure), an underemployed and pauperised mass of rural population came into being, eking out a precarious existence and vulnerable to the terrible famines which rocked rural India with far greater frequency under the new dispensation than ever before (Dutt 1985; Bhatia 1967).

Third, the commodity form in which the economic surplus was realised now consisted of the primary commodities needed by the colonial power. The peasantry, which was obliged by the pressure of revenue and rent demand to take advances from traders-cum-money lenders, had to grow such crops as the traders dictated, and they in turn took their cue from the conditions prevailing in the market. So the very control over the peasantry that traders-cum-money lenders began to exercise as a result of the colonial tax policy was utilised by the advanced country to get the particular commodities that it wanted. The possibility that the peasantry may not respond to the market signals, and may merely withdraw into subsistence production, was removed by first engineering and then utilising the control which commercial interests came to exercise over the peasantry.[7]

Finally, while in no earlier society were property rights, in the sense of a single integral right over land or other means of production, clearly defined or existent (Habib 1965), colonialism introduced modern bourgeois property rights. In earlier societies what existed were claims to shares in the produce, fixed customarily and administered with a degree of flexibility. The ultimate sanction behind the extraction of surplus was force, but force would take the form of bringing back fleeing peasants to the land, or punishing them physically, but not that of uprooting them from the land itself or

[7] Merely forcing the peasants to meet a fixed cash obligation runs the risk from the point of view of the metropolitan economy that in a period of favourable prices the peasants may in fact reduce their marketed surplus. This risk is removed to the extent that the peasants are not free to decide their production pattern which now gets dictated by the merchant creditors. This is an important difference between Latin America and India.

downgrading their legal status as a part of the enforcement of a legal contract. With an indebted peasantry which often had to pledge its land in order to get a loan, with the growth of commercial crops whose prices depended on international market conditions over which the peasants had no control, with a vast pauperised land-hungry rural mass, the introduction of bourgeois property rights inevitably meant the transfer of ownership over land away from the peasants into the hands of the new class of creditor landlords. The devaluation in the legal status of the peasantry was also inevitably associated with a decline in its economic position (Patel 1952; Dasgupta 1970; Utsa Patnaik 1991).

Colonialism created the very conditions, which not only gave rise to unequal interdependence during the colonial period itself, but which, once they had come into being, could be perpetuated even in the absence of explicit colonial control. It was the progenitor of modern mass unemployment and modern mass poverty (Raychaudhuri 1990). To be sure, poverty existed even before, but that was poverty engendered by low levels of productivity. It was not poverty associated with unemployment and social insecurity. The poor faced natural insecurity in the form of floods, droughts, and diseases, though whether to a greater extent than under the colonial period remains questionable, since natural insecurity itself is a societal category. But in addition to facing natural insecurity, they now had to face social insecurity as well. At the prevailing wage rate there was an excess supply of labour. Whether employment could be obtained for a sufficient length of time on a particular day or not, and consequently whether bread could be obtained on a particular day or not, became a matter of uncertainty. This poverty bred by the impersonal relationships of the market place, and associated with a specific kind of insecurity, which was itself not an 'act of God' but rooted in complex social relationships working themselves out through the processes of demand and supply, to which millions of people uprooted from their traditional means of livelihood were suddenly exposed, was a peculiar contribution of colonialism.

The other side of the coin was a new class, of merchants-turned-landlords, of bureaucrats and baboos, of traders engaged in colonial commerce, some of whom were to become the native capitalists, and all of whom were the creatures of the colonial system. This domestic bourgeoisie, which was accommodated into the colonial system, benefiting from the web of relationships that bound the colony to the metropolitan country, and yet chafing at the constraints imposed upon it by the systematic racial discrimination practised by the colonial regime in the first instance, and at the overall lack of opportunities that the colonial system entailed at some remove, developed a peculiarly contradictory character. It both envied as well as resented the metropolitan bourgeoisie, wishing to emulate the behaviour and life-styles of the latter, and yet bitterly resentful of the fact that despite this emulation it was never accepted as an equal.

The domestic bourgeoisie recruited from these diverse groups spawned by colonialism itself as well as from the native traders, engaged in particular in internal trade, whom colonialism never could or did supplant, was in due course to move into local manufacturing production and fight for a space of its own in opposition to metropolitan capital. But the basic groundwork of the imperialist system as we have described it, namely a mass of poverty-stricken agricultural workers and peasants on the one hand, and a stratum of the bourgeoisie occupying key positions in primary production and local manufacturing but desirous of emulating the life-styles of the metropolitan bourgeoisie on the other, was prepared under the aegis of the colonial regime itself.

Once this groundwork had been prepared, the necessity of colonial political rule for the perpetuation of the system of unequal interdependence no longer logically existed. This is not to minimise the tremendous political significance of formal decolonisation, which consisted in most instances of handing over power to the domestic bourgeoisies by the colonial representatives of the metropolitan bourgeoisie, nor to suggest any kind of a conspiracy theory whereby the metropolitan bourgeoisie made accurate calculations and predictions about how much decolonisation would damage its interests. It fought bitterly till the end and was compelled into decolonisation by the mass upsurge after the Second World War of the colonial peoples on the one hand, and by its own weakening by the very fact of this war itself on the other. Our argument is meant only to understand why the promise inherent in decolonisation, which in Gandhi's words (in the Indian context) was to 'wipe the tears from the eyes of every Indian', never materialised.

The fact that the domestic bourgeoisie had been on the ascendancy had been noted as early as the 1920s by M. N. Roy and the other proponents of the so-called 'decolonisation' thesis, who argued that the colonial ties were already loosening, that the domestic bourgeoisie was already being provided with space within the formal colonial system, and that consequently the target of the liberation struggle could not simply be the colonial regime alone but had to be widened to include the domestic bourgeoisie as well (see Dattagupta 1980).

Whether or not this was a correct assessment for the time, the 'decolonisation thesis' has been revived, much more plausibly, for the period after formal decolonisation by Bill Warren (1973). His argument is that after formal decolonisation, imperialism as a constraint upon the growth of productive forces in Third World societies, if it was such a constraint, has ceased to matter. This according to him was already evident at the time of his writing in the rapid rate of growth of Third World economies, rapid both in comparison with their own historical achievements, as well as in comparison with the advanced capitalist countries. If these rates were still not high enough to meet the urgent social needs of the Third World countries, the reason lay in the internal structures of these societies, and the constraints upon growth that these structures entailed. Imperialism should no longer be dragged in as an alibi for the Third World countries' lack of adequate progress.

Notwithstanding formal similarities, there is a difference between the original 'decolonisation thesis' of the 1920s, and Warren's thesis. The concern of the original thesis was really to define the class configurations and targets of the anti-imperialist struggle; the concern of Warren's thesis is to suggest that after formal decolonisation there is no need any longer for an anti-imperialist struggle. The problem with theses such as Warren's, which incidentally run completely counter to the thrust of this book, is their arbitrary separation of internal and external constraints instead of seeing the dialectical unity between the two (see P. Patnaik 1972b). The analysis of the Third World economy's predicament has to be done within a structure in which the dominant domestic class alliance exists neither independently, unrelated to metropolitan capital, nor in total subservience to the latter (which would amount to saying that the grant of independence to the colonies was of no consequence). The limits to social progress in Third World societies have to be located within this structure as a whole, not in any arbitrarily singled out element of this structure.

4. THE RELUCTANCE OF CORE
CAPITAL-IN-PRODUCTION TO MIGRATE

The outline of the structure which we have provided in the earlier chapters rests on three crucial assumptions. As long as these assumptions are fulfilled, the structure reproduces itself even in the absence of explicit political control of any kind. These assumptions are: first, the migration of labour *en masse* from the backward to the advanced segment of the world is not possible. Such migration as takes place is a regulated one (for which we have used the approximate formulation that the rate of growth of the work-force in the advanced economy is a linear function of its unemployment rate). Second, notwithstanding relative price variations, capitalists in the backward country (as well as large segments of 'the middle classes'— professionals, bureaucrats, white-collar workers, and so on—though they do not figure in our model) prefer the manufactured goods imported from the advanced country to the manufactured goods domestically produced and that there are limits to the rationing of the former. (This is an extreme assumption. It is quite enough for our argument if a fixed proportion of the surplus and not necessarily the whole of it is sought to be spent on the imported goods and there is a ceiling to the intensity of rationing of such goods). Third, despite the wage differential between the advanced and the backward economies, the rate of growth of the latter's exports cannot be raised beyond a certain limit. This third assumption has two distinct components. There is no *en masse* migration of capital from the advanced to the backward economy to take advantage of the latter's low wages for producing the goods that are being manufactured in the former. And the backward economy capitalists cannot also utilise the low wages to outsell the advanced economy capitalists across the board.

While the first two of these assumptions appear fairly plausible, the first in an obvious sense and the second by virtue of the continuous product innovation at the core, the last assumption is bound to cause raised eyebrows. The second part of the last assumption, namely the inability of the capitalists in the periphery to increase continuously their encroachment upon the production spheres of the advanced country capitalists, will be examined in detail in Chapter 12. The first part, namely the reluctance of core capital to migrate *en masse* into the periphery to take advantage of the latter's low wages, is discussed below.

That it represents what really happened during the colonial period can scarcely be doubted. Ragnar Nurkse in his classic article (1954) on capital flows during the nineteenth century drew attention to the fact that only about a quarter of the capital flowing out of the advanced countries went into the backward economies of the tropics; the remaining three quarters went into the temperate zones of white settlement. Why, despite the fact that labour was much cheaper in the backward tropical economies, capital did not flow into these economies to produce the commodities which it was producing with more expensive labour in the advanced countries remains however the perennial puzzle of development economics.

Arthur Lewis (1978b) who explains the wage difference between the underdeveloped world, consisting among others of India and China, and the developed countries in terms of the fact that the agricultural revolution occurred in Britain much earlier, so that labour had to be drawn out of a much more productive agriculture than in India and China, never addressed himself to this particular question. We shall discuss his argument in Chapter 14; but it should be noted here that his not addressing this question makes his overall explanation of the real wage difference curiously inadequate. Granted that the British worker came out of an agricultural sector where the income per head was much larger than in India or China, granted that he migrated to lands of temperate settlement such as Australia or Canada or the United States only at wages high enough to be in keeping with the agricultural productivity he had left behind, granted that Indian or Chinese migration into distant lands occurred at correspondingly low wages in keeping with the low productivities in their domestic agriculture, and granted also that trade union action in the advanced countries ensured that there was no cross-migration to upset the real wage difference, of cheap Indian or Chinese labour into either the European countries or into countries where European labour was migrating. Granted all these propositions, his answer is still insufficient since it does not even raise the crucial question: why didn't European capital migrate to India and China? Why didn't the Manchester mill-owners, instead going on producing year after year in Manchester where labour was far more expensive, shift their productive capacity to Bombay or Shanghai, in which case the real wage differential would have been wiped out over a period of time? After all it is not just labour mobility that wipes out real wage differentials; capital mobility from high-wage to low-wage countries can have logically an identical effect. Trade union action might have prevented the cross-mobility of labour; but surely it could not have prevented the cross-mobility of capital, and at any rate nobody has argued that it could have or did. Why then did European capital not migrate *en masse* to the tropical countries?

Nurkse himself underscored the complementarity between the migration of skilled labour from Europe and the migration of capital, and Brinley Thomas (1973) subsequently argued that capital from Europe tended to flow mainly to such regions where people from Europe had migrated. While this pattern is noteworthy it still does not explain why capital flows only took the direction complementary to labour flows. Baran's (1957) speculation that climate must have played a major role in determining the direction of migration of capital, though vindicated in a way by the complementarity noted by Thomas between labour and capital migration, still does not answer the question: Why? Maybe, as Bagchi (1986) argued more recently, racial factors play a far more important role in economic decisions than economic theorists, postulating pure profit-maximising behaviour, normally recognise.

Be that as it may, it can be argued nonetheless that capital in contemporary conditions is far more fluid, far more international than it has been historically. The product cycle theories which argue that at a certain stage in the development of new products, the location of their manufacture shifts away from the main demand centres to areas where wages are low, emphasise this point, as do several Marxist writers who see in the internationalisation of capital and the break up of production processes and the geographical scattering of their component parts, an altogether new phenomenon marking a qualitative break from the traditional international division of labour. Some Marxist economists have even seen the high levels of unemployment in contemporary capitalism in the context of such production shifts: capital, no longer rooted in and tied to particular nation-States, treats the entire world as its theatre of operations and locates manufacturing away from the high-wage centres which in turn creates unemployment in such centres (Froebel, Heinrichs, and Kreye 1980). The essence of all these theories is that the diffusion of capitalist production facilities across the globe is systematically undermining the continual reproduction of any development-underdevelopment dichotomy.[8] This is not to say that all under-developed countries are becoming developed, but rather that their lack of development, wherever there is such a lack, is attributable to factors specific to them which make them an inhospitable venue for international capital.

There can be little doubt that a tendency of this kind, towards a geographical diffusion of production facilities, did appear in a pronounced fashion at a certain time, and most theories mentioned above are based on an extrapolation of this tendency, even though the quantitative significance of what diversification has actually been achieved continues to remain meagre. For instance, the share of the underdeveloped world in total manufacturing exports, though it has gone up, continues to remain exceedingly low, and much of the increase is on account of a tiny handful of East Asian economies (Chandrashekhar 1986; Chapter 12 below also provides some evidence). In other words while some notable diversification of production processes towards the four East Asian economies has taken place, as far as the rest of the underdeveloped world is concerned, it continues to remain trapped in the traditional international division of labour, modified no doubt by the fact that it is not primary products alone which are the province of the Third World, but lower-level manufacturing activities which include a degree of value addition to primary products.

The division of labour in other words is not simply one between manufacturing and primary products, but between sophisticated manufacturing on the one hand and primary production together with lower-level manufacturing on the other. This division however, though not identical with the earlier division, is merely at one or two removes from it. For the bulk of the Third World a massive shift of production facilities from the advanced countries on to their territories, a shift overriding all inherited division of labour, and resulting in a tendency towards equalisation of wage differentials and elimination of the vast labour reserves, remains an improbable prospect.

What is more, there are even indications that the pace of relocation of production facilities, such as it was in the 1970s, may be slowing down in the 1980s and 1990s. There are three main considerations militating against any substantial degree of relocation.

[8] This may be an unfair attribution to the Marxist writers just cited, but others sharing a similar perspective have argued this way.

First, any such relocation tends to upset the logistics of a company's operation. If a part or the whole of the production process for a commodity is shifted to a Third World country, away from the main centres of demand, in order to take advantage of the low wages prevailing there, problems of co-ordination invariably come up. Larger inventories, for instance, have to be held to guard against unforeseen delivery delays, which partly or wholly offset the advantages arising from low wages.

Second, low wages are not identical with low labour costs. If there are low wages, but the workers are militant, or there is a high degree of absenteeism or indiscipline, then the labour costs may still turn out to be high. When one adds to it the social and political uncertainties typically prevailing in a Third World country, where riots, strikes (not just in one's own factory but elsewhere as well), changes of government and changes in the policy environment are much more frequent than in the advanced countries, it is hardly surprising that multinationals continue to be chary about shifting production facilities to the Third World despite the latter's low wages. Indeed a necessary, though by no means a sufficient, condition for attracting multinational corporations to locate production facilities on a country's soil appears to be the prevalence in it of military or other forms of authoritarian rule, which can deal with social unrest in an utterly ruthless manner and thereby create appropriate 'tranquil' conditions for capital.

This is a kind of vicious circle. Saddled with vast labour reserves, and a legacy of mass poverty and social unrest, which are themselves the result of decades or even centuries of colonial and semi-colonial oppression where economic surplus was shipped out but metropolitan capital was never interested in investing in the production of manufactures, the Third World countries are now in a state where even if metropolitan capital were to be belatedly interested in developing manufacturing capacities, the climate for it would be far from a hospitable one.

Third, the possibility of breaking up a production process and taking a part or the whole away from the centres of demand is not independent of the specific products and the specific technologies we are talking about. It can be argued that while the possibility was strong in the 1970s, the current trends in technology development and product innovation are against it (Kaplinsky 1984). If multinational capital locates production facilities within the Third World in the coming years, it would be more for meeting the local market than for servicing the international market. And investment for meeting the local market, which would have the effect of denationalisation of Third World industries, if not of deindustrialisation altogether, would hardly disrupt the reproduction of underdevelopment.

5. A CRITIQUE OF THE THEORY OF UNEQUAL EXCHANGE

The views on imperialism advanced in the present chapter, though reminiscent in some ways of the theories of unequal exchange, should be clearly demarcated from the latter. The theory of unequal exchange is vulnerable to the many serious criticisms which have been levelled against it (see for instance Bharadwaj 1986; Utsa Patnaik 1986; Menon 1986). First, any concept of unequal exchange presupposes a 'norm' of equal exchange. It is not easy to define what constitutes such a 'norm'. If we say that whenever the rates of profit between two activities located in different countries are identical but the wage rates are different for simple unskilled labour working with the same intensity for the same number of hours every day, then this constitutes an example of unequal exchange, as Emmanuel (1972) indeed would do under his 'weak concept of unequal exchange', then we get into a rather meaningless intellectual position: it is not only that the advanced countries 'exploit' the backward countries, but, say, the steel workers exploit the cotton textile workers within the backward country, the industrial workers exploit the construction workers, all of them exploit the agricultural workers, the agricultural workers of one region exploit the agricultural workers of another region, and so on. The theory ceases to be a meaningful explanation of anything apart from being a simple moral statement.

Second, even if we accepted the theory of unequal exchange as it stands it still does not provide an explanation of uneven development. If the rates of profit are equal in two countries, even if the real wages are different, if all profits are invested, then equal rates of profit must entail equal rates of accumulation, and hence, *ceteris paribus*, equal rates of growth. Why then do we have unequal or uneven rates of development, which, through decades of history, have

characterised the dichotomy between the advanced and the backward economies?

Third, quite independent of the above criticisms, how unequal
exchange is sustained remains unclear. Emmanuel argues as if capital mobility equalises the rate of profit across countries, while labour
mobility is required for equalising the wage rate. This however is
untenable. If capital is genuinely mobile in search of higher profits,
then even if labour is immobile, the wage rates should be equalised
across countries as well. We do not need both kinds of mobility: one
is quite enough. If manufacturing is undertaken at the core while
primary production occurs in the periphery, and the real wages are
different while the rates of profit are identical in the two activities,
genuine capital mobility would imply that manufacturing too would
shift to the periphery until the wage differential is eliminated. Or
even if core capitalists are reluctant to produce in the periphery,
whose climate let us say does not suit them, why don't capitalists in
the periphery, hitherto engaged in primary production move into
manufacturing, using the same technology as at the core and
outcompeting the core capitalists owing to the advantage they enjoy
of having to pay a lower wage? Since monopoly does not enter into
these unequal exchange models which are based on the assumption
of free competition, except that labour mobility is restricted, these
questions cannot be answered within the context of that theory
which remains therefore curiously incomplete.

Finally, the empirical calculations on the magnitude of transfers
through unequal exchange are usually so small that they inevitably
give rise to the question: is *this* all that imperialism is about? The
unequal exchange theories curiously therefore understate the total
impact of imperialism on the Third World.

The fundamental point about this impact is that it is part of an
overall structural constraint upon development. It is not reducible to
a certain figure of the amount of 'loot', which invariably creates the
impression that if this amount was not snatched away, the underdeveloped countries would be on the road to prosperity. The unequal
exchange theories therefore aim at providing a figure for transfers,
based on theoretical assumptions which are unsatisfactory and informed only by moral indignation. By contrast, our argument has
been explicitly concerned with the complexities of the structural
constraints, and that too in a dynamic setting. It does not presuppose
any notion of an equal exchange; it does not attempt to provide any

estimate of the magnitude of the 'loot' or the 'drain'; and it does not pretend to claim that if this 'drain' did not occur, or if an amount equal to it was restored to the Third World annually, then the problem of underdevelopment would disappear. Moreover, unlike the unequal exchange theories we attempt to suggest the mechanisms through which the structural constraints upon development actually operate, how these mechanisms reproduce themselves spontaneously over time, and what the dynamic tendencies of the coupled system are. Both methodologically as well as substantively therefore the view of imperialism presented in this chapter differs from that of the unequal exchange theories.

This also explains why our position is different from that of the so-called 'dependency' school. The 'dependency' school to be sure is not composed of a single strand of argument; there are significant differences among the different authors grouped under this tendency. But even if we take the view that is most comparable to ours, that of Frank (1975) and his followers, the distance between their position and ours is obvious. The basic mechanism underlying the 'development of underdevelopment' in Frank is a transfer of surplus. While Frank does not accept Emmanuel's theory of unequal exchange, postulating instead a mechanism for the extraction of surplus through the use of monopoly power, such an extraction nonetheless remains central to his analysis. Our focus however is not on the extraction of surplus *per se*; it is the structural constraints arising from the dialectics of interaction between the advanced capitalist world and the Third World, an interaction that involves the terrains both of technology as well as of consumer demand, which restrict the pace of Third World development. It is the total characteristics of a coupled system, and not the fact of surplus transfer as such, that we emphasise, which is why we recognise the hurdles to delinking, the fact that attempts at delinking are fraught with contradictions. It is not enough to say as Frank does that delinking is the solution to the problem of underdevelopment. The real question is how to delink. And this in turn requires an examination of how the links operate. It is in this examination, and in particular in recognising the texture and the thickness of the links in the real world, that our difference from the dependency theories lies.

11

The Market Question in a
Historical Setting

In the present chapter and the one that follows, we shall discuss certain historical aspects of the development of capitalism at the core in the light of our stylised picture of imperialism, both to establish that our stylisation has not been an altogether irrelevant or meaningless one, as well as to fill in certain gaps which a stylised picture inevitably contains.

1. A DECOMPOSITION OF THE DEMAND PROBLEM

Under the general rubric of the problem of aggregate demand at the core, one can distinguish between three quite distinct problems. The first is what might be called the aggregate expenditure problem, which states that given the mark-up, in any period at the desired level of capacity utilisation, $I+X$ must equal $S+M$. This was the problem, namely the possible insufficiency of aggregate expenditure to absorb the full capacity (or the desired capacity) output if it was produced, which was highlighted by Keynes and Kalecki.

The second is what one might call the problem of expenditure balance. Even if the desired capacity level output is absorbed, that is $I+X=S+M$ at this level, the composition of aggregate expenditure may cause a problem. There may be a trade surplus, or trade deficit, which, unless the asset preference pattern at home or abroad is suitably accommodating, may be unsustainable. In the extreme case, where nobody wishes to hold any claims upon a foreign country, trade has to be balanced: X must equal M and I must equal S.

A problem may arise in other words if aggregate expenditure does not have the correct balance. This was the problem highlighted by Kaldor.

The third problem is one of disproportionality. Even if exports are sufficient to cover the import requirements generated by the production of the desired capacity level output, and even if the savings out of this output are equal to what the capitalists wish to invest, the commodity composition of the investment may be quite different from the commodities released by the savings. The problem of transforming savings into investment would still remain. If this transformation is to be achieved through trade, then it is essential that the commodities in which savings are materialised should also be capable of being exported.

In the first of these problems, the *ex ante* aggregate flow expenditure is itself insufficient; in the second case, there is a mismatch between the composition of this *ex ante* expenditure and the desire to hold claims upon foreigners, at home or abroad. In the third case, there is a mismatch between the commodity demand generated by this expenditure, and the pattern of commodity availability. The distinction between the second and the third cases can be clarified as follows. Suppose both at home and abroad, there is complete indifference about the magnitude of claims (positive or negative) held upon foreigners. If the extra output of some domestic sectors (after meeting domestic consumption requirements) is required neither for investment nor for exports, then the economy can never achieve desired capacity use, even though in value terms *ex ante* investment and savings are equal.

In our model, we did not consider the third case, since we assumed that the core produces a composite manufactured good which can be consumed or invested: so by assumption the commodity forms of savings and investment could not be different. But the general conclusion of the model that the existence of unlimited export opportunities in the backward world solves for the core the problem of aggregate demand becomes even stronger when we take account of this third case.

The model assumed a single integral economy at the core. Once this assumption is dropped, it follows that not all the separate core economies necessarily have to undertake exports to the backward economies in order to solve individually their aggregate expenditure, or expenditure balance, or disproportionality problems. The task of utilising export opportunities in the backward economies in order to solve the possible aggregate demand problems which may arise at the core as a whole has usually devolved upon the leading core economy of the time. In the period up to 1914, this was the task fulfilled by Britain.

The nineteenth century witnessed a tremendous diffusion of capitalism, from Britain to Europe to the temperate regions of white settlement such as the USA, Canada, and Australia. Despite cyclical fluctuations of the Juglar or the Kondratieff kind, the inducement to invest at home or at the frontiers of the expanding core held up remarkably in consequence. The real problem which remained was to overcome disproportionality, to ensure that capital exports to the 'empty spaces' (which analytically are indistinguishable from investment within an enlarged core) did not suffer for want of availability of the right commodities in the original core countries. And this was overcome through the penetration into colonial markets.

Colonial markets were needed not so much for overcoming any persistent tendency towards over-production through an export surplus being run *vis-à-vis* them. They were made to absorb such commodities from the core for which there was insufficient demand within the core itself for purposes of either consumption or investment; and in lieu of these, they were made to export commodities for which the core had a use. The objective was to make them yield more in the form of exports to the core than they absorbed in the form of imports from it, so that even larger capital exports could be made to the regions of recent white settlement than were sustainable on the basis of the resources of the original core itself. And this was achieved without incurring any debt to the backward economies through the mechanism of the colonial 'tribute'. India, for instance, had an export surplus *vis-à-vis* the rest of the world almost throughout the colonial period, but it did not pile up any claims in the form of loans abroad as a result of this export surplus because the surplus was offset by the 'Home Charges', representing the element of unrequited exports from India to Britain.

When Keynes, in his *Economic Consequences of the Peace* (1919), drew a brilliant and vivid picture of the successes of pre-1914 capitalism, his judgement essentially was that expanding frontiers of capitalism had until then sustained an enormous boom of very long duration, which, according to Schumpeter's (1966) interpretation of Keynes, was no longer possible in the post-1914 epoch. But the role of the backward colonies in sustaining this boom did not figure in Keynes's analysis. This role consisted first, in a transfer of surplus without any quid pro quo (as Marx (1968) recognised) to the advanced capitalist world via Britain, and second, in their absorption of commodities which could not be absorbed in the core and yielding in return those which could. There were thus two distinct and separate processes going on under *Pax Britannica*.

2. SURPLUS EXTRACTION FROM COLONIES AND CAPITAL EXPORTS

The first of these processes was an extraction of surplus from the underdeveloped countries, its appropriation by Britain in particular, and its investment in Europe and the regions of white settlement.[1] India was a key source for this surplus extraction. From the earliest days of colonial rule in Bengal a drain of surplus from India had taken place through a variety of ways, such as monopoly over internal trade, the East India Company's monopoly position in international trade combined with its political dominance, the revenue system, and even straightforward fortune hunting by the Company's servants (see, for example, Sen 1992). For the period 1757–80—the two decades or so after the Battle of Plassey—J. C. Sinha (1927) put the total drain from Bengal at £38m., around £1.5m. annually. For the early years of the nineteenth century, around 1813, Tucker, a British merchant, and Hume, a British official, estimated the remittable surplus at £3m. to £4m. annually (Bagchi 1970; Chaudhuri 1971). For 1871, by which time the colonial administration had settled into a regular pattern, and the early days of loot, bribery, and crude grabbing had been left far behind, Dadabhai Naoroji (1871) estimated the 'drain' from India at £16m. annually.

Bagchi has compared these figures with Britain's net capital exports. According to Imlah (1958), these amounted to £67.2m, over the period 1820–9 and £292.2m. over the period 1860–9. Over 50 per cent of Britain's annual net capital exports therefore was financed by the drain from India, even on a conservative estimate, during both the earlier part of the nineteenth century and even the decade of the 1860s. These capital exports went in the earlier period to Europe,

---

[1] This section draws heavily on Bagchi 1972*a*.

where, according to Jenks (1963), the 'investment of her capital had given the wings to the migration of her industrial arts'. In the space of a couple of decades after the Battle of Waterloo, continental Europe was no longer importing British cloth, but was instead importing British yarn to feed its own thriving textile industry which had been set up with the help of British technicians and engineers.

The direction of British capital exports thereafter, as indeed of the capital exports from France, the other major lending European country, was towards the regions of recent white settlement, North America, Australasia, South America, especially Argentina and Brazil, and parts of Africa. An enormous migration of European labour took place into the so-called 'empty spaces' of the world through the nineteenth century, and together with this migration went European, and in particular British, capital. According to Matthew Simon's estimates, quoted in Bagchi, of all the new British portfolio investment between 1865 and 1914, as much as 68 per cent went to regions of recent white settlement. Of the outstanding long-term foreign investment of France in 1914, an almost identical proportion was held in Europe, the USA and Canada.

As the income from past capital exports would begin to flow in from the new areas of white settlement, while the empty spaces of the world would begin to get filled up, the realisation problem might raise its head again, but in the pre-1914 period, this did not happen. Perhaps the increase in rentier consumption that J. A. Hobson (1902) the moralist so strongly castigated was quite sufficient to forestall any realisation problem; otherwise the prosperity as well as the carefreeness of Edwardian Britain would have been difficult to explain.

The pumping out of an economic surplus without any quid pro quo from underdeveloped countries such as India, and its investment in expanding the frontiers of the capitalist core constituted one great pattern of the nineteenth century. It resulted in a massive diffusion of industrial capitalism: by the turn of the century, almost all the regions of recent white settlement which had begun as primary producers had no more than a third or so of their work-force engaged in agriculture (Kuznets 1971). The one notable exception was the USA where the proportion was still one-half, but agriculture in the USA had itself become a scientific, mechanised, and high-income yielding activity. By contrast, in the tropical colonies with enormous concentrations of population on land, more than 70 per cent of the work-force still struggled on in overcrowded agricultural activities that had by then become firmly linked to the international market.

3. THE FLIGHT OF BRITISH EXPORTS INTO COLONIAL MARKETS

The second important process throughout the century was what Hobsbawm (1969, 146) called the steady flight of British exports 'from the modern, resistant and competitive markets into the underdeveloped'. He draws a parallel between the changing direction of capital exports and the changing direction of commodity exports, that the former too went increasingly towards the underdeveloped world and the British Empire like the latter. There is however an important difference which gets blurred because of the classification used by Hobsbawm. While the direction of capital exports, once Europe had ceased to absorb them, was towards the USA and subsequently towards Latin America and the white colonies of the British Empire which were part of the expanding core, the direction of commodity exports was increasingly towards the Far East including India, towards economies that were and continue to remain backward. Since the Empire included both the white dominions as well as the backward economies like India, the similarities which Hobsbawm sees between the changing directions of capital and commodity exports in fact hide a basic difference. After the initial railway investment India did not see much capital exports for developing its production facilities coming its way, and the same can be said of the other tropical colonies and semi-colonies. On the other hand as British goods faced stiffer competition from its rivals, these were the very countries which became more and more important as markets for commodities. The distinction between 'advanced' and 'backward', or between 'regions of the expanding core' and the 'backward regions' is more significant therefore than his distinction between 'the Empire' and 'the non-Empire', which is why this work generally uses the term 'colonies' not in its juridical sense but to denote the politically dominated backward economies.

The very diffusion of capitalism through an expansion of the core also meant a decline in Britain's position as 'the workshop of the world'. British goods were increasingly unable to compete not only in the markets of the newly industrialising countries, which in any case were protected through tariffs, but even in Britain's own market. The 'flight' to the underdeveloped countries' markets that Hobsbawm talks about was the way out. ' Latin America . . . it is not unfair to say, saved the British cotton industry in the first half of the nineteenth century, when it became the largest single market for its exports—reaching 35 per cent of them in 1840, mainly to Brazil'. The East Indies ' soon became absolutely crucial. From 6 per cent of our cotton exports after the Napoleonic Wars, this region came to absorb 22 per cent in 1840, 31 per cent in 1850, and an absolute majority of them—anything up to 60 per cent—after 1873. India took most of this—about 40–45 per cent after the onset of the Great Depression. Indeed in this period of difficulty Asia saved Lancashire, even more decisively than Latin America had done in the early part of the century' (Hobsbawm 1969, 146–7). Considering the fact that textiles formed 72 per cent of Britain's manufactured exports in 1867–9, and as much as 51 per cent even on the eve of the First World War, the underdeveloped Asian, and in particular the Indian, market was clearly of crucial significance.

To see how the two processes gelled together, assume for a moment that the colonial markets were not available to Britain. It may appear at first sight that *ceteris paribus* (that is, if Britain's imports from the colonies remained unchanged), Britain would have made larger capital exports to the 'new' countries (assuming there was demand for them) which would have left its domestic level of activity unchanged. These larger capital exports would have entailed a correspondingly larger borrowing from the colonies (since the amount of 'drain' in any period was given and could not have been raised at will), which would have left the net capital exports unchanged, but there was no reason to expect any serious crisis as long as the colonies were willing to extend credit to the requisite extent.

This line of argument however is erroneous. It presumes that whatever was not sold in the colonies could be sold in the 'new' countries through capital exports. In fact however large segments of the British economy, notably the textile industry, produced commodities for which demand was comparatively small at the going prices both in the old as well as in the new countries of the core. Since the transformation of the production structure is not an instantaneous process, if the colonial markets were not available, not only would Britain not have been able to make the magnitude of net capital exports that it did, but would have experienced a recession owing to lack of markets for its traditional products. And such a recession would surely have had repercussions for other countries of the core as well. If in the face of such a recessionary threat, it had decided to protect its domestic industries, then the Gold Standard would have been undermined, curtailing the long period of prosperity which the core countries enjoyed. The availability of the colonial markets therefore, by providing a way out of a potential disproportionality crisis, located in Britain but with implications for the core as a whole, sustained the long Victorian and Edwardian boom. And in addition, the 'drain' provided, within this boom framework, extra resources for undertaking net capital exports to speed up the diffusion of industrial capitalism to the 'new' countries.

In retrospect, the manner in which economic historians have analysed the effects of the terms-of-trade movements upon the British economy would appear highly unsatisfactory. Since Britain had access to colonial markets, and since the possibilities of capital exports to the frontiers always existed throughout more or less the nineteenth century, neither the advanced capitalist economies taken as a whole, nor the British economy taken in isolation, could have been considered in any basic sense as being demand-constrained. Even after the nineteenth century was over, the Edwardian years did not witness any serious demand constraint. Now, if a system is not demand-constrained, then a favourable movement in the terms of trade is all to the good as far as it is concerned: the volume of exports paid for by the foreign primary producing sector's earnings may fall, but this would have no effect upon the domestic level of activity, and need have no effect even upon its actual volume of exports as long as capital exports (including export surpluses *vis-à-vis* the primary producers) can be made. Indeed it is a symptom of the absence of any serious and persistent demand constraint that net capital exports to the colonies (including export surpluses) from the core countries taken as a whole remained comparatively small throughout the nineteenth century.

Thus, if the actual volume of British merchandise exports declined relative to its imports in the late nineteenth century, not only was this fact itself of no great consequence, but must have owed its origin to factors other than the terms-of-trade movements themselves, such as for example the structural shifts in the economy in favour of the service sector. At any rate, the view held both by Lewis

(1949) and Hobsbawm (1969) that the relative decline in Britain's merchandise exports late in the century was a result of its favourable terms-of-trade movement, and was somehow responsible for undermining the strength of the British balance of payments represents an illicit injection of underconsumptionism into the argument where there is hardly any scope for it.[2] On the contrary, the favourable terms-of-trade movement had a role logically analogous to that of the 'drain', and, if anything, would have contributed to the sustenance of the long boom.

4. THE ROLE OF INDIA IN THE PRE-WAR BOOM

The role of tropical colonies like India is brought out vividly in Saul's work (1960) on the multilateral pattern of payments settlement. For 1880, by Saul's estimate, Britain's balance of payments deficit (current account plus gold) *vis-à-vis* Europe and the USA was approximately £70m. Its trade and bullion balance *vis-à-vis* the rest of the world (excluding India) was just over £20m. and its capital exports for the year, on Cairncross's estimate, were around £9.3m. The total requirement for meeting the current account-cum-gold deficit with Europe and the USA, the merchandise-cum-gold deficit with the rest of the world (excluding India) and the export of capital was thus of the order of £100m. A quarter of this was provided by its overall surplus with India, while the rest must have come from invisible earnings from the rest of the world excluding Europe and the USA. The surplus with India was made up of £8m of interest receipts, about the same amount for Home Charges and remittances, £6.9m of positive trade and bullion balance and about a couple of million pounds of other invisible earnings. India alone thus met more than one-third of Britain's total payments deficit (current account plus gold) *vis-à-vis* the USA and Europe, with Turkey, Japan, Argentina, Brazil, and British Africa chipping in with small contributions.

---

[2] So when Hobsbawm says that Britain's export-boosting mechanism was undermined by the favourable movement in its terms of trade, he is taking it for granted that capital exports to the colonies for boosting its exports could not have taken place. At the very least this amounts to assuming something which needs to be established. For the underconsumptionist argument mediated through the terms of trade movements see the Introduction to P. Patnaik 1986.

By 1910 however the picture had changed quite considerably. Taking into account the total British balance of payments position (current as well as capital account), Britain's total deficit (*vis-à-vis* countries with which it did have a deficit) was £145m., of which the USA (£50m.), Continental Europe (£45m.), and Canada (£25m.) alone accounted for £120m. As much as £60m. for financing this deficit came from India alone, which thus financed more than two-fifths of the total, and more than 60 per cent of Britain's deficit *vis-à-vis* the USA and Continental Europe. India's excess of exports was £15.8m. with the rest of the Empire and £48.6m. with foreign countries for the year ending 31 March 1911. From Europe it earned £30m., from China and Hong Kong £10m., and from Japan and the USA £7m. each. Out of its total deficit with the UK of £60m., £19.5m. was on account of trade and bullion movements.

The point of these figures is as follows: it is not that between 1880 and 1910, a whole series of independent and uncoordinated changes occurred which added up to a significant change in the overall picture; rather the easy accessibility of the Indian market, which was unprotected and where there was no independent and sovereign State deciding on tariffs and commercial policy, allowed Britain to use India as a fulcrum to support its position in the international economy. In Saul's words, 'it was mainly through India that the British balance of payments found the flexibility essential to a great capital exporting country'.

The source of this flexibility lay in Britain's having the Indian market on tap. The change between 1880 and 1910 does not fully bring out the extent to which this was the case. After all the increase in Britain's net exports to India between 1880 and 1910 was only £12.7m. But the last few years before the First World War saw a really massive increase in Britain's trade and payments balance to India. Between 1907 and 1913, Britain's trade balance with India (merchandise and bullion) increased by £16.8m., and overall payments balance (including invisibles and capital exports) by £29.2m. The balance of merchandise trade alone increased by £14m. in these six years. As Saul puts it, 'Had not British exports, and particularly British cottons, found a wide open market in India during the last few years before the outbreak of war, it would have been impossible for it to have indulged so heavily in investment on the American continent and elsewhere'. It is only necessary to add that without this 'wide open' market, Britain would also have gone into a deep recession, deep because in any such recession the incidence of demand decline would have fallen more heavily on the home-produced rather than on the imported goods which were the first preference.

The use of India by Britain for the purpose of settling its payments obligation through the framework of multilateralism was nothing new. In the earlier part of the nineteenth century, when Britain had a trade deficit *vis-à-vis* China, India had been made to grow opium and China had been made to consume opium so that the colonial 'tribute' from India could be taken out in the form of an export surplus *vis-à-vis* China with which Britain could balance its own trade deficit with that country (Greenberg 1969; Tan Chung 1973). In the late nineteenth century and right up to the war, India was again being used to settle Britain's balance of payments deficits *vis-à-vis* third countries by making herself a 'wide open' market for British goods, quite apart from providing as before a 'drain' of economic surplus to Britain. It is this fact of having 'wide open' markets such as India that, as we have emphasised in the theoretical chapters, was crucial for the success of pre-war capitalism.

The change between the early and the late nineteenth century in this respect was a change not in the essence of the relationship, but in the context. With the diffusion of industrial capitalism over other parts of the world, not only did British goods find it difficult to compete with the goods produced by its rivals, but, what is more, Britain's industrial structure remained weighted much more towards older industries like textiles than its rivals', especially in Europe. Gerschenkron (1966) has drawn attention to this aspect, especially in drawing the contrast between the classical case of Britain and the late-comers like Germany, in whose industrialisation producers goods played a far more prominent part from the very outset. Even if Britain had, let us say, borrowed from India instead of exporting to her, and had increased the export of capital in the form of finance so that the profile of its net capital exports remained unchanged, this would not have created towards the end of the century any additional demand in the 'new' countries for British textiles. The problem, as mentioned earlier, was one of disproportionality, and the 'wide open' market of India was vital to it both to prevent domestic recession as well as to make capital exports possible.

For this no doubt Britain paid a price. The very cushion of the availability of 'wide open' markets in India and China, which propped up its outdated and increasingly uncompetitive industrial structure, prevented a British and hence global recession, and kept the long boom going, also implied that this structure was never renovated.[3] If a crisis, as Marx emphasised, was a peculiarly capitalist way of lopping off obsolete and dead-weight activities, then the prevention of a crisis, though immensely beneficial for the system as a whole, makes the country, saddled with more of such activities (typically the leading capitalist country of the time) grow more and more vulnerable. This is one of the contradictions of the leadership position. By keeping its obsolete and dead-weight activities going, the leading country permits the entire system to grow without serious interruptions (and itself enjoys stability in the immediate sense), but this very growth undermines its own leading position, increasingly makes it vulnerable at the future date when the roller-coaster ride will come to an end, as it inevitably will.

5. THE COLLAPSE OF BRITISH HEGEMONY

The pre-war boom, precisely because of its prolonged and pronounced nature, had heightened these contradictions to a point where the crash, when it came, was all the mightier. There were no doubt many factors that merged to contribute to the conjuncture of the 1930s Great Depression, and different authors have emphasised different ones among these. For Schumpeter (1939, vol. 2, ch. 15, section G), it was the coincidence of the troughs of his three different types of historically observed cycles, a peculiar combination of circumstances produced by the ebb-and-flow of innovations. For Hansen (1938, 1941), it was the closing of the frontier, especially in the United States, the exhaustion of the empty spaces to which labour and capital could earlier migrate. For Fisher (1933), it was the inevitable sequel to the massive debt pile-up which had taken place in the preceding years. For Baran and Sweezy (1966, ch. 8), it was the outburst of the potential underconsumption crisis which had been building up from around the turn of the century because of the rise of monopolies, but which had been kept at bay by the

---

3 Those who use this to argue that the Empire was more costly than beneficial are committing a methodological error, making a cost–benefit analysis of a historical phenomenon which, like all such phenomena, has contradictory aspects. Such contradictions by their very nature cannot be telescoped into the single dimension required for a cost–benefit analysis.

automobile innovation that had played a role similar to that of the railways in the 1840s. For Kindleberger (1987), it was the upheaval in the sphere of international finance arising from the fact that Britain could no longer play the leadership role, while the USA demurred from assuming it. And for Kaldor (Kaldor and Mirrlees 1962), it was a drying up of the possibilities of technological progress.

These explanations are not necessarily mutually exclusive, and more than one of them captures some real factor contributing to the conjuncture. But one component of the picture which has scarcely been discussed sufficiently is the loss of British hegemony over Asia. Britain had been the lynch-pin of the earlier system, and had survived, and thereby contributed to the prolongation of the great Victorian and Edwardian boom, by going deeper and deeper into the Indian and Chinese markets. After the war, this was no longer possible.

British textiles declined sharply in the Far East and Indian markets after the war: local textile industries had arisen in both India and China, and Japanese competition began to be felt sharply. Under the combined pressure of local industries and Japanese imports (these two also competed fiercely against one another, with Japan increasingly gaining the upper hand until quantitative restrictions were imposed on Japanese imports in the 1930s in many Asian countries in the run-up to the Second World War),[4] Britain no longer had the 'wide open' markets of the pre-war years. Under the circumstances the Gold Standard was impossible to maintain after its resurrection, and, when the world went off Gold, a massive depreciation of the yen flooded Asian markets with Japanese goods, until the quantitative restrictions, just mentioned, were hastily erected. This marked a turning point: Japan decided to achieve by military means the penetration into Britain's Asian Empire that it had been denied while using aggressive economic warfare (see Lewis 1949).

Britain tried for a while through the Ottawa Agreement and by introducing a measure of protection in its colonies to form an alliance with the emerging local bourgeoisie against Japan as a rearguard action to preserve its tottering economic hegemony over Asia, but the British decline could not be halted. The Depression continued until preparations for the Second World War began.

---

[4] For Japanese incursions into the Indian market and the competition between Indian and Japanese producers, see Bagchi 1972.

Though the foregoing change would have produced a depression, would it necessarily have been the Great Depression? The collapse of British hegemony, which had sustained the Long Boom, and the inevitable uncertainties affecting in particular the export of capital, which the abandonment of the Gold Standard, another relic of *Pax Britannica*, entailed, would certainly have provided material enough for a serious slump. The fact that this slump became the Great Depression has to do with several of the factors mentioned earlier, in particular factors affecting the USA, which was the other main actor in the drama. But Britain's increasing difficulties in the colonial and semi-colonial markets, which, in the years of burgeoning capital exports to the expanding frontier, had been used to overcome disproportionality, and could now have been made to absorb British export surpluses, was an important element in its own right.

Looking at the matter from another angle, the technological distance between what Britain produced and what even backward economies like India and China could produce kept narrowing during the Long Boom. All the more so with Japan, which had neither been a colony or semi-colony, nor been a beneficiary of the British-led diffusion of industrial capitalism, but which had undoubtedly benefited from close economic links with the United States. The 'flying geese' pattern of technical change involving the advanced and the backward economies, whose necessity was underscored in Chapter 8, could not be maintained. The British goose kept lagging behind until a part of it was no more ahead than a host of others.

6. CONTRADICTIONS OF *PAX AMERICANA*

The fact that the post-war period has witnessed till now yet another sustained boom may be disputed by those who see the period after the mid-1970s as marking a break. The slowing down of the rate of growth in the advanced capitalist world as a whole, the much larger levels of unemployment than in the pre-mid-1970s period, the collapse of the Bretton Woods system and the re-emergence at the economic level of rivalries among the advanced capitalist countries (though far more muted than in earlier periods), would be cited by them as symptoms of a crisis, reminiscent more of the inter-war period than of the late-Victorian or Edwardian era. That there is a change is undeniable; nonetheless, unless we stretch the meaning of the word 'crisis' to an extreme degree, the post-mid-1970s period can hardly be so described. It is more useful to look upon it as a continuation, though with accentuating contradictions within it, of the post-war boom.[5] The important point however is that these contradictions are reminiscent of the contradictions of the Edwardian era that we have been discussing so far.

This may at first sight appear surprising; and indeed there is one crucial difference. The Long Boom of the earlier period was sustained by the fact that the British market was open to encroachment by the then newly industrialising countries, which had themselves put up tariff barriers, while Britain retreated into the colonial markets and relied upon its invisible earnings, not only to cover what would otherwise have been a large trade deficit, but even to keep making net capital exports right until the war. The current Long Boom is sustained by the fact that the market of the USA, the post-war leader of the capitalist world, has been open to encroachment by its rivals, Japan and Germany, but the USA has nowhere to retreat. Its current account deficit is met by an inflow of capital from abroad, but it is prevented from slipping into a slump, which would have repercussions over the entire capitalist world, by maintaining a huge budget deficit.

The implications of this crucial difference will be examined later. It is important however to see that the continuation of such a state of affairs merely entails a continuation of the uncompetitive industrial structure of the USA. To be sure, the USA still remains the world leader in basic research, and consequently in inventions. It also remains the world leader in introducing a host of frontier technologies. But despite spending large amounts on basic research, the USA does not have the highest rate of productivity growth in the capitalist world, and this fact manifests itself in the surprisingly large stock of old technologies in use in the USA, a point noted by Baran and Sweezy (1966, 96). The fruits of basic research do not remain

---

5 A discussion of the specific context underlying the boom, e.g. the greater coherence among the metropolitan powers in contrast to their inter-war rivalry (a coherence that made the Bretton Woods arrangement possible in the first place), and of its specific constituent elements, e.g. Keynesian demand-management policies, the burst of post-war innovations etc., lies outside the scope of this book. For a comprehensive discussion see Armstrong, Glyn and Harrison 1991. A synoptic view can be found in P. Patnaik 1986.

confined to the USA alone, but are appropriated by other capitalist countries, which also appropriate and improve upon US innovations. While the USA thus is in no position to derive exclusive benefit from such activities as basic research, where it is the world leader, its rate of investment is not high enough to give it a sufficiently high rate of productivity growth.

Since technology is generally of the embodied variety, a higher rate of capital accumulation raises the ratio of new capital stock with higher labour productivity to the old capital stock with lower labour productivity. With a given capital–output ratio, this amounts to saying that a higher ratio of investment in output is associated *ceteris paribus* with a higher rate of growth of labour productivity. It is not surprising then that the rate of growth of labour productivity in the USA with a lower investment ratio is less than in economies like Japan which have far higher investment ratios.

Even assuming the same wage–profit ratio everywhere and a constant ratio over time, higher productivity growth, since it is accompanied on average by a larger proportion of new products, also helps boost exports, a conclusion which is strengthened if the divergence between product wages and productivity is larger (or increases faster) in the high-productivity-growth country. Not surprisingly then, the US products have lost out to Japanese competition; and the threat of Japanese competition itself is perhaps one of the factors keeping the inducement to invest low in the US economy. The tax-cuts instituted in the Reagan era led for instance to a consumption rather than an investment boom.[6]

The USA is caught in the same syndrome as Britain was in the Edwardian era. While it keeps its market open for its rivals and keeps up its level of activity through a large budget deficit, and thereby sustains the entire advanced capitalist world economy, the price for doing so is a progressive loss of its competitiveness *vis-à-vis* its rivals. Against this background it is faced with the following dilemma, as indeed Britain would have been but for its colonies. If it continues in the same way, then quite apart from the progressive loss of competitiveness, it is piling up foreign debt at an amazing rate, which must mean over time a transfer of asset ownership to foreigners that the US bourgeoisie would not be too keen to witness. If it protects the

[6] The failure of the Reagan boom to stimulate investment in plant and machinery is underscored in Sweezy and Magdoff 1987.

domestic market, that would mean precipitating a world-wide economic antagonism among the capitalist powers which cannot but have dangerous repercussions for the health of the system as a whole, apart from holding serious recessionary possibilities. A currency depreciation, even with the consent of its rivals, has potentially inflationary consequences, apart from being ineffective, as experience has shown. Finally, if it cuts down the budget deficit, then this would unleash a recession that would be particularly severe for itself, since the American public would more readily cut down its consumption of home-produced goods than that of imported goods.

The other possible ways out of the predicament are also fraught with serious problems. The USA could cut down its budget deficit, and stimulate domestic investment at the same time. But, unlike Japanese-style capitalism where the relationship between the State and capital is very close, so that there is a greater degree of planning in the economy with the State influencing capitalists' decisions, in the USA the State can hardly induce the capitalists to invest more. These decisions are shaped largely by their own expectations which the State can stimulate only indirectly, and hence not necessarily successfully.

Inducing Japan to invest more domestically is unlikely to succeed since Japan has been operating close to full employment, and is not too keen on taking in migrant workers. Inducing Japan to boost its domestic consumption at the expense of its export surplus is also unlikely to bear fruit. If a rise in the share of wages in Japan is seen as an instrument for achieving a higher domestic propensity to consume, one cannot seriously expect Japanese capitalists to acquiesce in such a move voluntarily. On the other hand, raising the domestic propensity to consume with given income shares is not a very promising course of action over any short length of time. Getting Japan to spend more on militarism may appear feasible; and indeed Japan's military expenditure has been rising rapidly. But the fear of Japanese militarism still looms large, including within Japan where the growth of militarism, associated as it had been in the past with Japanese fascism, arouses opposition from large sections of the population, and is considered unnecessary even by sections of the liberal bourgeoisie since Japan enjoys unprecedented access to world markets anyway. After all, the triumph of militarism in Japan in the 1930s was not unconnected with its exclusion, as we have seen, from the cordoned-off markets of the British Empire (see P. Patnaik 1989).

7. THE LIMITATIONS OF GLOBAL KEYNESIANISM

One way out of the problem would be for the advanced capitalist world to export capital to the backward economies. A reduction in the US budget deficit through a cut in the State expenditure would, as we have seen, have a recessionary impact on the US economy. While reducing US imports, it would simultaneously reduce demand for domestically produced goods. But if the surplus of US goods as well as rivals' goods, which emerged because of a cut in State expenditure sufficient to maintain trade balance between the USA and its rivals, were both exported to the backward countries, then at one stroke the growth of US debt would have been eliminated, as well as the dangers of a recession. These exports to the backward countries would have to be financed by an export of capital, but it seems on the face of it to be an attractive way out.

If the US current account deficit is, say, $100, and if out of every $1 of State expenditure $0.8 is spent on US goods and $0.2 on imported goods, then a cut in State expenditure by $100 and an increase in US exports by $80 would eliminate its deficit and leave its level of domestic activity unchanged. If its rivals (we assume here for simplicity that all imports are from rivals alone) also exported $20 more to the backward economies, then they too would face no recession. Domestic consumption and investment everywhere would have remained the same. Even though capital exports to the backward countries would have risen by $100, since the US budget deficit would have simultaneously fallen by $100, all it would mean is that instead of holding US government bonds, the wealth-holders would be holding at the margin some other government's bonds which happens to belong to a backward country, or some other kind of claim on the backward country. And as many liberal writers argue, a further advantage of this is that with $100 of capital exports the backward countries can invest more and have a higher growth rate.

Schemes such as these have been put forward by many. A cut for instance in military expenditure by the US government, and a diversion of an equivalent amount to the backward countries as foreign credit, helps the latter, eliminates the US current account deficit, does not (apart from transitional problems of adjustment) create any unemployment anywhere, or any cuts in consumption or investment, and is altogether better for the world. What is more, it is not the USA, which has to bear the burden of the capital exports. If earlier the Japanese wealth-holders were giving loans to the USA worth $100, it is the same Japanese wealth-holders who can now finance the capital exports. The so-called Okita Plan (Okita *et al.* 1986) hinges on this: the Japanese surplus is invested in the Third World, may be with the backing of the Japanese government; for the plan to succeed there must be a cut in US expenditure (or unutilised capacity in the USA).

There are two distinct problems with such plans in capitalist conditions. The first is the assumption that capital exports to the backward country would necessarily raise consumption or investment there. They could equally well finance a process of deindustrialisation in the backward country, or be used for raising government armament expenditure there. The likelihood of such kinds of use is great because the commodities that would be released by cuts in US expenditure would not exactly be the ones needed for raising investment or consumption of the masses in the backward country. Instead of bringing about adjustments in the production structure, the capitalist producers in the advanced countries are more likely to use credits for off-loading the released commodities on Third World markets.

Second, even assuming that this does not happen, and that backward countries do possess, and wisely utilise, the freedom to spend the loan amount on, say, investment, the crucial question is: why should anybody make such loans available to them? Even assuming that the USA did cut State expenditure, no Japanese rentier would be as willing to hold claims on Brazil or India as he would be to hold claims on the USA. The whole problem of the Third World's debt would not be a problem if this was not the case.

Every country has natural resources, land and other obvious assets. If lenders could feel confident that by giving a loan they could get ownership over the country's assets in the event of a default, then they might be willing to give loans, at any rate as long as the country still had some non-foreign-owned assets. But in the absence of a degree of political control which ensures that the country 'plays the game', and that its next government does not simply repudiate the conditions of the loan, if not the loan itself, few lenders can have this confidence. The question of credits to the Third World in other words is inextricably linked to that of political control; it is on this issue that all well-meaning schemes, including those of 'Global Keynesians' such as the Brandt Commission, inevitably flounder.

In contemporary conditions, where the exercise of political hegemony over the backward countries is no longer possible, getting them under the discipline of the IMF, which ensures their conformity to the 'rules of the game', prevents any nationalist or radical policy alternatives being tried out, and removes hindrances to the transfer of asset-ownership to foreigners arising from considerations of sovereignty, acts as a surrogate for such hegemony. But IMF discipline is only a necessary, but by no means a sufficient, condition for the extension of large-scale credit to the Third World, even for the purpose of off-loading commodities.

Nonetheless, whether or not Third World markets offer a way out of the current contradictions of the advanced capitalist countries, whether or not the scale of credit required for undertaking sizeable sales in such markets would be forthcoming, the effort to prise open these markets for commodities from the core has of late become quite intense. The USA has been vociferously demanding that international trade in services should be liberalised, that intellectual property rights should be recognised, and that protectionism in the Third World should be rolled back. All these are measures which would result inevitably in a displacement of the local production of a variety of goods and services in the Third World by imports from the core.

8. THE ROLE OF BACKWARD ECONOMY MARKETS: A SUMMING-UP

To sum up the argument. The term 'capital exports' is a hold-all, and for that reason potentially misleading, category. One must draw a distinction between two quite different kinds of capital exports. The diffusion of capitalism through an extension of the core to the 'empty spaces', where local manufacturing capacity develops, is brought about by one kind of capital exports. At the same time, the deindustrialisation of economies where existing manufacturing capacity is supplanted by imports from the core can also result from capital exports, which are of our second kind.

The backward economies, notably the tropical colonies and semi-colonies, did not see much of the first kind of capital exports, which went predominantly to the temperate regions of white settlement. Whatever of such capital exports they did see was for the purpose of introducing railways, plantations and mines, for tying them into the international system as primary producers. The second kind of capital exports they may see from time to time, but even these historically have been rather limited. Commodity exports from the core leading to deindustrialisation in the periphery have of course been there, but such exports in general have been matched by (and where 'drain' has taken place, exceeded by) imports of primary commodities. The external stimulus which has visibly contributed to the prevention of general over-production (as opposed to disproportionality), has been either capital exports of the first kind to the frontiers, or, as in recent years, capital exports to the State of the leading capitalist nation. It is this situation of more or less balanced trade between the core and the periphery which our theoretical model took as a stylised fact. What it did not consider, though it has historically been of extreme importance, is the role of backward economy markets in overcoming disproportionality.

12

Diffusion of Activities and the
Terms of Trade

The theoretical discussion in chapters 7 and 8 assumed that the manufactured good produced in the backward economy could not be exported. Such an extreme assumption is not necessary for our argument. Even if the workers in the advanced economy spend a fixed proportion of their consumption expenditure on the backward economy's manufactured good, the argument remains unscathed, as indeed it does if the capitalists in the backward economy wish to spend a fixed fraction of their consumption expenditure on this good; this fraction does not have to be zero. In either case the growth rate of the backward economy gets tethered to that of the advanced economy, which is all that is needed for our argument. The argument would not hold, namely the growth rate of the former would get untethered from that of the latter only if the backward economy could keep expanding its *market share*. The present chapter discusses why it cannot do so.

1. LIMITS TO AUTOMATIC DIFFUSION

We can look at the matter in general terms as follows. There are, say, n number of activities in any period of time whose outputs are being demanded in both segments. Some of these are located in the backward segment, some in the advanced segment, and some in both. In this last case where there are overlapping activities in the two segments, an identical activity would have a different weight in the world market. Of these n, say k, l and m denote respectively the three different groups of activities. Let us also assume that as technological progress occurs, *n* remains unchanged. Some activities drop out completely as others take their place. (They drop out, that is, from the bundle of goods that is demanded by the advanced economy workers and the backward economy capitalists.) We use the term diffusion to denote any tendency *ceteris paribus* either for k to increase, or for l to decline, or for the weight of the backward segment's production to increase in m. Diffusion is necessarily associated with an increase in the share of the backward economy's manufactured goods in the total market for manufactured goods.

Three different types of diffusion should be distinguished. The first we shall call voluntary diffusion. It is nothing but a spatial expansion of the core itself, such as the diffusion of manufacturing from Britain first to Europe, and subsequently to the temperate regions of white settlement. The hallmark of this type of diffusion is that it is accompanied by large-scale migration of capital (and of skills) from the original core to new areas where it replicates activities embodying even frontier technologies, not only to meet the local market but even for exporting back to the original core. This is the type of diffusion which featured in the previous chapter. A special case of such diffusion which has attracted much attention in recent years is the voluntary relocation of activities from high-wage to low-wage areas, even when there is no compelling need to do so.

The second type of diffusion we shall call automatic diffusion. This entails the involuntary shift of certain activities, because of competition, from the high-wage core to the low-wage backward economies. Metropolitan capital may be coerced into making such a shift, but typically it is the ability of the local bourgeoisie to undertake successful production of certain activities within the backward economy and to outcompete the metropolitan producers that provides the basis for such diffusion. In conditions of free-market competition this is the type of diffusion that would be accompanied by the destruction of low-productivity-growth sectors at the core, and their supplanting by production in backward economies.

The third kind of diffusion we shall call enforced diffusion. It is where the backward economy uses its own State deliberately to protect its markets, and to undertake activities which had hitherto been the exclusive preserve of the core. It represents a snatching of space by the local bourgeoisie from metropolitan capital, though the latter may, and does, cut its losses, and participate in the process through collaborations of various kinds. This kind of diffusion, which was the object of the so-called import substituting industrialisation in the Third World, will be discussed in the next chapter.[1] It differs from the other two in the sense that it represents an intervention by the backward economy's State in the spontaneous working of the market, while the others occur within the market context itself. The second type differs from the first by virtue of the fact that it usually represents an involuntary concession of space by metropolitan capital in certain spheres rather than a voluntary decision either to expand the core, or to relocate a whole spectrum of operations. Such strategic decisions on the part of metropolitan capital to relocate its activities, or of the metropolis to allow large-scale capital transfers, while they may have benefited a few countries such as South Korea, Hong Kong, and Singapore, are unlikely to be of much help for the Third World as a whole, or at any rate for large Third World countries like India and China. But the second kind of diffusion, which metropolitan capital or the State cannot prevent, given a reasonable degree of free functioning of markets (the absence of deliberate protection) is of interest to large Third World countries, as well as to others. Let us look at it closely.

Two conditions must be satisfied for automatic diffusion to occur. The first relates to the configuration of relative prices, which, with given mark-ups, depend upon the configuration of relative wages. In Chapter 7 we had two manufactured goods, one produced by each segment. However we can visualise each segment having an activity producing its own variant of each of the n commodities. Let us assume for a moment that they do so with identical technology (so that innovations are instantaneously imitated), and have identical labour productivity for every activity. The actual bundle of n commodities which the backward segment capitalists and the advanced segment workers would like to choose at any given configuration of relative wages would consist partly of commodities produced exclusively in one segment or the other and partly of commodities produced in both and considered identical at the prevailing relative prices. Now, we argued in Chapter 7, for any pair of comparable commodity variants, there is a relative price range over which the

---

[1] Import substitution can logically occur, even without *any* diffusion, by the backward economy's State simply lowering ξ^* (see Chapter 7) through deliberate controls. Typically, however, it *has* entailed a change in the production structure; i.e. diffusion.

advanced segment's commodity is preferred; only if the relative price of the backward segment's commodity falls below this, would demand switch towards it. This range however is not identical for all pairs of comparable variants. In general, the more new the commodity, the greater would be this range, that is the lower would the relative price of the backward segment's variant have to be to overcome consumer resistance against buying from an imitator whose credentials are as yet dubious. Since innovations are occurring in every period, this preference pattern may be postulated to repeat itself through time.

It follows that for any given configuration of relative wages, there would be a given distribution of preferences across activities in the two segments, and hence a given distribution of activities in steady-state equilibrium. *Diffusion*, in the sense of an increasing market share for the backward segment, would occur only if its relative wages keep declining over time. An identical wage difference between the two segments persisting over time permits only the maintenance of a given distribution of activities across segments but not diffusion, not the growing encroachment of one segment over another.

The second condition, which we deliberately assumed to be satisfied above in order to concentrate on the first, is that the backward economy should be capable of imitating the technology of production in a range of activities. One of the weaknesses of Schumpeter's innovation-imitation discussion is the lack of recognition of any constraints upon the ability to imitate. By contrast, when Marx postulated a minimum scale of capital as being a precondition for the introduction of new technology, this precondition applied not only to the act of innovation but also to the act of imitation as well.[2]

---

[2] Marx (1974a, 262) wrote: 'Under competition, the increasing minimum of capital required with the increase in productivity for the successful operation of an independent industrial establishment, assumes the following aspect: As soon as the new, more expensive equipment has become universally established, smaller capitals are henceforth excluded from this industry.' In a model which has a family resemblance to ours, but which is essentially Schumpeterian in spirit, Dollar (1986) assumed no technological constraints upon imitation, and showed that, but for innovations, factor-price equalisation would take place between the North and the South. Our results differ from his because we assume constraints upon capital mobility from the North to the South, constraints upon the ability of the South to imitate North's technology across the spectrum, and an insensitivity of demand to changes in the relative prices of the manufactured goods produced in the two regions. In Dollar's model there is no scope for the South being the main repository of labour reserves, which in our view is the basic characteristic of the international economy.

Marx's comments related to *individual* capitals. In the context of countries we adapted Marx's proposition to postulate in Chapter 8 that a precondition for a country to be an innovator on the world market was the possession at any given point of time of a minimum capital stock per capita. This can also be taken as the threshold below which there is a technological limit to the extent of diffusion. For countries falling below this threshold, there is a maximum limit to the extent of *potential* diffusion. In the context of automatic diffusion however where conscious State action in the backward segment to snatch activities away from the metropolis is not being considered, the ceiling upon the extent of *actual* diffusion would be less than this: the *individual* capitals may be too small to achieve the minimum scale required for successfully imitating metropolitan technology, the risks associated may be prohibitive for private entrepreneurs, and so forth. The difference between what is maximally possible under spontaneous market operation and the technological maximum is what allows scope for enforced diffusion.

It follows that there are limits to automatic diffusion. For example even if computer technology were to become well-known, not all Third World countries would possess the necessary infrastructure to undertake competitive manufacture of computers; and even if they did, a spontaneous diffusion of computer manufacturing would not necessarily occur. The entrepreneurs could always import the components and assemble them domestically. But since their competitive edge lies in their comparatively lower wages, unless there is a significant element of value addition they are hardly likely to emerge as successfully competing producers.

There are however some areas where they can imitate with success. Where the minimum scale of production is not prohibitively large, where the size of the home market in which a footing must first be obtained is also correspondingly large, where the technology in question is relatively simple and does not require the use of sophisticated technology in a number of complementary spheres either, Third World countries can step into the shoes of the original innovators. The textiles industry provides the classic example of a case where all these preconditions are satisfied. But there are others as well.

Even so, in any given period there are only certain activities into which Third World producers can enter, and in which they can successfully compete, *no matter how low their wages are.* While over time

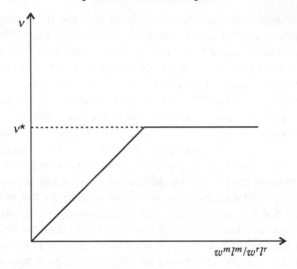

Fig. 12.1.

this list of activities expands, innovations at the core imply that a limit upon diffusion in our sense exists, quite irrespective of the wage rates, at every point of time.

The two points mentioned above can be put together as follows. The distribution of activities (for which we can take the index $v = (k + \sum_i^m \tau_i)/n$, where τ_is denote, for overlapping activities, the shares of the backward segment's manufactures in the total demand of the backward segment capitalists and the advanced segment workers)[3] is an increasing function over a certain range of the ratio of the wage rate in the advanced segment to that in the backward segment. At a certain value, however, v reaches a ceiling for reasons we have discussed and no longer responds to any further change in the wage ratio (Figure 12.1). Since there is nothing to indicate that over successive periods the pattern would be any different, Figure 12.1 can be assumed to hold over time as well.

The implications of this are important. Automatic diffusion can at best only be a transitional phenomenon. If wages in the backward economy rise *pari passu* with productivity, as they do in the advanced

---

[3] These weights can be taken as value ratios. It may of course be objected that for consistency's sake we should then be taking the index of distribution v as also a value ratio and not a ratio between numbers. But it makes little difference to our argument how we define this index; so we shall stick to the above.

economy, then lower wages can yield only a higher v, but not a rising one. We can in such a situation visualise for given parameters, i.e. for given mark-ups, given trade union strengths, given innovation-linked expenditure per unit of GDP in the advanced segment, and no tendency for a change over time in the core's import propensity for the periphery's products, a steady-state growth path for the coupled system with output, manufacturing productivity and manu-facturing wage rates rising at the same rate in both segments and the distribution of activities and the terms-of-trade constant. If on the other hand wages in the periphery do not rise with productivity, there can still be a steady state with v at its maximum possible level (under automatic diffusion), provided the underconsumption generated by the wages in the periphery not rising with productivity is somehow taken care of.[4] In either case then diffusion in the sense of a sus-tained rise in v is not possible.

Across steady states however the one involving a lower v has a lower proportion of periphery's output to core output. A reduction in this index then has the transitional effect of lowering the growth rate of the periphery. Such a reduction can come about owing to increased protectionism at the core. Protectionism at the core in other words can keep v below what is maximally possible through automatic diffusion. Even if it is at this maximum to start with, increased protectionism can have the transitional effect of lowering the periphery's growth rate.

In addition however we have seen that changes in the consump-tion pattern away from primary commodities and movements in terms of trade against the latter entail uneven development where the periphery's growth rate is kept below that of the core. It follows then that even in the absence of protectionism and even if the wages in the periphery relative to the core could be pushed down at will, the maximum long-run rate of growth the periphery can sustain (with v at its possible maximum under automatic diffusion) is below the rate of growth at the core. An increase in protectionism at the core can further reduce it from this level, though only transitionally.

If in the very process of reaching the maximum v, which is all the

---

[4] A steady state where v is at its maximum and wages are not rising with productivity in the backward segment, i.e. where the rates of growth of money wages in the two segments are divergent, cannot obtain with a fixed-mark-up-based pricing of the backward economy's manufactured goods. The mark-up is bound to increase along a steady-state path, which means that the rate of growth of product wages (not just money wages) remains below the rate of growth of productivity, entailing a potential underconsumption problem.

diffusion that is automatically permissible, the periphery's economy has not made any dent in its labour reserves, then it can scarcely hope to do so after its growth rate has become tethered to that of the core (though at a level below that of the core owing to changing tastes and terms of trade). And in case in the process of reaching the maximum v, the periphery's labour reserves do start getting used up rapidly, the State at the core can always intervene to prevent it (to preserve the stabilising mechanism of the system) by bringing down the maximum v through protectionism.

The foregoing is in sharp contrast to the optimism regarding the prospects of diffusion displayed by a number of authors including Arthur Lewis (1978*b*). In the changed context of post-war capitalism which has meant, according to him, an end of dual labour markets at the core and a greater importance of relativities in wage bargaining by workers in the sluggish productivity-growth sectors, Lewis detects a change in attitudes: 'The main purpose of nineteenth century foreign investment was to facilitate the exports of primary products. Indeed industrial countries took great pains to organise their tariffs so as to exclude manufactures from low-wage countries. Thus, there were low tariffs on raw materials, with high tariffs on the processed version of these same materials . . . And . . . even after the Kennedy round the tariffs of industrial countries on the kinds of manufactures imported from developing countries were much higher than the tariffs on goods they imported from each other. European and American investment in the developing countries to produce light manufactures for European and American markets is a new phenomenon of the second half of the twentieth century . . .'. This however is arguable on a number of counts.

Lewis's argument must be distinguished from that of the Starnberg group. He sees the phenomenon as arising from the fact of labour shortage, with the corollary that in a situation of high core unemployment it would presumably be reversed, if not spontaneously, then at any rate through State action. The Starnberg group sees this shift of capital elsewhere for export production destined for the core as an autonomous tendency resulting in high unemployment. Both however would differ from our perception of automatic diffusion. First, they see the diffusion of manufacturing as occurring under the aegis of metropolitan capital in Third World countries rather than of local Third World capital, aided by circumstances. However, the exports of simple manufactures from a host of countries such as Taiwan, India, or Brazil cannot be attributed to any significant direct investment from the metropolis. Second, and more importantly, despite the fact that a degree of diffusion of simple manufacturing to some backward countries has taken place, there still remain considerable hurdles to their import into the core. The Multi-Fibre Agreement of course is a classic example (Chandrashekhar 1986). Meant only as a transitional measure of protection in the beginning to enable an orderly and gradual structural shift away from the textile sector in the core countries, it has not only become a permanent fixture, but has over time even expanded its scope and coverage. And in the face of high unemployment rates in the core countries, and the clamour for protectionism in the USA, the Lewisian optimism appears altogether rather excessive.

The diffusion of manufacturing and other activities from the core to the backward countries, whether this diffusion occurs under the aegis of metropolitan capital itself, or whether it is enforced upon the core by the fact that in several spheres it becomes uncompetitive *vis-à-vis* backward country products, can play an extremely important role for particular countries, as indeed it has done for the four East Asian countries, Hong Kong, Singapore, Taiwan and South Korea. But its role as an engine of growth for the backward economies as a whole should not be overestimated. For example, the total manufactured exports from the underdeveloped world as a proportion of total manufactured goods exports in the world (excluding the centrally planned economies from both the numerator and the denominator), increased from 4.2 per cent in 1963 to only 7.6 per cent in 1977, a period of nearly a decade and a half during which diffusion of manufacturing was widely believed to have been rampant.[5] Much of this growth moreover was confined to the four East Asian small economies. If we exclude them from among the underdeveloped countries, the remaining countries' shares in the total manufactured exports of the capitalist world were 2.5 per cent and 3.1 per cent respectively on these two dates. It is true that the volume of manufactured goods exports grew at a much higher rate during the 1960s and the 1970s than ever before in the history of capitalism. Lewis's figures show that in the 1883–1913 period, world trade in

<hr>

[5] The figures given here are calculated from various issues of the World Bank's *World Development Report*; Nayyar (1978) gives similar figures. See also Chandrashekhar 1986.

manufactured goods had grown at the rate of 3.5 per cent per annum, compared to which between 1957 and 1969 the rate was 8.7 per cent per annum. But the bulk of this growth in trade was among the advanced countries themselves. TheThirdWorld's share, even including the Group of Four, increased only slightly, and continued to remain quite minuscule even up to the second oil shock, after which the growth of world trade in any case slowed down.

The argument often advanced that this minuscule share, far from showing the constraints upon diffusion, underscores on the contrary the tremendous scope for diffusion which exists, is a complete *non sequitur* as it stands. The neoclassical economists however make the additional point that the reasons for the Third World countries' inability to increase their share of manufactured goods exports in world trade is a result of their own policies, and that the successes of the East Asian four could have been replicated elsewhere if only the others had followed in their footsteps.

But what does 'following in their footsteps' mean? If it means, as many neoclassical economists suggest, pursuing a policy of 'liberal trade' and 'leaving things to the market', if it is this policy which is held responsible for their success, then such a policy regime is clearly replicable elsewhere, and has been and is being replicated. But it represents a complete misreading of the East Asian experience. On the other hand, any *sui generis* analysis of the East Asian experience suggests factors underlying their success which are intrinsically incapable of being replicated either in theThirdWorld as a whole or even in majorThirdWorld economies. So we turn to the East Asian experience and examine the question of its replicability, concentrating on South Korea and Japan, which provide the original 'model', and referring only occasionally toTaiwan.The two city-States, Hong Kong and Singapore, are so obviously special cases that the argument about replicating *their* experience carries little conviction anyway.

2. THE NATURE OF THE
EAST ASIAN STRATEGY

The basic development strategy pursued in Japan, and subsequently in South Korea, can be characterised as a 'neomercantilist' one. This has the following essential features: a bureaucratic–authoritarian State promoting the development of a class of domestic capitalists;

its nurturing and 'guiding' this class, especially the big capitalists, into being an internationally effective player, through influencing the flow of resources into targeted areas to take advantage of the possibilities inherent in the product cycle; a cordoning off of the domestic economic space for the domestic capitalists while a relentless export drive is undertaken for capturing export markets; and a utilisation of the market mechanism for this overall strategic end, supplemented of course by interventions in it and by-passing of it, where necessary, without making the market the determining factor in the process of resource generation and allocation (Jones and Sakong 1980; Bagchi 1987; Deyo 1987; Johnson 1982; Amsden 1989).

There are important differences between Japan and South Korea, notably the fact that South Korea relied heavily upon the inflow of external resources (though only marginally on direct foreign investment until much later) for boosting its rate of capital accumulation, compared to Japan. There are also important differences between South Korea and Taiwan, for which too the term 'neo-mercantilism' has been used (Haggard and Cheng 1987): in Taiwan for instance the role of direct foreign investment was significant from the outset, and the domestic bourgeoisie being nurtured by the State was a more widely dispersed class of small capitalists rather than anything comparable to the *chaebol*. Besides, in all these economies, the nature of the economic regime did not remain immutable: it changed through time as the economies themselves matured. Notwithstanding this however the main features mentioned above as constituting the neo-mercantilist strategy can be discerned in varying degrees in all three economies during crucial periods of their economic ascendancy.

This strategy is a far cry from the usual neoclassical interpretation which posits a simple dichotomy between dirigiste import-substituting regimes and outward-looking, 'market-friendly' open economies, and argues that starting in 1958 in Taiwan, and in 1961 in South Korea, a switch was made from one to the other. But the switch did not eliminate dirigisme. It consolidated it, though in a form different from India or Latin America of the 1950s, while giving it a purposeful neo-mercantilist orientation. Indeed, terms like 'Japan Incorporated' or 'Korea Incorporated', though drawing attention to the close links between the State and big capital, can be misleading on the nature of the neo-mercantilist strategy. They fail to highlight sufficiently the leading role of the State, the fact that the State was not just a malleable instrument in the hands of the dominant social class in civil society, but was instrumental in this class coming into being and guided and nurtured it into international significance as a part of a process of national industrialisation (Haggard and Cheng 1987).

While an extensive literature has grown up by now on the role of the State in East Asian industrialisation, so that any further dilation on the theme is unnecessary, the other aspect of the strategy, namely the drive for export markets *even while reserving the domestic market for the local big capitalists*, which is so different from the policy of 'trade liberalisation' advocated by the Fund and the Bank, has received less attention. In the case of Japan however the export boom began from within a regime of import controls, and the removal of import restrictions as well as the reduction of tariffs followed rather than preceded Japan's export success (Nakamura 1981). Moreover notwithstanding all these overt measures of import liberalisation, Japan still imposes stiff non-tariff restrictions on imports, which have been the cause of bitter complaint by its trading partners.

In the case of South Korea too the import regime has for long been 'essentially restrictive and full of hidden obstacles' (Luedde-Neurath 1986). This is in addition to the fact that the South Korean tariff structure itself was not lowered since 1953, the beginning of the import-substitution phase, until well into the 1980s, notwithstanding the transition to 'outward orientation' in the 1960s. Exports succeeded not because South Korea got its 'relative prices right' in the neoclassical sense, nor even because exporting was more profitable compared to home sales. Repeated exchange rate depreciations had the effect of jacking up raw material import costs in industries like textiles in the 1960s, and the State had to chip in with export subsidies in order to make textiles the chief export performer of the period. But even more important than subsidies, according to Alice Amsden, was the element of coercion by the State in pushing the private sector to export (Amsden 1989, 69). And indeed the relatively more profitable sales in the home market were a means of compensating firms for having to enter the less attractive avenue of exporting under duress. The cordoned-off home market was a logically necessary counterpart to the successful export drive.

This inevitably entailed an element of dumping. Major manufactured goods, even as late as 1980, were sold in export markets far below their actual costs of production. Hyun-Chin Lim quotes a report by the Ministry of Commerce and Industry according to which the export prices of TV sets, automobiles, steel products, fertilisers and cement were anywhere between 42 to 73 per cent of the actual costs of production in 1980, and adds: 'The loss to local firms caused by the dumping of exports was made up by doubling or tripling the domestic prices of those commodities' (1985, 96). Since the economy depended heavily on the imports of capital and inter-mediate goods, an export drive on this scale may well have worsened the trade deficit through over-exporting, as was the case perhaps with pre-war Japan. But this export thrust, together with the inter-national political-strategic factors which we shall discuss later, kept up South Korea's creditworthiness so that the neo-mercantilist strategy could be sustained.

While the South Korean success cannot be attributed to following the dictates of the market, the regime nonetheless was obviously dif-ferent from a command economy of the sort that prevailed in East-ern Europe. For one thing what was being built was capitalism where State ownership served the needs of capitalist development. Besides, the State undertook strategic intervention both through the market as well as outside of it, rather than through a set of commands. In an economy where export performance was impressive and foreign credits were available, it could afford to do so since the need for maintaining any detailed consistency in the production structure was obviated by trade possibilities.

What explains the successful pursuit of a neo-mercantilist strategy? The first precondition for such a strategy is the existence of a certain internal class structure. A close relationship between the State and big capital presupposes not only the weakness of the working class movement, so that the State does not have to make placatory bows towards the latter, but also the absence of alternative dominant classes, such as the landlords, demanding comparable concessions from the State. The first condition was obviously fulfilled in the East Asian economies. In Japan the Meiji State which was built upon the suppression of revolutionary peasant struggles was from its very inception authoritarian and anti-working class.[6] Even in the post-war period, notwithstanding sizeable support for the Left, the working class movement has never been strong enough to launch even a Social Democratic drive for power. In the rest of East Asia where anti-communism has been the staple for the regimes, and

---

[6] The classic work on this is, of course, Norman 1946.

hence by extension any form of liberal reformism has been suspect, the position of the working class movement has been even weaker.[7]

As for the second pre-condition, the post-war land reforms which eliminated the landlord class from the countryside effectively removed any alternative contenders for State power. The role of land reforms in the Third World is usually discussed exclusively in terms of its effect upon income distribution, size of the home market, and the development of agricultural production, all of which are important. But land reforms also have the effect of eliminating the landlord class, a major claimant for State power and State patronage, and thereby allowing the State to concentrate effort on capitalist industrialisation without having to look over its shoulders all the time for possible adverse landlord reaction.

Moreover, a hallmark of neo-mercantilism is not just a close relationship between the State and the big bourgeoisie, but a relationship in which the former has a leading role. It presupposes the State's ability to discipline the big capitalists themselves, which means that the latter's social base within the civil society must be weak to start with, so the process of class-formation within civil society should not have gone too far already before the neo-mercantilist strategy makes its appearance. And this precisely was another feature of the East Asian situation, where the class of big capitalists itself came up under State patronage and was always amenable to pressure exercised by the State in the name of 'national development'.

For the State to be able to speak in these terms and to coerce capitalists by invoking the 'national idea', there has to be both a degree of homogeneity in society to start with, and also some basis for the preservation of this homogeneity through an improvement within a reasonable period of time of the absolute living conditions of the working masses throughout the country, notwithstanding the suppression of organised workers' movements. In a relatively more homogeneous society, in ethnic and religious terms, the pursuit of a neo-mercantilist strategy by invoking the 'national idea' does not run into problems of inter-ethnic or inter-community tensions over the distribution of gains. The need for the State to arbitrate between communities, which necessarily distracts from its economic role, is

---

[7] The long hours of work of South Korean workers is an index of this. Chakravarty (1993) sees in this ruthless extraction of absolute surplus value an important ingredient of the South Korean success story.

much less. Likewise, to the extent that some basic improvement in living conditions is soon provided on a wide scale, a neo-mercantilist industrialisation strategy carries credibility with the people. In a small society where the adoption of such a strategy, if successful, can more easily make a palpable difference to the living conditions of the entire population, it has a better chance of being persisted with.

The East Asian economies were both sufficiently socially homogeneous as well as sufficiently small in size to be well-placed for embarking upon such a strategy. The provision of general literacy, apart from affecting the capacity of the work-force, also ensured a degree of credibility for the regime and its economic strategy; and this was enhanced by the rapid gains in terms of employment opportunities in manufacturing which the population could make within a relatively short time. To sum up: there are a set of internal factors in terms of size, social homogeneity and class-structure which constitute important preconditions for the successful adoption of a neo-mercantilist strategy.

This however is only a part of the story. It is equally important that such a strategy be allowed to succeed by the dominant capitalist powers of the time. If the international economy is already broken up into hostile blocs, if trade barriers are pervasive, or if the rate of growth of world trade is slow, then clearly a neo-mercantilist strategy by a group of newcomers would run into problems. But even when these conditions are all favourable, neo-mercantilism by a group of newcomers which enables them to expand aggressively by taking advantage of the relative freedom of trade existing elsewhere, can succeed only if it is tolerated. And for political-strategic reasons the East Asian strategy of development *was* tolerated. They were seen as a bulwark against the spread of communism in Asia; their foreign policies were completely in tune with that of the United States; they provided military facilities to the USA and were under its general military umbrella; and they supported the USA in the Vietnam War, in which some of them provided troops and from which all of them derived considerable economic benefits. Given this close strategic relationship, they also enjoyed unusual market access to the metropolitan economies, even while denying such access to others. They obtained large inflows of direct foreign investment (when they wanted it), being solid bastions of the 'free world'; and they were particularly well-placed to obtain enormous amounts of finance capital. The very impressive nature of their export performance certainly made them creditworthy, but an additional factor which also under-lay their export performance was their geo-strategic position.

The East Asian case in fact gives one a sense of *déjà vu*. While all historical parallels are problematic, nonetheless there is a parallel between the relentless export drive of East Asia and that undertaken in the period 1883–1913 by Germany. In the case of Germany too, as Hilferding had noted in *Das Finanzkapital*, there was deliberate dumping on the international market through the maintenance of a differential between domestic and foreign prices of the same com-modities. This was made possible by cordoning off the domestic market and charging high import duties precisely in the exportable commodities.

Some macroeconomic figures given by Arthur Lewis (1978*b*) also bear this out. Between 1883 and 1913, the index of money wage rates in Germany increased almost by the same proportion as labour productivity, leaving unit labour costs virtually unchanged in the manufacturing sector. But the prices of manufactured exports declined from 126 in 1883 (1899=100) to 108 in 1913. Primary product prices increased by 5.5 per cent over this period, and, even though we lack information on how the prices of the specific primary products used by Germany moved, they could hardly have fallen at all between these two dates. The unit labour cost in German manu-facturing was 86 per cent that of Britain in 1883, and climbed up to 91 per cent in 1913. Given the fact that in Britain over this period unit labour costs declined by 4.7 per cent (compared to 1.7 per cent in Germany), but British export prices rose by 9.6 per cent (partly because of the rise in cotton prices), the decline in German export prices is not explicable either in terms of raw material or labour cost movements, or in terms using up the 'slack' of low-unit labour costs earlier. Unless we believe that the share of profits in German manu-facturing declined across the board, and to a significant extent, we have to accept that German manufacturers were selling dear in the home market, and selling cheap in the export market. The fact that the cost of living in Germany went up by 26 per cent between 1882 and 1913, while that in the UK and France remained constant, lends some support to this view.

But the German export expansion drive too would hardly have succeeded if Britain had retaliated against Germany in the pre-First War situation by herself going protectionist. Britain however con-tinued running a trade deficit *vis-à-vis* Continental Europe and balanced its payments, and even made capital exports, by its invisible and investment-income earnings, and, as we have seen, by running a trade surplus with and extracting a tribute from colonies like India. Once the Gold Standard had collapsed, it did after all impose trade barriers against Japanese exports flooding its Asian colonial markets. Thus the international context within which a group of countries can successfully pursue a relentless export drive is exceedingly important. And the East Asian economies in the post-war period have enjoyed a peculiar advantage in this respect.

3. THE REPLICABILITY OF THE EAST ASIAN STRATEGY

When we talk of the possibility of replicating the East Asian experience in the Third World as a whole, two obvious points should first be taken note of. The first is the fallacy of aggregation. The export drive of the East Asian economies was so remarkably successful precisely because it was confined to a few. Had all Third World countries launched equally powerful drives for export expansion, then their collective success would have been far less significant than what was achieved in East Asia.

An example illustrates the point. Already by 1963 Hong Kong had an amount of manufactured goods exports almost as large as India, and Singapore an amount that was 52 per cent of India's. These two city–States merely ensured that their share in world exports of manufactured goods remained more or less unchanged between 1963 and 1977, going up from 1.5 per cent to 1.8 per cent. The more dramatic and also the more relevant examples (since they are not mere cities) are Taiwan and South Korea, whose share in world manufacturing exports increased from a mere 0.25 per cent in 1963 to 2.7 per cent in 1977. Surely a more than ten-fold increase in share such as this is unthinkable for the backward economies as a whole or even for a large enough segment of them. With such an increase the backward economies would have accounted for 45 per cent of total manufactured goods exports in 1977, and not just 7.6 per cent; they would have invited massive retaliation even before a fraction of such an increase could be achieved.

The second point relates to timing. The export drive of the East Asian economies was launched during a period when world trade was expanding at an unprecedentedly rapid rate and when world capitalism was in the midst of a pronounced boom. Even if the entire Third World today could institute East Asia-type economic regimes, they would still not be as successful because the international economic context has changed sharply. The growth rates of the advanced capitalist countries were far lower after the mid-1970s than earlier; and at the time of writing there is a serious recession. The growth of world trade too has slowed down perceptibly with threats of protectionism hanging in the air. A replication of the East Asian experience in the present context is impossible for the Third World as a whole, or even for large Third World economies, for this reason if for nothing else.

There is however a more substantive issue involved. Replicating the East Asian experience, as opposed merely to instituting Fund-Bank-style 'liberalisation' which is an entirely different thing altogether and which as we shall see later only perpetuates underdevelopment, presupposes the replication of a certain internal class configuration and a certain international geo-political relationship with the advanced capitalist countries. These conditions are not made to order; they cannot be created with the flick of a switch. If India for example persisted with a dirigisme quite different from what characterises the neo-mercantilist strategy of East Asia, the reason for it lies in the different class-structures in the two situations.

In countries like India where post-independence land reforms, while strengthening the rich peasants in the countryside, did not eliminate (except at the very top) the old landlord class, where the experience of pre-independence industrialisation (limited no doubt relative to requirements but still large enough in absolute terms) had thrown up a class of capitalists, and a working class, and where an articulate urban petty-bourgeoisie (including professionals and white-collar workers) exists and exerts considerable political influence, as underscored by Kalecki (1972b) for example, the State has to operate within a complex class-structure. It has to balance the interests of different classes and strata even while promoting overall capitalist development; the framework of parliamentary democracy makes such balancing, such arbitration, even more necessary. The apparently enormous web of regulations and controls is essentially a reflection of this complexity, this need for arbitration between classes and groups. The State is all-pervasive; at the same time it cannot have as close an identification with the capitalist class as in East

Asian countries, including Japan. It is more interventionist in one sense, if one looks at the plethora of controls, rules and regulations; it is less interventionist in another sense, if one looks at its ability to mould capitalists' decision-making, or more generally its ability to make the economy behave according to a plan. And precisely the same complexity, the same specificity of the historical trajectory of social evolution also entails that it would be difficult for an economy like India to replicate the geo-political pattern of relationship with the advanced capitalist world that East Asia has had. This does not mean that societies are mere prisoners of history; what it means is that the range of possibilities open to a society at any time is histor-ically conditioned.

The example of Dengist China is often invoked to argue that the East Asian strategy *can* be replicated in today's context. But there are two quite distinct elements in Dengist China's recent success in terms of rapid growth. One element has been the adoption of an East Asia-type strategy. While keeping its domestic tariffs high, it has sought to push out exports aggressively, by placating the USA *inter alia*, and to invite direct foreign investment to supplement very high rates of domestic savings and thereby maintain impressive rates of capital accumulation without undue worries about balance of payments. Until now, much of the investment it has drawn is from overseas Chinese (between 60 to 70 per cent) rather than from the advanced capitalist world.

The other element is a remarkable growth in agricultural output which has expanded the home market and brought about a spurt of rural industrialisation. This is in marked *contrast* to, say, the South Korean case where one of the points persistently made by the critics against the development strategy was the *neglect* of agriculture. The Chinese success therefore can by no means be treated as being due merely to a replication of the East Asian strategy, since the Chinese strategy in its totality is not such a replication.

Moreover while China's economic performance has no doubt been quite impressive, a question mark nonetheless hangs over its persistence for two reasons. The first is the tenuous relationship between China and the advanced capitalist world. In the event of the latter putting curbs on China's export thrust, on the proffered grounds, say, of human rights, its current economic strategy would suffer a setback. The second is the inevitable tensions being gener-ated within China despite its relative ethnic homogeneity on account of the rapid growth in regional inequalities that is taking place. The agricultural growth under the aegis of private farming has been regionally uneven. The linkage effects of the export thrust have also been felt in a regionally uneven manner with the coastal areas of Southern China doing much better on both counts than the interior. Even if the current strategy is persisted with, and parts of coastal China do succeed in following in the footsteps of the other East Asian economies, the basic proposition about the non-replicability of the East Asian strategy in the Third World as a whole would not thereby have been nullified.

Two conclusions follow from the foregoing. First, while we have in our theoretical discussion confined attention to the basic dichotomy between the advanced and the backward economies, each of these is not a homogeneous and unchanging category. There is both upward and downward mobility taking place within each, though Japan is perhaps the only firm example to date of an upward mobility across the divide by a nation of non-European origin. Even as the East Asian late-industrialisers have moved up within the Third World, large parts of Latin America have actually moved down during the decade of the 1980s. The moving up of the former therefore can by no means be construed as evidence that the basic dichotomy which is the focus of this book is breaking down.

Second, their moving up does not also mean that this dichotomy *can* be broken down if only other countries 'followed in their footsteps'. Certain specific conditions underlie their upward mobility which are not replicable elsewhere. Moreover their remarkable success in transforming their economies and societies has derived not only from the concentration of diffusion in their favour, but also from the small sizes of their economies. Even if the entire increase in manufactured goods exports from Taiwan and South Korea between 1963 and 1977 had come to India instead of these countries, so that India had tripled its share of world manufactured goods exports between these two dates, the transformation that this would have brought about in the Indian economy in terms for example of the reduction in the unemployment rate would have been much less than in the case of these countries.

To say all this is not to suggest that countries like India could not have or should not have raised their exports more than they did, or even, taking the backward countries as a whole, that the actual diffusion that occurred is all that could have been possibly tolerated by the core countries; it is not to say that there were no constraints arising from the side of the backward countries' own policies on the extent of the actual diffusion that occurred. The point is that, whether they made most of the opportunities or not, the opportunities themselves have been and continue to remain limited. If traditional radical analysis erred in assuming that the opportunities were zero, there is no reason now to go to the other extreme and assume that the opportunities are unlimited, that somehow capitalism at the core is so different today that the backward countries, if only they made things easy for capital to operate, could, because of their low wages, keep raising their share of manufactured goods exports and climb out of their backwardness.

Once we accept that the export opportunities are not unlimited, we are back with the following problem. Suppose the core countries grow at a rate as high as 5 per cent (which was true only of the boom period until the early 1970s), and suppose the backward countries' exports grow at this rate (which itself is rather optimistic), that their import propensity remains unchanged, and hence that GDP also grows at this rate. The structural shift within them towards manufacturing, together with the fact that within manufacturing itself new processes and new products would have to be introduced, would raise their productivity, let us say at the rate approximately of 2.5 per cent per annum. Labour demand then would grow at the rate of around 2.5 per cent per annum against a population growth rate of at least 2.25 per cent (outside of China). Even in these extremely favourable hypothetical conditions, the labour reserves would take a very long time to get used up (if labour reserves constitute 20 per cent of the work-force, then it will take 78 years), by which time the parameters of the discussion would almost certainly have changed for the worse.

This illustration should not be misunderstood. While it shows, on its own grounds, the facile nature of the argument often advanced these days that the backward countries would shed their backwardness if only they became more 'outward-looking', ours is not an empirical argument depending on the happenstance of a particular constellation of figures. The structural constraint upon the using up of labour reserves which we have emphasised goes deeper.

As our theoretical discussion has made clear, the using up of such labour reserves, since it would be accompanied by a rise in product wages in Third World primary production, would spark off via terms-of-trade shifts a process of accelerating inflation in the core countries, which can be settled by reducing either the wage share or the profit share in the core, and thus upset the social equilibrium underlying capitalism. Long before such a denouement came to pass, the core countries would have taken steps to prevent cheap manufactured goods exports from the Third World as they used to do earlier and bring down its growth rate to replenish its labour reserves.

We are so used to looking at growth at the core in dissociation from its relationship with the periphery that this last assertion would appear to many as being rather 'far-fetched'. In the case of the so-called 'exhaustible' resources, however, the fact that rapid Third World development, resulting in a correspondingly rapid increase in its consumption of such resources, would put pressure on their supplies and make current living standards at the core unsustainable, is often readily recognised. All that we are arguing is that what is recognised in the case of 'exhaustible' resources is also true, and far more plausible (since 'exhaustibility' is a rather questionable Ricardian legacy), for producible primary commodities. Indeed our argument is an extension of the use of Marx's concept of the 'reserve army of labour' to the international arena.

A using up of Third World labour reserves would entail the breakdown of the present system where its product wages relative to productivity in sectors providing inputs and wage goods to the core are a residue, and upon which the entire stability of the capitalist system depends. It is this which ultimately is the real constraint on Third World development; let us therefore turn to this aspect.

4. TERMS OF TRADE: DETERMINANTS OF SECULAR MOVEMENTS

The question of the secular adverse movement in the terms of trade obtained for the primary commodities has occupied much attention since the work of Prebisch (1950) and Singer (1950). Prebisch's position has been criticised on both theoretical and empirical grounds. We shall not discuss the theoretical critique except to remark that in this entire discussion the distinction between the short-run and the long-run determinants of the terms of trade has not figured the way it should, or, putting it differently, the distinction between the terms of trade when the primary sector output is given, as it is in the short-run, and when the primary sector output itself adjusts. In the short-run, for a given configuration of money wages, the terms of trade clearly depend upon the sizes of the two sectors, which are the major determinants of the demand for and the supply of primary commodities.[8] But in the long run, once supply adjustments are allowed, so that the relative sizes of the two sectors can be varied to bring demand and supply into balance, the terms of trade would depend on the state of technology in the manufactured goods sector, the wage rate of that sector in terms of primary commodities commanded (i.e. taking the latter as numeraire), and the magnitude of the mark-up in the manufacturing sector. Putting it somewhat differently, the long-run terms of trade depend on the primary commodity input per unit of the manufactured good, the manufacturing sector's wage rate per efficiency unit of labour, and this sector's mark-up.[9] The wage rate in the primary sector (again taking primary products as the numeraire) depends on the technology of that sector, the terms of trade, and the acceptable rate of profit to the capitalists engaged in its production.

The problem with Prebisch's original argument is that it does not provide a basis for secular movements in the terms of trade.[10] No matter whether productivity changes in the primary sector are 'passed on' while those in the manufacturing sector are not, and no matter what these rates of productivity change are, the terms of trade would not for this reason move in any direction.

Suppose there is an increase in labour productivity in the primary producing sector. With given money wages in this sector, the unit labour cost falls and *ceteris paribus* the price of the primary commodity falls. This would result in a fall in input prices for the manufacturing sector, and also a fall in the cost of living of its workers. The capitalists in the manufacturing sector would lower money wages in consonance with the decline in the cost of living of the workers, and

---

[8] Beckerman and Jenkinson's argument (1986) is confined to the short run: a deflation in the OECD economies (which amounts to a reduction in the size of the manufacturing sector) curbs inflation by turning the terms of trade against the primary commodities.

[9] This proposition which follows from our model was originally advanced by Kaldor (1978).

[10] For a critique of Prebisch along somewhat different lines from what follows see Spraos 1983.

this together with the decline in input prices would lower the unit prime cost for this sector. Since the mark-up is assumed given, the manufactured goods prices would fall *pari passu* with the primary commodity prices. The fact that productivity increases in the primary sector are 'passed on' in the form of lower prices therefore makes no difference to the terms of trade.

It may be thought however that money wages in the manufactured goods sector do not actually fall when the cost of living declines. But that is simply for the convenience of exposition: as a matter of fact money wages are normally rising. It is the degree of rise which would be higher or lower depending on whether the rise in the cost of living index is greater or smaller. The conclusion that whether productivity changes in primary production are 'passed on' or not is irrelevant to the terms of trade, remains unaffected.

Indeed, let us take the opposite case. Suppose productivity changes are not passed on by the primary sector capitalists. That means that with given money wages in the primary sector, as unit labour costs decline, the primary commodity prices do not decline. This can only happen if the primary sector capitalists enforce higher profit margins for themselves, if their acceptable rate of profit ($h^\star$ in our model) rises. Since neither the input prices nor the cost of living of the workers in the manufactured goods sector show any change, with a given mark-up the price in that sector too shows no change. Thus all prices remain the same and there is no change in the terms of trade despite the increase in productivity. Once again therefore whether productivity increases in the primary sector are passed on or not is immaterial for the terms of trade.

The other side of Prebisch's argument was that productivity increases in the manufactured goods sector are not passed on. If money wages rise together with productivity, which we accept, then the manufactured goods prices do not change at all and hence the terms of trade do not change at all. While this is what Prebisch asserted quite correctly, he thought that the passing on of productivity increases in the primary sector would keep changing the terms of trade against the latter. We have just seen that there is no reason to believe in this part of the argument.

Productivity increases and their effects on prices, whether identical in the two sectors or divergent, have nothing to do with terms-of-trade movements in the secular sense, which depend only upon three factors: the primary commodity input per unit of the manufactured

good, the wage rate (taking the primary commodity as the numeraire) per efficiency unit of labour in the manufacturing sector, and
the mark-up in this sector. We have not brought in State expenditure
in this sector so far. If such expenditure is brought in, then the last
two factors would have to be amended to the post-tax wage rate per
efficiency unit of labour, and the surplus per unit of output in the
manufacturing sector.

It is only changes in any one of these factors which can cause a
secular change in the terms of trade. It is the tendency for the share
of State expenditure to increase, which means that, for a given post-
tax wage rate per efficiency unit of labour in the manufacturing
sector, the share of surplus in the gross value of output (as also of
value added) rises over time. This provides the strongest basis for
believing that the terms of trade would move secularly against the
primary producing sector.

5. STATISTICS ON SECULAR DETERIORATION

If we go by the existing statistics on the terms-of-trade movements,
however, empirical support for such a secular movement does not
appear to be strong. Bairoch's (1975) estimates certainly show no
secular decline for the primary producers. And in any case the intervention of the two war periods, during which the terms of trade move
sharply in favour of the primary commodities, implies that even if
there were any underlying secular tendencies, they would never be
captured by a long and continuous time-series. The problem with
taking individual time segments, leaving out the war years, is that we
could well be comparing dissimilar years, such as peaks with
troughs. Moreover we have the task of separating out post-war 'normalisation' from underlying secular movements. We could take the
somewhat cavalier (and not altogether unjustified) position that if we
have a long time-series, no matter how punctuated by wars, where
post-war normalisation has had a chance to work itself out, and if we
compare more or less similar periods at the two extremes of the time-
series without worrying about the intervening years, then we are
entitled to derive some conclusions about the underlying secular
trend.

On this basis we could take Arthur Lewis's (1978b) continuous series on the prices of manufactures and of tropical crops and compare, say, the 1882–4 triennium which has a Juglar peak at its centre with the triennium 1968–70, which also has a peak at its centre, and which falls before either the currency instability or the oil price-hike, or the subsequent collapse of primary commodity prices intervened, and even before the wage-push acceleration in manufactured goods prices (which occurred between 1969 and 1972) had fully made itself felt. Between these two dates, the agricultural price divided by the manufactured goods price falls from 101.5 (1913=100) to 83.6. It is tempting to infer from this that there was an underlying tendency for primary commodity prices to decline relatively; but the result is so sensitive to the choice of end-points that one cannot claim this with any confidence. Indeed when looking at such long spans of time over which the nature of cycles itself has undergone considerable modification, it is difficult even to see what meaning can be given to 'similar periods' for purposes of comparison.

We could try another tack. We could divide the entire period into sub-periods leaving out the war and immediate post-war years, and compare the averages for comparable sub-periods making sure that within each sub-period we take comparable years as the end-points. The three obvious sub-periods into which the entire period can be divided are: 1883–1913; 1920–37; and 1948–72. Of these the middle sub-period was marked by the Great Depression during which the terms of trade were obviously unfavourable for the primary producers. But if we take the first and the last sub-periods, the latter of which was a far more pronounced long boom, and yet find that the terms of trade were worse on average for the latter than for the former sub-period, then there would be some basis for believing in a secular deterioration.

Using Lewis's data for tropical crops and manufactures once again, the ratio of tropical crop prices to manufactures' prices on average for the first period was (1913=100) 98.5. For the period 1948–72, the average ratio was 93.9. If even during the most pronounced and sustained boom in the history of capitalism, the terms of trade for agriculture at any rate have been worse than in the late 19th and early 20th century, then there is something to be said for the secular deterioration thesis even on the existing statistics. And if we remember the fact that the terms of trade have continued to deteriorate for primary commodities, other than oil, after the mid-1970s, and (again excluding oil) were worse in the late-80s than ever before in the last half-century, then the thesis gains added support (see Spraos 1980, 1983).

Even on existing statistics then, while the case for arguing the secular deterioration thesis is not strong, it cannot be ruled out of court. The whole purpose of our argument however has been to show that the existing terms-of-trade statistics are conceptually inadequate for shedding any light on this thesis. This is because any index number, being a weighted average of price-relatives, cannot, by its very nature, do justice to that part of the relative price change which comes from changing composition, notwithstanding what particular weights we take. It is the shift from higher-priced to lower-priced raw materials which has been the essence of the process, not so much the decline in the relative price of a given basket of raw materials. Thus the secular deterioration thesis cannot, even in principle, be captured entirely through movements in any index of barter terms of trade. We saw earlier (Ch. 8, fn. 7) that if the world conformed to our description that all primary production takes place exclusively in the periphery, then the ratio of the value of primary products used up in manufacturing at the core to the gross value of its manufacturing output (including primary products used up but excluding intra-industry transactions) would provide a reasonable proxy for our concept of the terms of trade. But since primary production is not confined exclusively to the periphery, the problem arises of what to take as the numerator. In view of our proposition that the prices of core primary producers move in sympathy with world prices we would be better off taking the total primary products used up rather than merely what is imported from the periphery, since then we would not have to worry about possible diffusion of primary production from the core to the periphery.

This, it would be commonly accepted, has been falling over time.[11]

11 While this proposition would be commonly accepted, and was highlighted in the classic discussion between Nurkse (1959), Cairncross (1960), and Maizels (1963), we do not have any consistent long-term series on it. The UNCTAD has been bringing out apparent consumption data for the advanced countries in recent years for both primary commodities as well as manufactures. But the country coverage of the data has been changing and apparent consumption of primary commodities includes not only productive but also final consumption. The ratio of apparent consumption of primary commodities to the gross value of output of manufactures (calculated from the same data) for EEC 6, UK, USA, and Japan moves as follows: 1959–60: 24.06%; 1971–2: 18.64%; 1973–4: 22.57%. For EEC 10 (though figures of Greece are not included), USA–Canada, and Japan, the ratios are: 1968: 17.63%; 1974–5: 18.46%;

If the fall was on account of a reduction in the physical amounts of given raw materials required per unit of output, then the cause would have been technological rather than directly social. But since it is not physical input-saving but the shift to lower-valued inputs that largely explains the fall,[12] we can say that this is the form taken by the secular deterioration of the terms of trade.

6. THE POST-WAR DEMAND FOR PRIMARY PRODUCTS

In retrospect one of the remarkable features of the post-war situation has been the decline in the barter terms of trade of the primary commodity producing sector of the world during the boom itself.[13] This marks a major departure from the historical pattern. From the early 1880s to the middle or the end of the 1890s, when core industrial production growth tended to slow down, there was a Kondratieff swing in the terms of trade against agriculture. The revival in the rates of industrial growth thereafter was accompanied by a swing in the terms of trade in favour of primary commodities generally, and tropical agriculture in particular, which continued through the war years right until 1920. While the shift in the terms of trade against primary commodities predated the onset of the Great Depression in the industrial nations, the slump itself of course took the terms of

1976–7: 18.81%; 1978: 19.21%. For the expanded EEC, USA–Canada, and Japan, the ratios are: 1982–3: 17.72%; 1984–5: 16.37%; 1986–7: 12.81%. Keeping in mind the fact that the oil-price hike introduced a bulge right in the middle of the period, we can clearly discern a downward trend in the ratio.

12 Maizels (1963, ch. 15) adduces three reasons for the slowing down of the growth in imports of primary products into industrial countries, namely, shifts in the pattern of demand, technological change, and fiscal and protectionist policies in these countries. It is the second of these which is relevant for us for explaining the terms-of-trade movements as we have defined them. But what Maizels calls 'technological' refers not to the reduction in physical consumption of particular raw materials per unit of gross output in particular lines of production but to the substitution of one kind of material by another, and the material 'saving' in such cases by our argument is tantamount to a terms-of-trade shift, i.e. it is a social rather than a technological phenomenon.

13 The boom itself was the most pronounced in the history of capitalism. Maddison (1982, 91) gives the following average annual growth-rate figures for the advanced capitalist countries for different periods: 1820–70: 2.2 %; 1870–1913: 2.5%; 1913–50: 1.9%; 1950–73: 4.9%.

trade to an unprecedented low level. With the beginning of the post-war boom, the terms-of-trade shift in favour of primary commodities which had started during the Second World War continued, but, from around the mid-1950s, even though the boom continued un-abated, the terms of trade, though fluctuating, moved generally against the primary commodities (Spraos 1980), a movement that has gathered momentum (if we keep oil out of the picture) in the years of relative stagnation in the advanced capitalist countries.

Further, it can be argued that the reason why the capitalist countries could experience such a long boom after the Second World War lies partly in the fact of the adverse terms-of-trade movement for primary production. To be sure, the boom was linked with a tremendous burst of innovations, so significant and pervasive that some have used the term the Scientific and Technological Revolution to denote this period of rapid technical change. Lewis (1978*b*) talks of the accumulated stock of potential innovations during the years of the 'Great Depression' (1913–48) suddenly sparking off a burst of investment and growth; Baran and Sweezy (1966) refer to the resumption of the interrupted automobile boom; others talk of the scientific breakthroughs during the Second World War creating the conditions for a whole range of new innovations. But no matter what the specific alchemy of the post-war burst of innovations that underlay the tremendous boom, surely the boom would have been truncated much sooner, if primary commodity prices had increased earlier, sparking off an inflationary upsurge. After all, even Schumpeter thought inflation to be a hindrance to the process of innovations that brings the boom to an end. By implication, the ability of the capitalist economies to maintain remarkable price stability right until 1969, when it was in fact wages rather than primary commodity prices that triggered off the inflationary spiral, must be held as an important factor contributing to the length and the strength of the boom (see Kaldor 1978). Estimates by Spraos actually show a substantial decline in the primary commodities' terms of trade (including oil) by 1972 which must have kept inflation in check.

How was this made possible? One can only offer a suggestion here. The post-war period also saw a burst of industrialisation in the underdeveloped world. This was not just a result of market-based diffusion, whether 'voluntary' or 'automatic', which we have been discussing so far. Much of it was the result of a deliberate, State-induced process of import substitution. The process which had started in Latin America and India during the 1930s, vigorously in the former and tentatively in the latter, was carried forward; other underdeveloped countries joined it after political decolonisation. In the conscious effort to speed up the rate of industrialisation, they had to negotiate foreign exchange constraints, and there was a frantic effort to exploit the existing export opportunities, which meant pushing out as much of the primary commodities and semi-finished products as possible. Not only was there a significant increase in the supplies of primary products, an increase which in itself may not have mattered since the capitalist countries' industrial production too was growing at an unprecedented rate, but a plethora of multiple exchange-rate arrangements, and outright currency devaluations by each country to help it to outcompete its rivals.

The implications of this increased competition can be seen theoretically as follows. In the short-run, a profit inflation is the mechanism for eliminating the *ex ante* excess demand for primary commodities. It squeezes the workers both in the core as well as in the periphery, and has the effect ceteris paribus of tilting the terms of trade in favour of primary commodities. Since this also raises the profit rate for the capitalists in this sector, they raise production over time which should eliminate the profit inflation unless demand continues to keep outstripping supply *ex ante*. The reason why terms of trade move in favour of primary commodities in a boom lies in this phenomenon of *ex ante* demand continuously outstripping supply.

Exchange-rate adjustments in the Third World acted in the direction of insulating the core workers from the effects of profit inflation. If this insulation is complete, if commodity prices in the international market move *pari passu* with the (post-tax) wage rate per efficiency unit of labour at the core, and if the ratio of (post-tax) product wage to labour productivity remains unchanged, then (given unchanged primary commodity input per unit of output) the terms of trade should remain unchanged. But rising State expenditure at the core meant an increasing surplus per unit of output, the effect of which was an adverse terms-of-trade movement for primary commodities. Despite such a shift, however, profitability in primary production improved owing to profit inflation which brought about notable increases in supplies. In short, the adverse movement even during boom conditions was due to a combination of two factors:

increased competition among Third World countries, and a rise in the share of surplus at the core.[14]

Evidence can be adduced for both these factors. For the latter we can cite Baran and Sweezy's estimate of the growing share of surplus in the US economy. As for the former, several examples come readily to mind. Within South Asia itself, this increased competition (which was of course not confined to primary commodities alone but encompassed semi-manufactures and simple manufactures as well) was evident in the rivalry between India and (the then united) Pakistan in the market for jute manufactures, and between India and Sri Lanka (or Ceylon as it then was) in the market for tea. Owing to this increased competition, and the exchange rate arrangements devised for the purpose, new entrants to the market no doubt gained, but the prices of primary commodities, taking the market as a whole, remained subdued even while there was a gentle rise in the prices of core products accompanying the rise in the share of surplus.

A point should be clarified here. From the argument that competition between the underdeveloped countries in their drive to earn more foreign exchange for industrialisation kept the terms of trade subdued during the boom, it does not follow that a slowing down in the pace of their industrialisation would push up the terms of trade. The increased competition represents a parametric shift. It may have accompanied the increase in the pace of their industrialisation, but insofar as a reduction in this pace does not *ipso facto* reverse this parametric shift it only adds further to the decline in the terms of trade.

The policies advocated by such international organisations as the International Monetary Fund and the World Bank are aimed at keeping up the intensity of competition among Third World

---

14 Cairncross (1960) had argued that Third World industrialisation, by putting pressure on primary commodity prices, was responsible for the restriction in the growth of demand in the advanced economies. In fact the absolute price increase between 1953 and 1971 was small and we are arguing that Third World industrialisation may have contributed towards keeping it so. If we assume the supply profile remains unchanged then it is a truism to say that the larger demand profile on account of Third World industrialisation has a price-raising effect; but this industrialisation also raises the supply profile which did increase to an extent not anticipated in the early 1950s (Kaldor 1976). The substitution of synthetics for primary commodities in many spheres therefore was quite independent of whether prices of the latter were rising or not.

countries. The Fund for instance suggests currency devaluations to every country as a part of its stabilisation policy, including to predominantly primary producing countries, even though the effects of such devaluations, pursued by all, cancel each other out as far as getting larger market shares are concerned, and even though demand in the international market for the commodity as a whole remains price-inelastic. At the same time it suggests restrictions on the pace of consciously planned industrialisation, and frowns upon the imposition of import restrictions. The upshot of such measures pursued by all is to maintain the fierceness of competition among Third World countries, prevent any coming together on their part for commodity agreements (since each is under IMF tutelage), and slow down their collective industrialisation drive, all of which contributes towards keeping commodity prices low for the advanced capitalist countries.

There is a specific reason, apart from the general one discussed in this work, why this is now important for the advanced capitalist countries. Kaldor (1976) had argued in the context of the commodity boom of the early 1970s that the introduction of a system of floating rates, by implying the absence of a stable currency (as good as gold) in terms of which wealth could be held had made wealth-holders rush to commodities as their prices rose, thus compounding the price rise. While at the moment the capitalist economies are free from inflationary worries, the level of activity in the core as a whole is none too high. Should a concerted and significant boom begin, it is quite possible that inflation would fairly quickly make its appearance. While there may be no inflation, the capitalist economies' greater proneness to inflation remains. In addition, the danger of price stability being upset through Third World producers getting together, even at the current level of activity, is ever present. But each being held in thraldom to the IMF prevents any possible co-operation, and subverts even such agreements as already exist. And restrictions on Third World industrialisation, by keeping down demand for the primary commodities, reduce the inflationary threat to the core even in the event of a significant concerted boom taking shape there.

There is a logic to the Fund conditionalities from the core's point of view, no matter how detrimental they may be for the Third World countries. This flows from the fact that they attempt on a world scale at what Marx called centralisation of capital. By eliminating smaller industrial capitals, they attempt to create the conditions for a resumption of the rapid onward march, free from fears of inflation, of metropolitan capital. The crucial question, however, is why the Third World countries get into the clutches of the IMF in the first place. Or, putting it differently, what are the contradictions in the path of consciously planned, State-initiated development, which at one stage had aroused so much hope, that force these countries into the tutelage of the IMF, which is after all a proxy for accepting the policies laid down by the very countries from whose economies they had sought to distance themselves at the time of decolonisation? This question will be taken up in the next chapter.

13

The Limitations of
Enforced Diffusion

The question of State intervention to promote development in the periphery has not so far been considered, except with reference to the neo-mercantilist strategy which, we argued, constituted a special case. The possibilities of 'voluntary' and 'automatic' diffusion of activities from the core to the periphery were discussed in earlier chapters. This chapter examines the limitations of an 'enforced' diffusion of activities away from the core through the conscious intervention of the Third World State in the form of the usual import-substituting industrialisation strategy. It focuses on the problems of the so-called 'mixed economies'. The problems of Third World socialist economies, though in some ways overlapping, need to be discussed separately, but except for a few brief comments in the next chapter that is beyond the scope of this book.

1. THE CONTEXT OF
ENFORCED DIFFUSION

By 'enforced' diffusion I mean an implantation of activities in the Third World economy which if it relied entirely on the market would not necessarily occur. Such diffusion is predicated on conscious State intervention, both in setting up production units itself, and also in nurturing private production. State intervention of this sort usually pre-supposes political upheavals leading to a change in the class nature of the State. Intervention by the State in the economic arena or its withdrawal from it are not simple matters of discretion for a particular State, but represent political responses to class pressures, and hence political conflicts which also change the character of the State itself.[1]

In the Latin American countries, for instance, the initiation of import-substituting industrialisation marked not merely a change of policy in the context of the Great Depression; it signalled a shift in the nature of the dominant class alliance behind State power. The old alliance of comprador bourgeoisie and large land-owners, backed by foreign capital, had either to surrender power to a new alliance dominated by the manufacturing bourgeoisie which had developed in the interstices of the old division of labour, or to make significant concessions to the latter (see Furtado 1972). In colonial economies like India, the introduction of tariff protection on a far more limited scale also represented a concession to the domestic bourgeoisie by British colonialism trying to keep the empire intact and using it as a means to ward off rival powers, and to protect itself against the effects of the Great Depression. The import-substituting industrialisation which occurred in India was much narrower in scope and less profound in its impact, because the colonial State, far from attempting to expand the domestic market simultaneously, pursued the very opposite policy of cutting back expenditure (which resulted in a running down of the infrastructure), and even choosing that very time to pay back some of India's external debt (Bagchi 1982, 123–4). A deliberate policy of import-substituting industrialisation, together with State efforts to expand the domestic market through large-scale public expenditure and investment, had to wait till the achievement of independence from colonial rule.

In Latin America however the industrial sector expanded rapidly, as the following figures from Lewis (1978*b*) show: industrial output (1960=100) in 1929 was 38 in Chile, 23 in Honduras, 30 in Argentina, 12 in Brazil, 15 in Mexico, and 9 in Colombia. The State did not just protect domestic industry; it kept up domestic demand by

---

[1] A pre-condition for the adoption of policies for enforced diffusion is not only an appropriate domestic political conjuncture, but also an appropriate international conjuncture. The disunity among metropolitan powers was also an important factor allowing several Third World countries to embark upon this path. When Hirschman (1971, 25–6) suggests that for maximising growth 'the developing countries would need an appropriate alteration of contact and insulation, of openness to trade and capital of developed countries, to be followed by a period of nationalism and withdrawnness' (pp.25–6), what he misses is that this flicking on and off cannot be done at the government's pleasure; these policy shifts are historically conditioned.

running large budget deficits, with which it simultaneously financed investment in infrastructure and in basic industries. In the period after decolonisation this became the official development strategy of a large number of underdeveloped countries in Asia and Africa as well, many of which gave the public sector a leading role in the development process and even claimed to be building 'socialism' of one kind or another.

The fact that this strategy has run into serious contradictions can hardly be denied today by even its most ardent admirers. Whether the strategy of significant State ownership, substantial increases in State expenditure and investment, the preparation of National economic plans (no matter how seriously these were implemented), an insulation of the economy from foreign competition through tariffs and quantitative restrictions, and the imposition of a plethora of domestic controls and regulations over capital (even though these may have been flouted with impunity), was adopted in the name merely of nationalism, or of a journey towards some version of socialism (though scarcely towards socialism of the Marxist-Leninist variety), it certainly has had to yield ground today to a new wave of thinking which sees virtues in the privatisation of State enterprises, in a more open-door policy towards foreign capital, in a decontrol of the economy, in a reduction of subsidies to curtail budget deficits, and in trade liberalisation involving a dismantling of the regime of quantitative import restrictions and a gradual lowering of tariff rates.

This new wave may be temporary; this new wave would create its own contradictions (after all we have been underscoring the relationship between the spontaneous operation of the system and the state of underdevelopment); this new wave has undoubtedly been dictated by the metropolitan countries (who were opposed to 'enforced diffusion' from its very outset) and agencies such as the Fund and the Bank dominated by them; this new wave has been influenced by the apparent success of East Asian capitalism which has often been attributed to the wrong reason, namely the operation of the free market; but there have obviously been objective contradictions in play within the domestic economy itself which have contributed to the emergence of this new wave. What were these?

2. ENFORCED DIFFUSION AND THE
CAPITAL—OUTPUT RATIO

'Enforced diffusion' almost by definition entails a higher capital—output ratio in the activities implanted in the periphery than in the corresponding activities in the core, at least in the short-run. We are after all not talking about activities for which the periphery already has (or can easily acquire) technological competence and a cost advantage: that is the province of 'automatic diffusion' which is feasible within the context of the free market itself. We are talking about activities catering to the domestic market, erected behind protectionist barriers, and the technological mastery over which takes time to acquire. The domestic market for such activities may be too small in the beginning relative to the minimum efficient scale of operation; the quality of output in complementary activities as well as of the infrastructure would be much poorer in comparison to the core; the appropriate skills may be immediately lacking; and 'learning by doing' effects initially absent. One does not have to go beyond Frederich List to conclude in such circumstances that for a while at any rate production would be relatively inefficient compared to the core, in the sense that per unit of capital good (which would necessarily have to be imported to start with) the output in such activities would be less in quantity or poorer in quality.

Making such activities export-worthy would, under the usual circumstances, take a considerable length of time. With a higher capital—output ratio than in the core, such activities would yield products whose exportability may require a reduction in product wages to inordinately low or even negative levels, which are politically unsustainable. And even if product wages are squeezeable, successful exporting takes a considerable length of time, the establishment of appropriate trade channels, an image and reputation, and so on. Finally, the established exporters in the world market, which would typically be the core countries, would not sit back and watch their market shares getting eroded. They would resist with all the strength at their command (and we are not talking here of activities which are getting 'marginalised' at the core and which are amenable to 'automatic diffusion', though even in their case there is resistance). The least one can say is that unless the country is 'adopted' by some section of core capital (in which case we are talking about 'voluntary' and not 'enforced' diffusion), it would take considerable time for the new activities in the periphery to begin exporting, if at all. It follows that 'enforced' diffusion is almost invariably associated with a process of 'deepening'. Since the rate of export growth does not rise, even as the rate of growth of the economy increases because of the combined effects of 'enforced diffusion' and the expansion of the home market owing to larger State expenditure, an attempt is made to reduce the import propensity by deepening the production structure, by going from an 'initial stage' of import substitution when only a range of final consumer goods are domestically produced, to a 'later stage' of import substitution when capital and current inputs also begin to be produced in the domestic economy. This has the effect of raising the capital–output ratio in the economy.

One reason for this rise in the capital–output ratio has already been mentioned. If in each activity which is shifted to the periphery the capital–output ratio is higher than in the core, it follows that a process of deepening of the production structure through time must be associated with an increase in the capital–output ratio. But there is a second reason as well which contributes even more powerfully towards this end. And that is the following.

So far we have treated the periphery as if it constitutes a single economy. In reality, however, the periphery is split into a number of distinct economies each of which embarks upon this process of 'enforced diffusion' in isolation. Each however is linked by its history to the core with which it has the bulk of its trade relationship. With the increase in its growth rate each needs a larger volume of current inputs in the form of natural resources, such as coal, oil and other minerals and raw materials. Even though the periphery as a whole produces these commodities, and, if it constituted a single unit, could increase production of all of them without much significant increase in marginal costs, since each is called upon to pay the others in hard currency which is scarce, each attempts to increase its own domestic production of as many of these materials as it can, resulting in an increase in marginal costs, and hence in the capital–output ratio. Bilateral trade agreements are not really a solution for this; what are needed are multilateral agreements among countries sufficiently diversified in their primary commodity production structure. In the absence of such agreements, a rise in the capital–output ratio for this reason, which is additional to the one mentioned earlier is inevitable.

Even the possibility of any one country buying more manufactured goods from another in lieu of the raw materials which it supplies is limited since each would rather buy such goods from the core: even between identical goods produced by the core and some other countries in the periphery, the preference in most countries in the periphery is for the core good.

There is a third reason for the rise in the capital–output ratio. An increase in the rate of growth in the countries of the periphery creates a larger demand not only for the primary commodities currently being produced in other countries of the periphery, as in the above case, but also for agricultural goods in each country. The technology on the basis of which output in this sector expands to meet the enlarged demand is not a given, as we assumed in our theoretical discussion, but is dependent upon how the agrarian relations change in the new situation. If the land concentration remains as before, no matter what adjustments are made in the composition of the top land-holding stratum, the expansion of output occurs within the context of an emerging tendency towards landlord-capitalist development (see U. Patnaik 1987 for a discussion of the Indian context). Such a tendency which has manifested itself in several underdeveloped countries, is associated with an increase in the capital–output ratio.

The reliance of an agriculture developing along capitalist lines upon energy sources such as oil is much greater, and this, as we have seen above, contributes to a rising capital–output ratio. Moreover, by substituting machinery for human labour, it not only contributes to a perpetuation of labour reserves, but also directly raises the capital–output ratio, and adds to the demand for new sources of energy. Likewise to the extent that a given rate of growth in agriculture has to be sustained on a smaller land area, namely the land upon which the capitalists are employing yield-raising methods of production, while a part of the total cultivated land where the tenants and poor peasants operate remains unaffected by such methods owing to the disincentives which the latter have in applying them, the capital–output ratio would rise even faster. In other words, if as the technology within the agricultural sector is changing in favour of a higher capital–output ratio owing to the fact of large holdings being run on capitalist lines, the share of such holdings in total output also increase, then the rise in capital–output ratio is even greater.

The above should be distinguished from the Ricardian argument, which is essentially that the capital–output ratio increases in agriculture as output increases because of the so-called 'diminishing returns'. Our argument does not presume any diminishing returns. It asserts that the behaviour of the capital–output ratio as agricultural output increases depends upon the structure of agrarian relations within which this increase takes place. If this growth takes place on the basis of an emerging tendency towards capitalist development, then the capital–output ratio does necessarily increase. On the other hand, it is perfectly conceivable to have alternative agrarian relations and methods of production organisation which can yield the same order of output increases without raising the capital–output ratio at all, for example by employing more human labour than machinery (as long as unemployment exists), by making more intensive use of smaller-scale rain-harvesting systems rather than large irrigation projects, by using more renewable energy sources.

A number of writers have emphasised the constraining role of the agricultural sector in the process of development of Third World economies. When we look closely at the matter however the so-called agricultural constraint appears to be nothing else but a constraint of a rising capital–output ratio in agriculture, and this in turn is not independent of the structure and the form of organisation of the agrarian sector. Kalecki (1972c) was explicit about this. When he located the constraint upon the overall growth of such economies in the growth rate of the agricultural sector, the fact that this sector's growth rate could not be increased beyond a certain low level was attributed by him to the prevalence of usury, landlordism and land concentration, in short to the extant agrarian relations. While one may disagree with Kalecki's postulation of a maximum rate of growth in agriculture (he was after all discussing a medium-term plan), and with his belief that the extant agrarian relations remain unchanged even as pressures on agricultural supplies build up; while one may invert the Kaleckian conception to assert that agrarian relations do undergo a change (towards a socially narrowly based form of capitalist development) even within the pre-existing pattern of land concentration in order to meet the requirement of capitalist industrialisation, the fact that the concentration of landownership still extracts a price in the form of a rising capital–output ratio entailed in the resulting capitalist development can scarcely be denied. One has only to look at the rapid rise in the requirement of non-renewable energy per unit of output in Indian agriculture in the period of the so-called Green Revolution, which greatly accelerated the tendency towards capitalist development in the countryside, to convince oneself of this (see Chakravarty 1987 on the growing energy-intensity of Indian agriculture).

An important implication of the foregoing argument should be noted. What appear at first sight to be natural phenomena often turn out on closer examination to have social roots. The rising capital–output ratio in agriculture may at first sight appear to be a natural phenomenon, arising from Ricardian diminishing returns. On closer examination, however, we cannot dissociate it from the process of capitalist development in agriculture. Likewise the fact that countries pursuing a path of 'enforced diffusion' have to experience rising capital–output ratios in meeting their raw material and energy needs appears at first sight to be a natural phenomenon arising from the scarcity of such resources. In fact the proximate cause lies in the inherited pattern of international relationships whereby the Third World countries trade with one another through core currencies which are in short supply for each of them. Whether or not there are diminishing returns owing to the existence of scarce resources on a global scale, whether or not mankind as a whole can continue to experience output growths of the order that it has experienced in recent history, is a deep and profound question. If the answer to this question is negative, then the whole issue of sharing these resources equitably among the entire people of the globe has to be squarely faced. But, more importantly, the immediate constraints upon Third World development cannot even be said to arise from such natural scarcities. They have their roots in a certain social order taken in its totality, i.e. in its international as well as in its internal aspects.

3. PRIMITIVE ACCUMULATION AND RISING SHARE OF SURPLUS

We have been focusing on capital–output ratios for a good reason. It used to be argued in the 1950s that the capacity for savings and in-vestment in the underdeveloped countries was low on account of their poverty (Nurkse 1958). This argument was logically faulty to start with. The potential savings and investment ratios in an economy depend upon the proportion which its economic surplus bears to its total output, a rough indication of which is given by the proportion of property incomes. This proportion was no less in underdeveloped countries like India at the time of their independence than in the advanced capitalist countries. If the actual savings and investment ratios in the former appeared nonetheless to be lower than in the latter (many in retrospect have questioned the veracity of the figures themselves), the difference clearly had nothing to do with poverty and per capita incomes *per se*, but had rather to do with the manner of deployment of the surplus, as Baran (1957) argued long ago.

It turns out however that the savings and investment ratios in many underdeveloped countries in recent years have been higher not only than the corresponding ratios in virtually all the advanced capitalist countries, with the exception of Japan, but also compared to what these ratios were for the advanced capitalist countries during any stage of their development. These ratios moreover have been rising over the last few decades since the deliberate introduction of development policies. In 1951, when the UN brought out its well-known document on *Measures* to achieve development (which was authored by a group of distinguished economists, including Arthur Lewis), it was thought that starting from around 5 per cent or so of national income, if the savings ratios could be pushed up to about 15 per cent in the underdeveloped countries, then they would be well on the road to development. Today a large number of underdeveloped countries would exceed the 15 per cent target by a long shot; and yet the problem of development remains as elusive as ever.

To be sure, compared to the historical experience, along with the increase in the savings ratio, there has been—in the former colonies and semi-colonies at any rate—an increase of a considerable magnitude in the growth rate. But this increase, impressive in absolute terms though it may be, appears nonetheless insufficient either to remove the problems of mass unemployment and poverty, or even to close the gap noticeably between the rich and the poor nations. It has not moreover been anywhere near what one might have expected from the increase in the savings rate.

To say that the reason why higher savings have not raised growth rates correspondingly is because of a rise in the capital–output ratio is by itself a mere tautology. Neoclassical economists attribute this rise in the capital–output ratio to inefficiency of resource use caused by the regime of domestic controls and restricted trade (especially through quantitative restrictions). Apart however from the problems associated with the concept of efficiency (on which more later), the case for inefficiency has to be independently established and not deduced from the observed rise in the capital–output ratios. Since the observed movements in the capital–output ratio are merely derived from observed movements in the investment ratio and the growth rate, any thing that constrains the growth rate in the face of an increase in the investment ratio (including even Ricardian diminishing returns) would manifest itself as a rise in the capital–output ratio, which may not have anything to do necessarily with efficiency or inefficiency of resource use. It is in this context that some discussion of the plausible reasons for the observed rise in this ratio becomes relevant.

We have discussed so far some of the reasons from the production side why a rise in this ratio occurs under conditions of enforced diffusion. That these reasons are pertinent is attested to by studies such as the Raj Committee in India (1982) which attributed the increase in this ratio to the rapidly growing need for new sources of energy. But apart from these there is a second set of reasons having nothing directly to do with production which also contributes to the increase in this ratio. And this is to do with the fact of the use of the State exchequer for private enrichment by the emerging bourgeois and proto-bourgeois class in such mixed economies.

Consider an economy that is growing at a certain rate of growth. Because of the reasons mentioned above the investment ratio is rising over time to maintain this growth rate. Since private investment more or less responds to the growth of the market (using Hicks's (1950) terminology, it is of the 'induced' variety), the active role in maintaining the growth process is being played by State investment. In order to maintain the growth rate then without raising the share of the budget deficit in GDP, State revenue as a proportion of GDP must increase. But if there is evasion of direct taxes so that the proportion of direct tax revenue to GDP does not increase, or there is a growing share of transfers in the form of subsidies to the capitalist farmers, rich peasants and the urban bourgeoisie (and for protecting the interests of the vocal salariat and the organised workers), then in the absence of a sufficient decline in the ratio of product wages to productivity in the State enterprises, the growth rate can be maintained only by a growing squeeze on the urban and rural poor through indirect taxes or a budget deficit-induced inflation. In short, the share of economic surplus in GDP would be rising faster than

the share of investment, with growing luxury consumption accounting *inter alia* for the difference.

Now a part of luxury consumption, especially consumer durables
and residential construction, gets included in estimates of investment. The distinction between the two is difficult to capture by any
method of estimation, but where investment is calculated by the so-
called 'commodity-flow' method, by calculating in each period the
magnitude of commodities whose end-use is supposed to be investment, the latter is likely to be overestimated. Consequently the
increase in the capital–output ratio is also likely to be overestimated.

Exactly the same happens if private enrichment at the expense of
the State exchequer takes the form of inflating the costs of State
investment projects. Here, as well as the fact that the constant-price–
investment ratio would be overestimated because of the estimation
procedure mentioned above, the current-price–investment ratio will
increase faster than the constant-price–investment ratio. And if the
investment deflator used is such that it does not fully eliminate the
element of cost inflation owing to private enrichment, this will
constitute a second reason for the overestimation of the constant-
price–investment ratio. In short, in the actual figures of investment
and capital–output ratios, we are not necessarily confronting the
phenomena that these ratios are supposed to capture conceptually,
but a variety of refracted consequences of what one might call
primitive accumulation of capital.[2]

But apart from these refracted consequences, which cannot be
eliminated for statistical reasons, there is a genuine economic reason
why such primitive accumulation raises the observed capital–output
ratio. The pressure on the State budget on account of bourgeois
enrichment, which we have hitherto assumed to be getting fully
'passed on' to the poor through inflation or higher indirect taxes,
leads more realistically to a situation where the 'passing on' itself is
partial, and State investment is also partially pruned. Such pruning,
by upsetting the phasing of State investment is likely to raise the
capital–output ratio, as the following example shows. Suppose a
project requires $10 of investment and, once completed, yields $4 of

---

[2] The fact of such private enrichment at the expense of the State exchequer, or
rather through the instrumentality of the latter, has been widely discussed, though it
is located within divergent political economy frameworks. See for instance Bardhan
(1984) and P. Patnaik (1988) for two different approaches in the Indian context.

output annually. If capital stock is growing in the sequence $100, $110, $120, $130, $140, the output stream, starting from the second year, would be $40, $44, $48, $52, and $56. If because of a fiscal crunch the sequence of cumulated investment becomes $100, $110, $118, $124, and $129, then the output stream would be $40, $44, $44, $48, and $48. The observed incremental capital–output ratio in the second case would be 3.625 instead of 2.5 in the first stream, even though there has been no change technologically. The same kind of result would arise if the State raises indirect taxes to finance its investment, but the commodities released by such taxation are different from those required for investment, and the latter are in short supply because increased luxury consumption on account of budgetary transfers to the bourgeoisie has pulled such commodities away. Such disproportionalities resulting in shortages of some commodities, which hold up investment, and unsold stocks of others (which are counted as investment), would also manifest themselves as increases in the capital–output ratio.

Some of the contradictions inherent in the growth process in such mixed economies pursuing a policy of enforced diffusion, are obvious from the foregoing. An increase in the growth rate compared to its historical trend requires in any case an increase in the investment ratio, and to the extent that the end-use of the pre-existing surplus is not altered to bear the brunt of this increase, some increase in the ratio of surplus to output becomes necessary, relative to the comparison path that would have obtained in the absence of deliberate development, at the very outset of the development process. This increase is correspondingly less to the extent that the 'drain' of surplus to the core ceases, or some 'slack' exists in the agricultural sector, or fiscal instruments are utilised to alter the end-use of the domestically retained pre-existing surplus. Insofar as the capital–output ratio increases from the production side, for reasons discussed in the last section, the increase in the proportion of surplus is still larger. To the extent that the process of private enrichment, or what we have called the process of primitive accumulation of capital, intervenes, the increase in the proportion of surplus is larger still. And the disproportionalities resulting from such private enrichment via the budget give rise to a still larger increase in the ratio of the economic surplus.

Moreover, until now we have implicitly assumed that in the absence of the three reasons for increasing surplus along a particular growth path mentioned above, namely, the rise in the capital–input ratio from the production side, the process of private enrichment through the budget, and the disproportionalities that come in its wake, the ratio of surplus to output would remain unchanged. But if in the absence of these factors, the surplus would still have been increasing owing to the decline in the ratio of product wages to productivity in the private sector, the difference between private surplus and private investment being absorbed by growing luxury consumption, so that the three factors mentioned above act over and above an already existing tendency of the surplus to increase, then the overall increase in the share of the surplus would be greater still.

The upshot is that even though the rate of growth of output is maintained at a higher level than historically, the conditions of the bulk of the population do not show any significant improvement compared to the past, while a small stratum at the top (which may be quite large in absolute numbers in countries like India), a stratum we have labelled as the bourgeoisie and the proto-bourgeoisie, enriches itself noticeably. To be sure, the recruitment to this stratum being more open than before, that is the growing differentiation in society being at a stage where significant upward mobility is still possible, moderates to an extent the threat of any revolt from below. The main threat to social stability arises from an altogether different source, the competing claims among the various sections of the bourgeoisie and proto-bourgeoisie, who often mobilise regional, caste, ethnic, and religious loyalties to advance their claims. But the enthusiasm for such economic development among the poor soon evaporates.

4. NON-ABSORPTION OF LABOUR RESERVES

A manifestation of this increasing surplus is the continued non-absorption of the existing labour reserves. To see this let us assume a one-commodity world. A rise in the share of the surplus is synonymous with a decline in $w.l$, where w is the real wage per unit of labour and l the labour coefficient per unit of output. A decline in l therefore is one form which the rise in surplus takes. And with a certain rate of output growth, a declining l may entail a rate of employment growth, which is insufficient, given the rate of growth of the work-force, to make any dent on the magnitude of labour reserves.

That this has actually happened in several underdeveloped countries is obvious.We shall confine ourselves to citing some figures from India. According to the decennial census data, the organised sector consisting of factory industries, the State apparatus, and registered trading and financial enterprises had an employment growth rate between 1970–1 and 1980–1 of 2.4 per cent per annum, which was barely above the natural rate of growth of the work-force already employed in this sector. Its growth in other words was in no position to absorb the labour reserves existing in the countryside and in the so-called urban 'informal' sector.

When we look at the agricultural sector, the picture is no better. Notwithstanding larger doses of fertiliser and energy inputs in the wake of the Green Revolution, the rate of growth of agricultural production (not value added) was just short of 3 per cent per annum in India during the 1970s and the 1980s. The main achievement of the Green Revolution therefore lay not in any acceleration of the growth rate already experienced in the post-independence period (which itself was far higher than during the last half-century of colonial rule that witnessed a virtual stagnation in output),[3] but in simply sustaining that growth rate, which in its absence would have petered out within the prevailing agrarian relations. If labour requirement per unit of output had remained constant, an output growth of this order would have caused labour demand to grow slightly faster than labour supply in agriculture. But three additional factors intervened in this situation.

First, the Green Revolution had an extremely uneven regional impact. Though the overall growth rate of agriculture in the Indian economy was maintained at a slightly higher level than the rate of population growth (2.25 per cent per annum), this growth was concentrated mainly in the north-western part of the country comprising Punjab, Haryana and Western U.P. Even such growth as occurred elsewhere was also confined to irrigated tracts especially in the coastal delta regions. As a result, in at least nine states covering more than half of the country, agricultural growth has fallen behind the rate of population growth in the 1970s and the 1980s, and even

---

[3] For output trends in agriculture during the last half-century of colonial rule in India see Blyn 1966; Sivasubramonian 1965. Heston (1983) has produced a set of estimates contradicting Blyn's conclusions. For a critique of his method see Habib 1984.

within the backward states such growth as has occurred has been confined to pockets (U. Patnaik 1991*a*). The growth of labour demand in other words has itself been regionally concentrated. One would expect in such a situation some migration to occur from the laggard to the fast-growing regions; and it did occur. But the tendency to mechanise agriculture to reduce dependence on migration would be strong, and this indeed has been happening. Some writers have noticed an inverted U-shaped curve linking labour use (in mandays per gross cropped hectare) on the Y-axis with time on the X-axis in the early Green Revolution regions (see Chandrashekhar 1993). The first stage of the Green Revolution consists not only of an increase in cropping intensity, but also of higher yields in traditional crops like wheat, both of which entail a significant augmentation of land productivity. In this phase there is a rapid increase in labour use per net cropped area, and also an increase, though a less rapid one, in labour use per gross cropped area, since labour coefficient per unit of output does not decline much. In the second phase however while the growth of land productivity slows down, that of labour productivity accelerates, bringing down labour requirement per unit area. This is the phase when mechanisation to save on labour is introduced. The motive is to remove uncertainties in labour availability which acquire particular significance because the high cropping-intensity means that harvesting one crop and preparing the soil for the next must be completed within a certain time.

Second, as the Green Revolution spreads to newer areas within what we have called the dynamic belt, these new areas do not necessarily replicate the inverted U-structure. They do not pass sequentially through the two stages, but telescope the two, so that right from the beginning labour and land augmenting technical change proceed together. By starting late, they learn directly from the experience of the pioneer regions and straightaway introduce the technology package which the early developers had come to acquire in stages (Bhalla 1987). For both these reasons, if we take the period as a whole, we find that notwithstanding the maintenance of the agricultural growth rate through the so-called Green Revolution, the growth of labour demand in agriculture lags progressively behind the output growth rate until even the dynamic regions cease to absorb anything more than the natural increase in their own agricultural work-force, if even that. In the backward regions, even this is not possible, so that taking the country as a whole, agricultural growth becomes insufficient to absorb even the natural increase in the agricultural work-force.

Third, the spread of capitalist relations, precisely in the context of a situation where large labour reserves exist, has resulted in a growing casualisation of the labour force. Earlier, workers in the rural areas fell into two categories: the attached workers who were tied to a particular household and did a variety of work including agricultural operations for the household, and casual workers who worked not for one household but for many and who might or might not get work on a particular day on a daily wage basis, or a piece rate basis. In the initial years after the Green Revolution in Punjab when localised labour shortages developed, certain forms of tying workers also sprang up. Of late however there has been a significant shift towards casualisation (Vaidyanathan 1985). Precisely when agriculture's capacity to absorb even the natural increase in its work-force has been undermined, the agricultural sector has begun to witness a greater proletarianisation of the work-force. What this means for the workers is a 'cordoning off' of the agricultural sector: they are thrown to their own devices without the cushion of the old patronage system, and increasingly appear, even in the statistical data, as belonging outside the agricultural work-force. Even as the labour reserves have grown, or at any rate remained undiminished, they have come more into the open, so that their location is no longer confined to agriculture alone.

Let us go back to a theoretical point. What we have been saying runs counter to Ricardo's classic argument on machinery. That argument was based on the proposition that an increase in the share of the surplus, by raising the investment ratio, also raises the growth rate, so that over time employment with the use of machinery must overtake what would have prevailed on the original path without machinery. Ricardo was talking about a single innovation, while we are discussing a sequence of changes which raise the capital–output, as well as the capital-labour ratios. More importantly, Ricardo assumed that all surplus, in excess of a certain fixed level of capitalist consumption, was invested; we on the contrary, while assuming away like Ricardo any deficiency of aggregate demand, have postulated that all surplus coming into private hands, which is in excess of what they decide to invest on independent grounds, in particular the growth of the market, is consumed. Even assuming constant real wages and a steadily rising labour productivity, we can well have a situation where the rising share of surplus is so dissipated through a rising capital–output ratio and a rising share of luxury consumption in output that the resulting growth rate of employment does not reduce the proportion of labour reserves any more than the original path would have done.

5. THE DEMAND FOR 'NEW' GOODS

The threat to the path of enforced diffusion however comes from an altogether different source. Its inability to absorb labour reserves or to increase significantly the living standards of the bulk of the population creates only the conditions for general disillusionment among the people leading to a loss of crucial social support, but it is not the common people that put pressure for its abandonment. That pressure comes from within the ranks of the very beneficiaries of such development.

Even if enforced diffusion makes an economy produce a whole lot of commodities and absorb a whole lot of technologies prevalent at the core at a certain time, these technologies and commodities do not remain unchanged at the core. In the underdeveloped country the capacity to generate technologies and commodities which would be used at the core is, as we have seen, limited. And given the nature of taste formation among the upper echelons of such a society, any other innovation which the underdeveloped country may make on its own resources is considered by them to be at best a second preference, an inferior substitute for the 'genuine' products available at the core. Among large segments of the new rich middle classes in the periphery, therefore, the demand for foreign goods, temporarily satisfied by the process of enforced diffusion, re-emerges as word spreads of the appearance of new 'foreign' goods at the core. And once unsatisfied demand for such commodities builds up, resentment mounts against the economic regime which limits access to their imports. To this is added the pressure from a whole new section of businessmen, often expatriates, who see in the prospects of being able to produce such goods locally (which would amount in effect to assembling them), or of acting as trade intermediaries, a means of gate-crashing into the charmed circle of domestic capitalists, of getting rich quick almost overnight.

In the face of such pressures, there are three different possible courses of action open to the peripheral economy, given its overall social parameters. It can permit the imports of the 'new' goods; it can permit the local production of such 'new' goods on the basis of a fresh round of capital goods and technology imports. Or, finally, it can continue with the restrictive regime banning both the imports of such goods as well as their local production on the grounds of their having a low 'priority'. Of these the last one is the least realistic. It presupposes an intransigence on the part of the State, an immunity from the social pressures of the new rich middle classes (including elements of the bureaucracy), which is just not there. Moreover even if the State perchance showed such an intransigence, the restrictive regime is always sufficiently 'porous' for imports of such commodities to slip through it, and to a growing extent. Finally, even assuming that the restrictive regime can be sufficiently rigidly enforced, insofar as in the absence of 'new' goods the domestic rich simply refrain from consuming the 'inferior' home-produced ones (as we assumed in the model of Chapter 7), the State would have to hold (or subsidise the holding of) increasing amounts of unwanted stocks of unwanted goods to maintain over time a certain desired level of capacity utilisation in the economy. This kind of a phenomenon, which we christen as 'neo-Tugan Baranovskyism', is quite palpably unsustainable.[4]

Either of the first two possibilities however entails a regime change, whose logical corollary is a tethering once again of the growth process of the economy to the growth of exports. The whole point of 'enforced' diffusion was to delink the economy from being a plaything of the operation of the world market, to initiate a growth process which to a significant extent is independent of the growth prospects of exports and does not depend either on enticing larger flows of private capital from the core. This gets lost when under pressure the economy gets opened up to imports, either directly or through local assembly, of every fresh round of 'new' goods being innovated abroad. Some of these 'new' goods being domestically produced may in the course of time emerge as export goods from the periphery itself, but then that is nothing else but a version of

---

[4] This christening is provoked by the work of the Russian economist Tugan-Baranovsky who argued that a realisation crisis can always be averted under capitalism even in the face of a rising surplus through an appropriate increase in investment. His work has been much discussed; see for instance Lenin 1960; Luxemburg 1963; Sweezy 1942; Kalecki 1971.

'automatic' diffusion, whose limits we have already looked at in the previous chapter.

In fact whatever scruples the State in the periphery may have, even while allowing the imports of 'new' goods, or of the wherewithal for its local production, soon become irrelevant as matters are taken out of its hands. In other words, even if it is the case that allowing such imports with every fresh round of innovations at the core, would logically entail the abandonment of enforced diffusion, and would logically create the conditions implicit in our model of Chapter 7, this logic is not even allowed time to work itself out. Such imports immediately give rise to acute balance of payments difficulties (which in any case under conditions of enforced diffusion are never much below the surface), and necessitate recourse to the IMF, both for short-run bailing out as well as for providing the 'cover' for commercial borrowing. And once the Fund has come in, its conditionalities provide the coup de grace for enforced diffusion.

The 'opening-up' of the economy, and the dismantling of the economic regime which had been associated with 'enforced' diffusion is accompanied by a swelling of the labour reserves. The very fact of 'opening-up' gives rise to a process of deindustrialisation: a number of activities which had come up behind protectionist walls are swept aside by the imports that now come in. Even when imports are of commodities different from those domestically produced, the switching of demand from the latter to the former has an exactly analogous effect. This deindustrialisation moreover is financed by foreign credit, in the form of loans from the IMF and commercial loans. The servicing of these brings in its train a further deflation of the economy which adds to unemployment. This increase in unemployment in the traverse from one kind of economic regime and growth strategy to another does not necessarily disappear within any definite period of time. After all, there is no reason why the time-profile of employment even when the economy has got fully launched on the so-called export-led growth path would be any higher than that on the path of enforced diffusion. Why then should the swelling of the labour reserve during the traverse be merely a temporary phenomenon? Indeed the whole experience of the colonial period, and the experience hitherto of a host of Latin American countries that made the switch (not to mention the experience, though brief, of several Eastern European economies) suggest the contrary.

The real contradiction in the strategy of enforced diffusion thus arises from a basic asymmetry. While innovations in the periphery cannot gain currency at the core, innovations in the core do gain currency both at the core as well as at the periphery. Or, putting it differently, whatever gains currency at the core also gains currency at the periphery, but the periphery, being hamstrung by its low per capita capital stock in the matter of successfully innovating for the core, also finds itself incapable of innovating for its own market. Any strategy of relatively autonomous development flounders on account of this, which is ultimately linked to a deeper cultural hegemony exercised by the core over the periphery. The bourgeoisie in the periphery (using the term in the wider sense that Fanon (1974) did), has a contradictory attitude to the metropolitan bourgeoisie. On the one hand, it wishes to carve out a space for itself in opposition to metropolitan capital, which after all is what underlies the strategy of enforced diffusion. On the other hand, it prefers the commodities produced at the core to the commodities produced under its own aegis, because its ultimate ambition is to imitate the life-styles of the metropolitan rich. It cannot suggest to the latter an alternative life-style based upon its own innovative capacity; it can only hunger for a life-style which is outside its own innovative capacity.

6. THE LIMITS TO INNOVATIVE CAPACITY IN THE BACKWARD ECONOMY

Let us briefly recapitulate the argument why the backward economies cannot innovate for the core market. All innovations occur first of all at the fringes of a production structure which is based on a certain technology. They are based on a certain minimum expenditure of resources on research, development, and marketing. The backward economy has neither such a production structure, including the associated infrastructure, over its economy as a whole (even enforced diffusion creates only an island of 'modern' production superimposed on layers of production structures belonging to earlier epochs), nor the capacity to undertake the expenditures needed for innovation. No doubt large countries like India and China have large capital stocks in absolute terms, and large pools of skilled manpower on the basis of which, it might be supposed, they could develop the capacity to innovate for the core market. But they also have large populations, for whose employment a part of this capital stock must be earmarked, and for whose requirements a part of the expenditure, which if devoted exclusively towards innovating for the core might have been productive, has to be diverted. What is crucial is a minimum capital stock per capita. It is this that we singled out in an earlier chapter as the main determinant of innovative capacity for the core market, and hence the world market.

Two conclusions follow. First, it is not that the backward economy is incapable of innovating; it is just that it is incapable of innovating commodities for the core market, a distinction which is important. Second, it is not inconceivable that in large economies if the State could turn its back completely upon the bulk of the population, ignore its needs, bring about over time a concentration of the country's capital stock in a small region, then perhaps that small region, endowed with modern means of transport and communications, modern scientific establishments, and a range of modern industries, could emerge as an innovator for the core market, since for all practical purposes it would be indistinguishable from the core itself. But then this would require a really ruthless process of internal colonialism; no doubt all underdeveloped countries are characterised by 'dualistic' structures, but then this would constitute much more than dualism, and would necessitate even internal curbs on population mobility lest the modern infrastructure gets damaged by the inevitable influx of destitutes from outside. And even if such successful islands of 'export-led growth' could be created within the underdeveloped country, what purpose would it serve for the development of the country's population as a whole? Just as the fact of Germany 's being a developed country is of little use to the Indian poor, likewise a scenario in which Bombay becomes a developed island, on a par with the core economies but by totally insulating itself from the rest of India even while drawing upon the latter's resources, would be of little consolation to the Indian poor. Our focusing on a certain minimum level of per capita capital stock in a country as a precondition for its being able to innovate for the core market, presumes therefore that the country remains reasonably integrated, and that there are no completely insulated and highly privileged islands within it exercising an internal colonial relationship with the rest of it, sucking out the latter's resources.

7. ON THE NEOCLASSICAL CRITIQUE OF ENFORCED DIFFUSION

It is worth distinguishing our critique of the strategy of enforced diffusion from the neoclassical critique. The essence of the neoclassical critique is that the strategy of enforced diffusion involves an inefficient resource use, which a framework of more open trade and less domestic controls would avoid. Of late a whole new 'political economy' has been propounded within this approach to explain why such inefficient economic regimes come into being and survive (see Krueger 1974).

Interestingly, the proponents of this political economy do not adopt a consistent political economy approach in all matters. If the policy of enforced diffusion is sustained in the interests of certain social groups, whose interests does the policy of opening up the economy serve?[5] Even if they believed that it was in the interests of the overwhelming bulk of society, the question still remains: which particular social groups agitate for it? Are they merely the embodiment of reason? Or do they have some specific vested interests? And if they are merely the embodiment of reason, then how is it that while some social groups represent vested interests, others including the Fund and the Bank who advocate 'liberalisation' are untainted by such interests and become the embodiment of pure reason? And so on.

Likewise, this political economy makes no effort to provide a political economy explanation of successful cases of development, and is altogether lacking in any historical dimension. Is the development of Germany, Japan, South Korea, the United States the result of the pursuit of 'free trade', 'free market' policies? If Japan was as protected in the 1950s and saw as much State intervention as India did, then wherein lay the *differentia specifica* between the two cases? Is the level of corruption any higher in India than in Japan, where a Prime Minister had to relinquish office for having accepted bribes? And how is it that despite having pursued 'free trade' 'free market' policies, in fact to the maximum extent ever actually recorded, during the colonial period, countries like India find themselves in an abject state of underdevelopment today?

---

[5] This criticism can be levelled against the argument of Bardhan 1984 as well.

In short, one cannot take this political economy seriously, nor any seemingly radical political economy that discusses only the political economy of the so-called 'inward-looking' development, but not that of 'liberalisation' or of the tendencies towards it. Let us however consider the logic of the neoclassical economic argument entirely on its own.

There are two distinct kinds of inefficiency that tend to get lumped together in such discussion. One is what I would call the inefficiency of 'indiscipline', the fact that in the absence of the coercion exercised by the market, motivation suffers all around. The market 'keeps everybody on his toes', and in its absence there is no other spontaneously disciplining device. Essential to this concept is the view that any system must have idle resources, of workers thrown out of work and factories closed down on account of inefficiency, to act as a deterrent to such inefficiency, not just the threat of idleness (for that alone would be insufficient in practice) but actual idleness. The second concept of inefficiency refers to 'wrong choices'. Even in a society with no laxity of the first kind, if decisions are made on the basis of incorrect, wrong or partial information, they are bound to result in an output loss. In terms of a military analogy, the soldiers, the Generals, and every other military agent may be as highly motivated as is possible, but the intelligence on the basis of which the strategy is worked out is wrong. The market is a comprehensive purveyor of information on the possibilities open to an economic agent or to a country for that matter, and interference with the prices distorts this information, leading to wrong choices, both at the macro as well as at the micro level. It is this concept of inefficiency, for which the prescription usually advanced is: 'get prices right'.

The distinction between these two concepts of inefficiency is important if only to underscore the fact that any society that wishes to transcend the coercive discipline of the market and organise itself on more humane lines, must develop an alternative work-ethic and work-culture. And if it does so, then the need for having real markets and real free trade on the basis of which decisions are made by dispersed agents need not logically arise (see P. Patnaik 1991). But we are concerned here with the neoclassical argument, and not the ideal alternative to the market; so we shall not pursue this question further.

Even if we eschew all basic considerations regarding the realism of the neoclassical view, such as the fact that underlying the market are unequal power relationships, that the actual prices are the result of strategic decisions, that market shares do not depend only upon 'efficiency' however defined, that the empirical evidence for the so-called inefficiency of 'inward-looking' strategy of development is by no means as overwhelming as is made out, there still remains a curious superficiality about this view.[6] Consider a world characterised by universal free trade and free markets, which is in equilibrium in the sense that, even though the countries are producing an overlapping mix of commodities, the costs of production of each commodity everywhere are equal and that each country attains full capacity output. In such an ideal world, there is nothing to determine where capitals, accumulated everywhere, would be invested. True, in such a world, real wages everywhere would have the same ratio with productivity (assuming that the same technology is available to all), but the geographical location of the world's unemployed would be indeterminate.

The only argument against this can be that the countries saddled with large-scale unemployment would witness a lowering of wages which would entice capital from everywhere else into these countries until the wage–productivity ratio is equalised everywhere on the basis of a more even distribution of unemployment. In other words, the only consistent neoclassical story one can tell about a world in which there is capital mobility at all, is one in which capital must move from high-wage to low-wage (per efficiency unit of labour) countries. But in such a case, there would be no underdevelopment at all to start with. Thus the neoclassical prescriptions either constitute a *non sequitur* (if capital movements are governed by some other factors), or are offered against a malaise which they cannot even theoretically recognise—which cannot exist by their theory.

Notwithstanding the fact that the neoclassical economists devote much time to elaborating upon the empirically obvious facts about private enrichment from the existence of the system of controls in underdeveloped economies, the theoretical structure within which they locate these facts is neither rounded in terms of economics, nor

---

[6] The literature on strategic trade theory runs counter to the *simpliste* neoclassical positions; see Krugman and Helpman 1986. On the empirical side, Chandrashekhar (1988) shows on the basis of case studies that the so-called inefficiency of Indian industries by international standards is an exaggerated view. Interestingly a study by the World Bank of the Indian capital goods industry came to the similar conclusion that the industry is by no means inefficient by international standards.

conversant with history, nor concerned at all with sociology. If they ever treated the real world not as an arbitrary deviation from the ideal state in their minds, but a phenomenon in itself which requires an analysis *sui generis*, then perhaps there would at long last be a meeting ground between them and the others who have been struggling to make sense of it.

14

Socialism and Third World Development

1. THE DIFFICULTIES OF DELINKING

When Paul Baran named the last chapter of his book *The Political Economy of Growth* 'The Steep Ascent' he could scarcely have imagined how steep that ascent would turn out to be in practice. The fact that many underdeveloped countries pursuing what then appeared to be a promising path of self-reliant development, among whom Baran had high hopes in India, would, instead of pressing forward towards socialism as a means to sustain self-reliance, slide back into IMF conditionalities, may not perhaps have surprised him. After all these were countries with fairly entrenched bourgeoisies that would have made such an advance difficult. But the fact that there would be a slide back even among socialist countries, not just the extraordinarily poverty-stricken, embattled, and fragile countries, opting for socialism, but even among countries such as China which had witnessed some of the most heroic revolutionary struggles of this century, to a point where they too would have to listen to the 'advice' emanating from the Fund and the Bank would certainly have come to him as a surprise. To say this is not to trivialise the experiments in China, or to pre-judge the course of the current reforms, but merely to underscore the fact that the belief which many had that, once the revolution had triumphed, progress towards a society without want would be along a more or less well-charted course, and would be a more or less uninterrupted one, has turned out to have been simplistic.

Paradoxically, the difficulties of this transition, instead of being seen as testifying to the immense strength of imperialism, which has the capacity to win the peace even after losing the war, are being seen by many as constituting proof of the intrinsic unworkability of socialism. As a reflex, even the existence of imperialism is being doubted. In fact, the dominance of imperialism has never been as strong as it is today; even its ideological hegemony today is so overwhelming that few believe in its very existence.

The purpose of the preceding chapters has been to provide a sketch of the mechanics and the role of imperialism, and this would be a convenient point to summarise the overall argument briefly. If capitalist economies, where overall investment is the sum of the investment decisions of individual capitalists and prices reflect the claims upon aggregate output of different social groups, such as the workers, the rentiers, and the entrepreneurs, were characterised by organised labour *en masse* confronting organised capital, then they would not have been able to maintain both steady output growth and steady inflation over long stretches of time. This indeed has been the case historically. The reason why these economies have been able to do so is that a large segment of the workers who work for capital remain unorganised, or sufficiently weak in terms of their ability to bargain, so that they cannot enforce in a sustained manner their *ex ante* claims upon output. Had these unorganised workers been located within the capitalist economies, their role as a cushion for the economic stability of the system would nevertheless have jeopardised the social stability of the system. But they are located outside, in the outlying regions of the system from where capitalism in any case has to obtain much of its primary commodities, and their *ex ante* claims are kept in check by large labour reserves which exist in such regions. The polarisation of the world into a core of advanced capitalist countries with social and economic stability, high rates of productivity growth (through innovations in manufacturing) which yield high rates of real wage growth and hence rising standards of living, and a periphery coupled to this core which produces primary commodities and those manufactured goods from whose production the core is moving away, but whose growth rate is ultimately limited by the rate of growth of its exports, thus not only works to the capitalist countries' advantage, but also tends to reproduce itself spontaneously. The reproduction of labour reserves in the periphery is an essential component of this process. What Marx had written in *Capital* about the reproduction of wealth at one pole and poverty at another holds at the international level (no matter what its relevance within the domestic economies of the core capitalist countries)[1] in much the way he had described but with different mediations.

Any conscious efforts on the other hand by the Third World States to break out of this trap flounders for an obvious reason. The domestic bourgeoisie (including the upper layers of the bureaucracy and the professional classes) which gets strengthened by such deliberate development (what we have called 'enforced diffusion') is keen to emulate the life-styles prevailing at the core demands commodities which are being innovated at the core but which are beyond the capacity of the underdeveloped country to innovate on its own. The pressure to import such commodities or components for their local assembly mounts. Since in any case, during the process of 'enforced diffusion', the rise in the capital–output ratio, coupled with the rise in the share of private surplus, means a negligible increase if at all in the living standards of the bulk of the working population, such a strategy loses crucial social support. A reversal of it, pressed for all along by the core countries and the agencies dominated by them, and now desired by the domestic bourgeoisie for its own reasons, becomes inevitable. This brings the economy immediately under the umbrella of IMF-conditionalities, and tethers its growth rate in the long-run once again to the rate of growth of its exports of primary commodities and early-stage manufactured goods. The process of delinking the economy from the relationship of unequal interdependence flounders because the social groups that preside over such delinking are unequal to the task. Trapped within the cultural hegemony exercised by the core, insensitive to the plight of their poorer fellow-countrymen, they first bring the strategy of 'enforced diffusion' into disrepute with the masses by using the State for private enrichment, and then use this very fact of disrepute to press for a reintegration with the core, again for their own ends.[2] The period over which such a double-switch occurs may be more or less

[1] Whatever illusions some may have entertained about its declining relevance within the core capitalist countries should be dispelled by the developments of the recent years. This however is a matter lying outside our present concern.

[2] From this however it would not be legitimate to draw any conclusions about the 'comprador' character of the Third World bourgeoisie. Our discussion is not concerned with this question, partly because the social groups we are talking about are not co-terminus with the bourgeoisie in the strict sense (though somewhat closer to Fanon's conception), and partly because the contemporary context appears to us to require concepts transcending the traditional national-comprador dichotomy within the bourgeoisie.

protracted; but most Third World countries appear inexorably to be heading towards it.

2. ON SOME LEWISIAN THEMES

The themes touched upon in this work have been identical with or parallel to those which Arthur Lewis has discussed in several of his writings (e.g. 1978*a,b*). A further word on the difference between his position and ours may therefore be in order here. Lewis's basic argument relates to the factoral terms of trade. Europe had an agricultural revolution while the tropics did not. An average European farmer grew more on the plot of land he had than an average Indian farmer did. When the former migrated he did so at higher wages than the latter. These two belts of population have been kept separate by preventing the migration of the huge labour reserves of India and China to the temperate lands. It follows from Lewis's analysis that tropical development can occur not through trade, but through a continuous and self-sustaining increase in output per head by 'imitating the agricultural and industrial revolutions' at the core, for which trade can at best provide a kind of launching pad.

Our differences with Lewis relate both to his analysis as well as to his prescription. First of all, the so-called agricultural revolution was a bit of a myth. Even in England, where it is supposed to have been the most pronounced, between 1700 and 1850 the yield per unit area of cereals went up by less than 25 per cent (Mingay and Chambers 1966; U. Patnaik 1991). The idea that even prior to the industrial revolution, the average European farmer enjoyed a standard of living substantially higher than say the Indian farmer in 1700, can scarcely be supported with reference to a presumed agricultural revolution. (And if it is argued that labour productivity in agriculture went up noticeably in Europe even though land productivity did not, then the obvious rejoinder would be that the wages at which migration took place should then be related to the incomes of the unemployed rather than of the farmers). On the other hand, there exists no particular reason to believe that in 1700 itself the average European farmer enjoyed a higher living standard than his Indian counterpart. Given the fact that multiple cropping was more prevalent in India than in say England, and that cultivable land was not in short supply, the only other plausible basis for such an assertion would be a higher rate of surplus extraction in India, for which there is no obvious evidence. And yet assertions such as this are by no means uncommon, and are based invariably on presumption rather than any evidence.[3]

In explaining the difference in wages at which the different streams of migration took place in the earlier part of the nineteenth century, we have to look not towards any technological differences in the inherited agricultural sectors, but to the fact of colonial penetration. This led on the one hand to deindustrialisation and hence an overcrowding of agriculture. On the other hand, it resulted in significant changes in the cropping pattern and production practices, and in a neglect of traditional irrigation facilities, all of which contributed to a retrogression of agriculture in the tropical colonies. European labour, coming from an agriculture which was not necessarily any more advanced to start with, occupied the 'empty spaces' in the temperate regions from which the 'natives' were driven off, and hence enjoyed a higher standard of living than was possible back home. Tropical labour coming from the colonies where it had become impoverished was kept in an impoverished state in its new settlements as well. It was the fact of domination rather than any prior technological breakthroughs in agriculture which accounted for the difference in the wages of the two streams of migrants. And not only were the streams kept separate, but, as we have discussed earlier, capital did not flow into the tropics to take advantage of the wage difference. If it had flowed in, then no matter what obstacles were placed in the way of labour migration from the tropics to the temperate regions, the wage differences could not have persisted. Moreover, local capital which could have taken advantage of the wage difference to outcompete the metropolis in industrial products was systematically discriminated against. Thus at the origin of the dualism on the world scale lies the fact of coercion which colonialism entailed, but which does not figure in Lewis's analysis.

It follows that even today when coercion in the form of explicit political control no longer exists, the core countries would not merely sit back and watch the labour reserves in the periphery dwindle, if, as we have argued, such dwindling stiffens the *ex ante* claims of Third World primary commodity producers upon the core products. The Third World's implementation of its own 'agricultural and industrial

---

[3] An example of this kind of presumption, Bagchi (1972) shows, can be found even in Kuznets 1971.

revolutions' in imitation of the core is not a matter of its merely making up its mind to do so; the core would certainly attempt to prevent such a denouement.

Even leaving this aside however, there remains a more immediate tangible problem. What would prevent such attempts at imitating core technologies from creating the same kind of dualism within the Third World countries as exists internationally? If implanting core technologies was a one-shot affair, then with real wages kept down by the existence of labour reserves and surpluses devoted to investment, the periphery could experience a high rate of growth in the manner outlined by Lewis himself in his famous model of development with 'unlimited supplies of labour' (1954). But, as we have seen, the core technologies do not remain static. Unless the Third World countries are in a position to innovate the new technologies, which they palpably are not, the process of implanting core technologies becomes a continuous one. This means that labour productivity keeps increasing, not just because of the transition from traditional to modern production which would happen in the Lewis model too, but within the modern sector itself. If wages in the modern sector rise together with productivity, then the rate of employment growth in the modern sector may be too small ever to absorb the 'unlimited supplies of labour', perpetuating the dualism in the peripheral economy.

But the case of rising wages in the modern sector perpetuating dualism in the economy, though it constitutes one possible scenario (referred to as the savings constraint in the literature), is not the essence of our argument. Our argument presupposes neither rising wages (it holds equally well if wages are kept at some 'subsistence' level) nor even any conscious policy decision to implant continuously every successive innovation in core technology. The State cannot resist the domestic pressure from the 'elite', at any rate in conditions where the economic trajectory is one of bourgeois development, and make this implantation of core technologies a once-and-for-all affair. Now, it may be thought that if technological progress is a continuous affair, based on successive borrowings of innovations from the core, then, with real wages remaining unchanged, the growth rate should accelerate, as a larger and larger proportion of the modern sector's output accruing as surplus enables the economy to maintain a progressively increasing investment ratio in this sector. This however is not the case. Unless the domestic economy has the capacity to produce the equipment associated with the new processes or the new products that constitute the fresh round of innovation, which it obviously does not have since it is not the innovating economy, the accelerating growth, if it were to occur, would invariably be associated with a corresponding growth of import demand.

Export growth on the other hand cannot increase correspondingly to pay for the growing import demand. The exports of traditional commodities have obvious limits to their growth rate. The exports of modern sector goods are hamstrung initially by high capital–output ratios, the time taken for 'learning-by-doing' effects to materialise, and the time taken to establish markets and reputations abroad in commodities which one has not innovated. And when such exports do materialise after a lag, still newer commodities and processes have been innovated abroad. This is not to say that exports of modern sector goods cannot or do not occur, but simply that there is a limit to the export growth rate. The fact of low wages *per se* does not mean that the periphery would become an exporter of the latest goods, immediately upon implanting their production in the domestic economy. And if so, then this sets a ceiling upon the overall growth rate of the modern sector itself, no matter what the gap between its rates of growth of product wages and productivity is.[4]

Since the growth even of the modern sector depends on the rate of growth of exports, a configuration of output and productivity growth rates in this sector may get established which perpetuates the dualism in the economy by failing to absorb the labour reserves from outside, irrespective of how wages in this sector move in relation to productivity. A simple illustration (which is in conformity with what is mentioned above, but constitutes a slight modification of our model in Chapter 7) will make the point. Suppose the growth rate of exports, assumed to be independent of the ratio of product wages to productivity in the modern sector, is x, and a given fraction m of investment in the modern sector has to be imported each year. Then the long-run rate of growth of investment and hence also of output

---

[4] See Chapter 12 for an elaboration of the argument that there exists a limit to the extent of automatic diffusion and hence the long-run rate of growth of the backward economy's manufacturing sector which is independent of the relationship between the rates of growth of its product wages and productivity. The only additional point being made here is that the limit to diffusion arises not only from the factors mentioned there, namely the country's technological capability, the capacity of individual capitals, and protectionism in the metropolis, but also from the sluggishness with which exports adjust.

in the modern sector (we are assuming in line with standard growth theory that all technical progress is of the Harrod-neutral kind) cannot exceed x. The growth of labour productivity, which would be a function of x (despite the technology being generated abroad) may be such that together with the magnitude of x, the growth in employment demand it generates is insufficient to absorb the labour reserves at the prevailing rate of growth of the working population. Now, whether wages in the modern sector rise at the same rate as productivity or do not rise at all affects only the distribution of consumption between the wage earners and the surplus earners, but not the growth rate.

This case also illustrates why the proposition that if only the Third World countries could bring down their population growth rate, they would be on the road to prosperity is a facile one. The point at issue is not the desirability of a lower population growth rate, though any such lowering must be based on voluntary decisions in a society where health and education facilities, and more generally opportunities for leading a more meaningful life, are made available to all. Coercive measures to bring down the birth-rate are offensive to human dignity. When viewed as a prerequisite of development, they are theoretically a *non sequitur* as well. True, *ceteris paribus*, a lower rate of population growth implies a better chance for the labour reserves to get used up; this is but an arithmetical truism. But there is no reason why *ceteris paribus* should hold. The possibility of labour reserves getting used up in the periphery depends, as we have seen, also upon the prospects of export growth to the core since a continuous process of implantation of innovations from the core is an unavoidable feature. If together with the decline in the population growth rate in the periphery, there is also a decline in the rate of export growth to the core, then there is no reason why the labour reserves should ever get used up. If, as we have argued, a using up of labour reserves in the periphery jeopardises economic and social stability at the core, then the latter has an instrument for preventing such a denouement, namely a regulation of the periphery's exports into its economy of commodities which are competitive with its own products, which is in fact what did happen in the colonial period. The need for the use of this instrument may not occur in practice for long periods of time, if the parameter values are such that the labour reserves are not being used up. But from this it would be erroneous to conclude that if only we arbitrarily adjusted one of the parameter values, namely the rate of population growth, the using up of labour reserves would automatically follow.

The persistence of dualism within backward economies despite a growing modern sector has been attributed in the literature to a variety of phenomena, such as rising wages in this sector, and the existence of demand constraints owing to its oligopolistic nature (see Spaventa 1959). Interestingly however the role of imitative technological change in the persistence of dualism has scarcely figured in the literature. And yet it is perhaps the single most significant factor. Rising wages *pari passu* with productivity can hardly be said to characterise the modern sectors of the peripheral economies in general. No doubt, the workers in the modern sector get much higher wages than those working in the traditional sector, and constitute in many instances a privileged elite within the working class. Even this elite however cannot be said in general to be obtaining wage increases in tandem with productivity growth. In India for example, the share of the wage bill in the gross value of output of the corporate manufacturing sector, whether State-owned or privately owned, has declined steadily in the post-independence period. Likewise, the demand constraint which makes itself felt under oligopolistic conditions because investment decisions are linked to the expected growth of the market and in turn determine the actual growth of the market which shapes expectations, can always be countered through active State intervention. If these were the critical factors underlying the persistence of dualism, then this persistence would be difficult to explain. But the fact of imitation of core technologies as a continuous process, which the State typically is unable to prevent, and which is quite irrespective of the wage movements, produces a dualism that has deeper roots. It follows then that contrary to the Lewis prescription, the periphery, if it wishes to chart a trajectory of development that genuinely improves the conditions of the mass of population by absorbing the large labour reserves, must avoid the continuous replication of the technological change occurring at the core.

3. COMPONENTS OF A NON-IMITATIVE STRATEGY

There are at least four crucial components of a non-imitative strategy of development. The first relates to the fact that structural and technological change in the Third World has to be planned. Instead of the imports and/or domestic production of new goods being willy-nilly a resultant of private preferences (backed by purchasing power), which polarises the developing country into one sector where modern, sophisticated and ever changing processes and products are appearing at a rapid rate to cater to the demands of a small segment of the population while in the rest of the economy large numbers remain unemployed and hungry, the decisions about the rate of technical change, the spheres in which new goods and processes prevalent at the core should be introduced and where they should not be, the appropriate mix of commodities, new and old, that should be made available to the people, are decisions that must be socially controlled. This requires not bureaucratic controls, but regulations which have social sanction, as we discuss below.

To say that structural/technical change should be planned, and that planning should be based on a social consensus, does not mean dooming the economy to what someone called 'a home-spun vegetarian paradise'. While a higher rate of productivity growth in a situation where the overall rate of growth of the economy is not very sensitive to this productivity growth does mean a lower rate of growth of employment, we cannot conclude from this that a freeze on technological progress represents an optimal social policy. (The case can be made out for instance that in the provision of public facilities like health, the underdeveloped countries should have access to modern technology for the entire population.) While the actual change in technology and the composition of commodities, dictated as it has been by private interests even in economies with substantial State regulation, has been too rapid and pervasive to overcome unemployment and poverty (a classic example is the use of combine harvester in Indian agriculture), the opposite course of freezing all technological change till full employment has been achieved is equally questionable. For one thing, when full employment is achieved, the need to raise productivity for achieving further growth would immediately reassert itself, but society would lack the wherewithal for achieving such productivity growth on the basis of the equipment, skills and technology at its command at that point of time. Besides the people of the Third World must also derive immediate benefits from modern technology. It is the people as a whole, and not just a small section, that should derive these benefits and this calls for a careful evaluation of the benefits against the possible adverse employment effects of such technology in order to introduce it selectively.

The second component of a non-imitative strategy relates to the need for having an independent trajectory of innovations in the Third World. Most process and product innovations today originate in the first world; the point just made above related to how much of these the Third World countries should adopt and at what pace. But that is only a part of the story; the more important issue relates to the need for the Third World countries to generate their own innovations. This is necessary for at least three reasons. First, the typical process and product innovations at the core take the character of what Marx called substituting 'dead labour for living labour'. Technical progress at the core is typically labour-saving; even if it is sufficiently all-pervasive (encompassing the production of the means of production as well) not to raise the capital–output ratio over time, it usually entails that for a given capital–output ratio, the capital–labour ratio keeps increasing, or, what comes to the same thing, for a given growth rate of output, the growth rate of employment is lower. When this technical progress is transplanted to the Third World, it has the effect, since the growth rate is insensitive to productivity growth, of keeping the vast labour reserves unutilised.

This particular character need not inhere in all innovations however. As Oskar Lange (1946) argued long ago, under conditions of monopoly capitalism, there is a selectivity in favour of labour-saving innovations. In other words, among a range of possible innovations, only those are selected under conditions of monopoly capitalism which are labour-saving. There is no reason then why in the Third World innovations should not be tried out, which, while maintaining the capital-labour ratio, lower the capital–output ratio, so that for a given rate of growth of capital stock it is not the rate of growth of employment that is lower but the rate of growth of output that is higher.

Second, an independent trajectory of innovations, no matter whether it is labour-saving or not, might give the Third World countries a better chance in first world markets than a mere imitation of the first world's goods. By the time the production of such goods has become sufficiently established in the Third World economy for it to launch itself as an exporter, product innovation at the core has moved ahead and these goods have become 'out of date'. Even if they are produced cheaper and can replace the core's own production of such goods, a ceiling nonetheless exists on the rate of growth of exports under what we have called 'automatic diffusion'. On the other hand, products innovated within the Third World itself are in a sense 'new products' in the core markets, and as such could conceivably command larger export markets.

Third, it can be argued that tastes do not remain static. Innovations to develop new products are therefore necessary in any society today; the crucial question then becomes whether such innovations should originate at the core or whether the periphery should have its own trajectory of innovations, and the answer must lie in the latter direction.

This however brings us immediately to the third component of a non-imitative strategy. If technological and structural change is to be planned, if innovations are to occur along an independent trajectory, then it follows that the economy cannot pursue a capitalist path of development. Socialism in the sense of social ownership of the means of production constitutes the necessary condition for initiating the kind of development which alone can overcome mass unemployment and poverty in the Third World. This, to be sure, would appear to many as a strange thing to say at a time when socialism appears to be in a profound crisis, and socialist structures have collapsed over large parts of Eastern Europe. A few words on that crisis are contained in the next section. But the argument for turning one's back upon socialism would be more credible if only it could be shown that the problems of the Third World were amenable to solution within the framework of a capitalist order. Not only has nobody shown this, apart from pointing a finger yet again in the direction of the East Asian four, but the entire history of the Third World in the colonial as well as in the post-colonial epoch is a proof to the contrary. The argument of the last several chapters of this book have been devoted to showing on the basis of that historical experience why capitalism provides no answers to the fundamental social problems of the Third World. On the one hand, the success of capitalism at the core has been predicated upon the maintenance of a system of unequal interdependence. On the other hand, within this system of unequal interdependence which perpetuates the existence of large labour reserves in the Third World it is scarcely conceivable that there would be a spontaneous elimination of these reserves. This last proposition, which, judging by his remark that 'the option of trade was of limited value', even Arthur Lewis would accept, is not nullified by the example of a few small countries (or city-States) rising almost to the status of developed countries under an exceptional combination of external and internal circumstances.

As regards the option of a self-sustaining (not export-led) growth ushered in through the development of a relatively autonomous capitalism helped by the active intervention of the State, this tends merely to reproduce an internal dichotomy within the underdeveloped country between advanced and backward strata and sectors and fails in absorbing the labour reserves, given the nature of the bourgeoisie and the historical context in which it makes its debut. It cannot escape the cultural hegemony of the core; and domestically it has to share power with the landed rich which helps only in hastening the reintegration of the economy into the metropolitan orbit and denies the mass of the rural population the fruits of even such development as occurs.

If capitalism then has no answers to the burning social issues confronting the Third World, it clearly becomes necessary to transcend it. Socialism, no matter what other problems it may give rise to, has indeed brought about enormous transformations in such underdeveloped countries as China, where it has been tried, transformations which have significantly improved against heavy odds the living standards of vast masses of the poor.[5] The fact that the socialist order has also displayed serious and obvious limitations by way of bureaucratisation, absence of political freedom and democratic institutions for the political intervention of the people, and also the fact that the contradictions within the socialist societies have become accentuated to a point where privatisation is being resorted to in a number of spheres of economic life, should not blind us to the achievements of even such socialism as we have had. The deformities and contradictions are arguments for learning from the past and attempting to build better socialist societies in the future but not for a reversion to capitalism. It is only by exercising their collective will rather than by leaving their fates either to the spontaneous operation of a free

---

5 By the mid-1980s, China, despite a more adverse ratio of arable land to population than India and an initial base of far more intensive cultivation, had achieved a per capita foodgrain production that was 50 per cent higher than India's. Given the more equal distribution of food in China then, this almost certainly would have eliminated mass poverty, though in the more remote and arid regions pockets of poverty might have survived; see U. Patnaik 1986. Even the subsequent agricultural growth in China after Deng's reforms owes much to the foundations laid in the pre-Deng period; see Mitra 1988.

market based on unequal interdependence or the play of private interests within a regime of State-sponsored capitalist development that the people of the underdeveloped countries can overcome the enormous odds that are placed against their advancement and climb out of their current miserable conditions of life.

But simply saying socialism is not enough. The fourth component of a non-imitative strategy must be a social redefinition of the conceptions of use-value. Socialist societies too can well recreate within themselves the same contradictions which obtain in the 'mixed economies' where State-sponsored capitalist development has been tried out. The cultural hegemony of imperialism, the passion for the life-styles it creates at the core, the rampant consumerism it promotes affects the Third World bourgeoisie in an immediate palpable sense. But even if the society opts for socialism, the professionals, the bureaucracy, the white-collar workers who get thrown up by the process of development, and even the workers, who, freed from their subsistence level existence, can now aspire for something better, are not immune to the dream of a 'Western life-style'. Now if it were possible for all within the Third World to achieve the average life-style of the core, then, while one may lament the craze for the glittering and the synthetic, and brood over the deeper implications of the consumerist passion, one would have little against it from a narrowly economic point of view. But such is by no means the case. Neither under capitalism, nor under socialism, can all in the Third World hope to enjoy in any foreseeable future anything like the average life-style prevailing in the advanced capitalist countries. To pretend otherwise would be sheer hypocrisy.

Even assuming that we are talking of the living standards of the core as they are today and not what they might become, and that the available reserves of natural resources in the world can permit it, the achievement of such living standards in the Third World would require a scale of investment that is enormous. Even assuming that the domestic savings rate can be jacked up to finance such investment over a certain definite period of time, these savings have to be transformed into investment via trade to obtain the requisite technology, equipment and even the natural resources (whose availability on a global scale we have assumed). This means that the core would have either to absorb much larger exports from the periphery for some time (causing domestic unemployment) or to allow adverse terms of trade against itself (causing domestic inflation). Even if the core had no long-run interest in ensuring the existence of unutilised labour reserves in the periphery, and even if the sociological pressures for a continuous emulation of the changing core living standards could be resisted, both of which are assumptions we have rejected, quite apart from global natural resource constraints and domestic savings constraints in the periphery, there remains the sheer fact of a serious conflict between the core and the periphery in the latter's traverse from its current living standards to those enjoyed at the core. (This conflict would disappear if the core voluntarily reduced its domestic expenditure and exported capital to the periphery instead, but we have already discussed in an earlier chapter the impossibility of such altruism). The other problems which we have assumed away only make matters worse.

While the achievement of core living standards for all is thus impossible in the foreseeable future, initiating a policy of free imports of technology and equipment in the name of achieving this serves the interests of a few and succeeds only in recreating internally the dualism between high living on the one hand and poverty on the other. The advocates of capitalism often claim as if all that stands between the poor in the Third World and 'Western' living standards, or for that matter between the relatively worse off in Eastern Europe and their better off counterparts in the West is the lack of free trade and free markets in the former, as if a mere decree announcing the lifting of internal controls and trade restrictions is all that is required for any country to lift itself to 'Western' living standards. If this indeed were all there would be no problem of underdevelopment to start with, since for a good deal of their recent history countries like India did have free markets, free trade and freedom for capital.

Once we recognise that hankering after core living standards and the core commodities constituting them has only the effect of preventing the removal of mass poverty or of recreating it all over again after it has been removed or ameliorated, it follows that a redefinition of the social conception of what constitutes use-value must be a part of any successful strategy of development. If this strategy to be successful must be non-imitative, then it must be non-imitative of Western-style consumerism as well. It should be clarified however that the point being made is not that some authoritarian socialist State should determine for the people what they should or should not hanker after; the point simply is that a social consensus must evolve among the people, on which alone State policy can be based, regarding the type of society and living standards which should be aimed at.

4. THE PRODUCTIONIST CONCEPTION OF SOCIALISM: A CRITIQUE

Much has been written about the authoritarianism of the socialist States. What is not often appreciated however is that the genesis of this authoritarianism lay in imperialist encirclement. The leaders of the Bolshevik Revolution did not plan to set up an authoritarian State. On the contrary during the Revolution and its immediate aftermath Russia witnessed the boldest democratic experiment in its history (Deutscher 1954, ch. 10). The imperialist powers' intervention on the side of counter-revolution during the Civil War not only resulted in a setback for the experiment in Soviet democracy, but also brought about a decimation in the ranks of the revolutionary proletariat that led inevitably to a substitution of the Party for the class. The process of bureaucratisation of the Party and the State noted by Lenin (1975a), the snuffing out of democracy and democratic intervention by the working class, the gradual depoliticisation of the working class, all of which characterised the trajectory of development taken by the Soviet Union shortly after the Revolution under the extra-ordinary circumstances of a bloody Civil War and imperialist intervention, were strengthened by the trauma of collectivisation and the Nazi invasion. The almost continuous struggle for survival of the Soviet State shaped the trajectory of its development which in no way represented a realisation of the socialist vision.

The personality factor was certainly important, as was the immense strain of industrialising a backward country at a hectic pace by a Party whose roots among the peasantry had been weak to start with. And there is undoubtedly a tension between the belief that the vanguard of the proletariat has a deeper scientific understanding of the historical process and the convention that it must step aside from power if more votes are cast against it than in favour of it. But the scope for these tensions to get resolved in practice did not exist because of the exceptional circumstances of Soviet development. And in the rest of the socialist world facing identical encirclement the Soviet 'model' found ready acceptance.

We know now that the fight against imperialism is better conducted in democratic conditions in which the political energies of the working people are activated, that the suppression of democracy which appears necessary in the short-run for winning battles against imperialist encirclement weakens socialism in the war as a whole. Democracy is necessary for the survival of socialism and its necessity is in no way dependent upon socialism having made peace with imperialism; on the contrary, its necessity is paramount precisely when socialism is engaged in struggle.

The fact that socialism would grope its way towards evolving, both in the realm of ideas as well as in practice, the democratic institutions and political conventions appropriate for a society where the opaqueness of social structures is meant to disappear over time can scarcely be in doubt, except perhaps by those who see an irresolvable contradiction between collective forms and individual freedom, which makes all collective forms in their eyes arbitrary impositions that are fundamentally anti-democratic. But the logical weakness of their basic premisss was exposed by none other than Keynes in 1926:

Let us clear from the ground the metaphysical or general principles upon which, from time to time, laissez-faire has been founded. It is not true that individuals possess a prescriptive natural liberty in their economic activities. There is no 'compact' conferring perpetual rights on those who Have or those who Acquire. The world is not so governed from above that private and social interests always coincide. It is not so managed here below that in practice they coincide. It is not a correct deduction from the Principles of Economics that enlightened self-interest always operate in the public interest. Nor is it true that self-interest is generally enlightened; more often individuals acting separately to promote their own ends are too ignorant or too weak to attain even these. Experience does not show that individuals, when they make up a social unit, are always less clear-sighted than when they act separately. (1951, 312)

Since the individual is not reducible to a mere member of the collective, since he or she is an ensemble of individual and class instincts, there would always be a tension between collective action and individual instincts in socialist societies. But there is no reason why this tension should be any greater than in bourgeois societies (where actions taken in the name of society are neither collectively arrived at, nor serve social interest in any definable sense beyond class interest), and why this tension should not be a creative one pushing society towards greater perfection of its democratic structures.

There is a further point of substance. If we paraphrase Marx's remark that no society can be free if it oppresses others as no society can be democratic if it subjugates others, then one can scarcely be impressed by the democratic nature of the societies of the core capitalist countries, whose record in 'carpet-bombing' other societies 'back into the stone age' is unrivalled. Democracy in its essence, not as a formal mode of governance, is incompatible with imperialism. The institution of genuine democracy is possible only with the dismantling of the structures of imperialism, only in a socialist society. The pusillanimity of social democracy, as indeed of many of the current reformers in Eastern Europe, consists in their failure to recognise this.

But the argument advanced here is an altogether different one. The fundamental conception which has informed the movement until now is that it is superior to capitalism in developing the productive forces, a conception which has inevitably got transformed into the notion that it would be able to raise the production of the same goods (or the same use-values) which capitalism produces, to a much greater extent. This conception emerged out of a reading of Marx to the effect that capitalism in the course of its development gets progressively enmeshed in crises resulting in underutilisation of productive forces, while socialism would be a superior productive system. An extreme form of this understanding was a belief in the breakdown thesis, but those who did not believe in the breakdown thesis merely shifted the argument on to a different plane: capitalism would have remained stuck in a morass of stagnation and underutilisation of productive forces had it not been for greater State intervention, and that too in a manner which is both dangerous and wasteful. In either case it was an actual or potential production failure that was supposed to be the argument against capitalism.

Overlapping this no doubt was a distinct second argument, namely that capitalism has brought us to a stage in human history where wars, both global and regional, are inevitable, and that for the survival of mankind it was essential to get rid of capitalism and build a socialist order.[6] But the conclusions drawn from this second argument never transcended the narrow vision of socialism drawn from

6 This was essentially the Leninist argument; see Lukacs 1970.

the first, namely as a superior system for producing the same use values. Generations of Marxist writers felt compelled to demonstrate the virtue of socialism in the higher growth rates it had achieved. And the growth rates were impressive; but the question was never asked: is socialism supposed to have the same conception of use-values, the same consumerist life-styles as capitalism? There was at any rate little discussion of it in socialist societies (except during the Cultural Revolution in China, which provided answers that were untenable).

Even critics of socialism would agree that one area where the extant socialist societies did achieve remarkable success was in using up their labour reserves (Kornai 1982). They did so because of very high rates of accumulation combined with low rates of productivity growth. It was an essential accompaniment of their using up of labour reserves that process and product innovation was not as rapid as under capitalism. As a result when they did reach full employment, not only did their growth rates slow down (that was to be expected), but, more importantly, there was a large gap in living standards between them and the capitalist countries, which in any case never carried large internal labour reserves (at least in Western Europe) owing to a number of circumstances operating over a long historical period, such as emigration, transfer of unemployment to the Third World via deindustrialisation, and the peculiarly labour-intensive character of machine-building in its early stages.[7]

Given the fact that socialism had always prided itself on being a superior productive system ('We can give you all that the West gives and even more', itself a paternalist attitude), the awareness of this gap in the context of the pervasive presence of the same kind of consumerism as prevails at the capitalist core, created insurmountable contradictions. This is not to gloss over the deficiencies of the bureaucratically managed economic systems that characterised the socialist countries, nor to adopt a moral stance against consumption *per se*. The idea is not that people should have foregone their access to goods in order to accommodate the inadequacies of a particular system of economic management (that would be a singularly repugnant idealist position). But it is a distortion of socialism to consider it as being identical with a more successful satisfaction of consumerism, and any future socialist experiment, in the Third World context

---

[7] This peculiarly labour-intensive character of machine-building, an awareness of which perhaps underlay Marx's postulating a falling tendency of the rate of profit the way he did, was drawn attention to by Hobsbawm (1975).

at any rate, must be conscious of the fact that it is neither possible to achieve for all within any foreseeable future the Western living standards, nor necessarily desirable. Socialism must address itself to the task of evolving a social consensus on a redefinition of the concept of use-value, for which again the existence of democratic structures is a paramount necessity.

While the problems of mass poverty and unemployment in the Third World cannot be resolved by capitalist development of any variety (whether export-led or import-substituting), the kind of socialist development which can resolve them must chart out for itself an entirely different trajectory, in which the deepening of democratic structures and institutions, and through these the development of a social consensus on alternative life-styles to the consumerism of the capitalist core must play a crucial role. The case for this is not merely an abstract moral one; the removal of mass poverty and unemployment is impossible otherwise.

5. THE TRAVAILS OF TRANSITION

There remains nonetheless the crucial hurdle. To say that Third World socialism must create alternative life-styles may sound fine, but as long as imperialism exists the task remains extraordinarily difficult. The idea that a part of the world, such as India, will simply be allowed by imperialism to detach itself from the system of unequal interdependence upon which capitalist stability is founded, and to pursue its own socialist course using up its labour reserves and shunning Western-style consumerism, is entirely unrealistic. There would be encirclement, fomenting of civil war, a trade embargo, and all manner of covert action; this may over time escalate into overt intervention. More subtle, but perhaps even more important in the long-run, there would be the continuous barrage of propaganda about the 'joys of Western-style living' which supposedly would become available to all in socialist countries if only they embraced free market capitalism. A world in which one part witnesses continuous process and product innovation and promotes an ideology of consumerism to sustain it, a part that is already affluent, while the other part, the poorer one, makes a virtue out of necessity and attempts to define alternative life-styles, cannot possibly remain so dichotomised for long. One vision must inevitably and eventually swamp the other.

But while the effect of one kind of swamping would be a more egalitarian, a more purposeful and more co-operative form of living for mankind as a whole, the effect of the other kind of swamping is merely the perpetuation of the existing misery and poverty. This however is another way of saying that socialism, the only possible answer to its problems, cannot succeed in the long-run in the Third World unless it can get generalised to the developed world as well.

No matter what the process of this transition, and the travails associated with it, the fact that such a denouement would eventually come about can scarcely be doubted by anyone who looks upon the future of mankind with hope, who believes in its capacity to use reason for building a better collective future for itself. And the use of reason must entail the acceptance of two propositions. First, that the problems of the Third World are not those of its own creation, but are a result of its being dragged into an international system whose spontaneous operation keeps it where it is, and which uses the coercion of force and ideology to resist all its genuine attempts to break out of it. And second, that the world cannot remain frozen in its current dichotomy for ever. Many have argued that the natural resources of the world are a legacy for mankind as a whole, and what a small minority considers its 'natural liberty' to use up for maintaining ever increasing living standards, is effectively, within any meaningful time-horizon, denied to others who are thereby prevented from attaining similar living standards. But whether or not one takes the 'exhaustibility' argument seriously, the awareness surely would grow that attempts to perpetuate the current dichotomy in the world through coercion, as capitalism does, represents a diminution of living within the core itself. The triumph of socialism in parts of the Third World, apart from what it can achieve even during the difficult period of transitional coexistence in terms of overcoming mass poverty and misery where it has triumphed, can play a crucial role in developing this awareness.

BIBLIOGRAPHY

Amin, S. (1979). *Unequal Development*, New Delhi.

Amsden, A. (1989). *Asia's Next Giant*, New York, Oxford.

Armstrong, P., Glyn, A., and Harrison, J. (1991). *Capitalism Since 1945*, Oxford.

Arrow, K. J. and Debreu, G. (1954). 'Existence of an Equilibrium in a Competitive Economy', *Econometrica*, July.

Baer, W. and Kerstenetzky, I. (eds.) (1964). *Inflation and Growth in Latin America*, Homewood, Illinois.

Bagchi, A. K. (1972*a*). 'Some International Foundations of Capitalist Growth and Underdevelopment', *Economic and Political Weekly*, special number, August.

——(1972*b*). *Private Investment in India 1900–1939*, Cambridge.

——(1976). 'Deindustrialisation in India in the Nineteenth Century', *Journal of Development Studies*, January.

——(1979). 'The Great Depression and the Third World with Special Reference to India', *Social Science Information*, 18(2).

——(1982). *The Political Economy of Underdevelopment*, Cambridge.

——(1986). 'Towards a Correct Reading of Lenin's Theory of Imperialism', in P. Patnaik (ed.) *Lenin and Imperialism*, Delhi.

——(1987). *Public Intervention and Industrial Restructuring in China, India and the Republic of Korea*, ILO/ARTEP.

Bairoch, P. (1975). *The Economic Development of the Third World since 1900*, London.

Baran, P. A. (1957). *The Political Economy of Growth*, New York.

——and Sweezy, P. M. (1966). *Monopoly Capital*, New York.

Bardhan, P. K. (1984). *The Political Economy of Development in India*, Oxford.

Barro, R. (1974). 'Are Government Bonds Net Wealth?', *Journal of Political Economy*, November–December.

Beckerman, W. and Jenkinson, T. (1986). 'What Stopped Inflation? Unemployment or Primary Commodity Prices', *Economic Journal*.

Bhaduri, A. (1983). *The Economic Structure of Backward Agriculture*, London.

Bhalla, S. (1987). 'Trends in Employment in Indian Agriculture, Land and Asset Distribution', *Indian Journal of Agricultural Economics*, October–December.

Bhatia, B. M. (1967). *Famines in India*, New York.

Blyn, G. (1966). *Agricultural Trends in India 1891–1947: Output, Availability and Productivity*, Philadelphia.

Cairncross, A. K. (1960). 'International Trade and Economic Development', *Kyklos*, 13, fasc. 4.

Chakravarty, S. (1982). *Alternative Approaches to a Theory of Economic Growth: Marx, Marshall and Schumpeter*, Calcutta.

——(1986). 'Reflections on the Present World Economic Conjuncture', in P. Patnaik 1986*a*.

——(1987). *Development Planning: The Indian Experience*, Oxford.

——(1993). 'Marxist Economics and Contemporary Developing Economies', reprinted in *Selected Economic Writings*, New Delhi.

Chandrashekhar, C. P. (1986). 'Imperialism and Industrialisation in the Underdeveloped Countries', in P. Patnaik 1986*a*.

——(1988). 'Investment Behaviour, Economies of Scale and Efficiency under Import-Substituting Industrialisation', *Economic and Political Weekly*, annual number.

——(1993). 'Agrarian Change and Occupational Diversification: Non-Agricultural Employment and Rural Development in West Bengal', *Journal of Peasant Studies*, January.

Chaudhury, K. N. (ed.) (1971). *The Economic Development of India under the East India Company*, Cambridge.

Chowdhury, B. B. (1964). *The Growth of Commercial Agriculture in Bengal*, vol. 1, Calcutta.

Dandekar, V. M. (1981). *The Worker–Peasant Alliance*, Calcutta.

Dasgupta, R. (1970). *Problems of Economic Transition*, Calcutta.

Dattagupta, S. (1980). *Comintern, India, and the Colonial Question*, monograph 3, Centre for Studies in Social Sciences, Calcutta.

Degras, J. (ed.) (1971). *Communist International 1919–1943: Documents*, London.

Deutscher, I. (1954). *The Prophet Armed: Trotsky 1879–1921*, vol. 1, Oxford.

Deyo, F. C. (ed.) (1987). *The Political Economy of New Asian Industrialisation*, Ithaca, NY.

Dobb, M. H. (1940). 'Imperialism', in *Political Economy and Capitalism*, London.

——(1972). *On Economic Theory and Socialism*, London.

Dollar, D. (1986). 'Technological Innovation, Capital Mobility, and the Product Cycle in North–South Trade', *American Economic Review*, March.

Dutt, A. K. (1988). 'Inelastic Demand for Southern Goods, International Demonstration Effects, and Uneven Development', *Journal of Development Economics*, July.

Dutt, R. C. (1985). *Famines and Land Assessments in India*, Delhi.

Emmanuel, A. (1972). *Unequal Exchange: A Study of the Imperialism of Trade*, London.

Engels, F. (1954). *Anti-Duhring*, Moscow.

—— (1967). 'Preface', in Marx (1967)

Fanon F. (1974). *The Wretched of the Earth*, Penguin.

Fisher, I. (1933). 'The Debt–Deflation Theory of Great Depressions', *Econometrica*, 1.

Flavin, M. (1985). 'Excess Sensitivity of Consumption to Current Income: Liquidity Constraints or Myopia?', *Canadian Journal of Economics*, February.

Frank, A. G. (1975). *Capitalism and Underdevelopment in Latin America*, Penguin.

Froebel, F., Heinrichs, J., and Kreye, O. (1980). *The New International Division of Labour*, Cambridge.

Furtado, C. (1972). *The Economic Development of Latin America*, Cambridge.

Galbraith, J. K. (1968). *American Capitalism*, New York.

—— (1973). *Economics and the Public Purpose*, Boston.

Gerschenkron, A. (1966). *Economic Backwardness in a Historical Perspective*, Cambridge, Mass.

Goodwin, R. M. (1967). 'A Growth Cycle', in C. H. Feinstein (ed.) *Socialism, Capitalism, and Economic Growth*, Cambridge.

—— (1991). *Chaotic Economic Dynamics*, Oxford.

Grandmont, J. M. (1982). 'Temporary Equilibrium Theory' in K. J. Arrow and M. D. Intrilligator (eds.) *Handbook of Mathematical Economics*, vol. 2, Amsterdam.

Greenberg, M. (1969). *British Trade and the Opening of China 1800–1842*, Cambridge.

Habib, I. (1963). *The Agrarian System of Mughal India*, Bombay.

—— (1965). 'The Social Distribution of Landed Property in pre-British India', *Enquiry* (Delhi), reprinted in Habib 1995.

—— (1975). 'Colonialisation of the Indian Economy', *Social Scientist* (Delhi), reprinted in Habib 1995.

—— (1984). 'Studying A Colonial Economy Without Perceiving Colonialism', *Social Scientist*, December, reprinted in Habib (1995).

—— (1995). *Essays in Indian History: Towards a Marxist Perspective*, Delhi.

Haggard, S. and Cheng, T. (1987). 'State and Foreign Capital in East Asian NICs', in Deyo 1987.

Hahn, F. H. (1984). *Equilibrium and Macroeconomics*, Oxford.

—— and Matthews, R. C. O. (1964). 'The Theory of Economic Growth: A Survey', *Economic Journal*, 74.

Hansen, A. H. (1938). *Full Recovery or Stagnation?*, New York.

—— (1941). *Fiscal Policy and Business Cycles*, New York.

Harrod, R. F. (1939). 'An Essay in Dynamic Theory', *Economic Journal*, 39.

—— (1948). *Towards A Dynamic Economics*, London.

Hayek, F. A. von (1946). *The Road to Serfdom*, London.

Heston, A. (1983). 'National Income', in *Cambridge Economic History of India*, vol. 2, New Delhi.

Hicks, J. R. (1950). *A Contribution to the Theory of the Trade Cycle*, Oxford.

Hilferding, R. (1910). *Das Finanzkapital*, Vienna.

Hirschman, A. O. (1971). *A Bias For Hope*, New Haven and London.

Hobsbawm, E. J. (1964). 'Introduction', in Marx 1964.

—— (1969). *Industry and Empire*, Penguin.

—— (1975). *The Age of Capital 1848–1875*, London.

Hobson, J. A. (1902). *Imperialism: A Study*, London.

Imlah, A. H. (1958). *Economic Elements in the Pax Britannica*, Harvard.

Jenks, L. H. (1963). *The Migration of British Capital to 1875*, London.

Johnson, C. (1982). *MITI and the Japanese Miracle: The Growth of Industrial Policy 1925–1975*, Stanford.

Jones, L. and Sakong, I. (1980). *Government, Business and Entrepreneurship in Economic Development: The Korean Case*, Cambridge, Mass.

Kaldor, N. (1961). 'Capital Accumulation and Economic Growth', in F. A. Lutz and D. C. Hague (eds.) *The Theory of Capital*, New York.

—— (1964). *Essays on Economic Stability and Growth*, London.

—— (1968). *Causes of the Slow Rate of Growth of the United Kingdom*, Cambridge, reprinted in Kaldor (1978).

—— (1976). 'Inflation and Recession in the World Economy', *Economic Journal*, reprinted in Kaldor (1978).

—— (1978). *Further Essays on Economic Theory*, London.

—— and Mirrlees, J. A. (1962). 'A New Model of Economic Growth', *Review of Economic Studies*, June.

Kalecki, M. (1954). *Theory of Economic Dynamics*, London.

—— (1962). 'Observations on the Theory of Growth', *Economic Journal*, March.

—— (1968). 'The Trend and the Business Cycle Reconsidered', *Economic Journal*, reprinted in Kalecki 1971.

—— (1971). *Selected Essays on the Dynamics of the Capitalist Economy*, Cambridge.

—— (1971*a*). 'Class Struggle and Distribution of National Income', *Kyklos*, reprinted in Kalecki (1971).

—— (1972). 'Fascism of Our Time', in *Last Stage in the Transformation of Capitalism*, New York.

—— (1972*b*). 'Intermediate Regimes', in *Selected Essays on the Growth of Socialist and Mixed Economies*, Cambridge.

—— (1972*c*). 'Problems of Financing Economic Development in a Mixed Economy', in *Selected Essays on the Growth of Socialist and Mixed Economics*, Cambridge.

Kaplinsky, R. (1984). 'The International Context for Industrialisation in the Coming Decade', *Journal of Development Studies*, October.

Kennedy, C. (1964). 'Induced Bias in Innovation and the Theory of Distribution', *Economic Journal*, 74.

Keynes, J. M. (1919). *Economic Consequences of the Peace*, London.

—— (1949). *The General Theory of Employment, Interest, and Money*, London.

—— (1951). *Essays in Persuasion*, London.

Kindleberger, C. P. (1967). *Europe's Post-War Growth*, Oxford.

—— (1987). *The World in Depression*, Penguin.

Kornai, J. (1982). *Growth, Shortage and Efficiency*, Oxford.

Krueger, A. (1974). 'The Political Economy of Rent-Seeking Societies', *American Economic Review*, 64(3).

Krugman, P. and Helpman, E. (eds.) (1986). *Strategic Trade Policy and the New International Economics*, Cambridge, Mass.

Kuznets, S. (1971). *Economic Growth of Nations*, Cambridge, Mass.

Lange, O. (1941). 'Review of Schumpeter's *Business Cycles*', in *Review of Economic Statistics*.

—— (1946). 'A Note on Innovations', in W. Fellner and B. F. Haley (eds.) *Readings in the Theory of Income Distribution*, Philadelphia.

—— (1964). *The Theory of Reproduction and Accumulation*, Warsaw.

Lenin, V. I. (1960). 'A Note on the Question of the Market Theory', *Collected Works*, vol. 4, Moscow.

—— (1975). *Selected Works*, 3 vols., Moscow.

—— (1975a). 'Better Fewer But Better', in Lenin 1975, vol. 3.

—— (1975b). 'Imperialism: The His=ghest Stage of Capitalism', in Lenin 1975.

—— (1975c). 'What Is to Be Done?', in Lenin 1975.

Lewis, W. A. (1949). *Economic Survey 1919–1939*.

—— (1954). 'Economic Development with Unlimited Supplies of Labour', *Manchester School*, vol. 22.

—— (1978a). *The Evolution of the International Economic Order*, Princeton.

—— (1978b). *Growth and Fluctuations 1870–1913*.

Lim Hyun-Chin (1985). *Dependent Development in Korea 1963–1979*, Seoul.

Luedde-Neurath, R. (1986). *Import Controls and Export-Oriented Development: A Reassessment of the South Korean Case*, Boulder, Colo.

Lukacs, G. (1970). *Lenin*, London.

Luxemburg, R. (1963). *The Accumulation of Capital*, London.

Maddison, A. (1982). *Phases of Capitalist Development*, Oxford.

Magdoff, H. (1969). *The Age of Imperialism*, New York.

Maizels, A. (1971). *Industrial Growth and World Trade*, Cambridge.

Marx, K. (1964). *Pre-Capitalist Economic Formations*, London.

—— (1967). *Capital*, vol. 1, London.

—— (1968). *Theories of Surplus Value*, part 2, Moscow.

—— (1970). 'The Civil War in France', in Marx and Engels 1970.

—— (1974). *Capital*, vol. 3, Moscow.

Marx, K. (1976). 'The Poverty of Philosophy', in Marx and Engels 1976.

——and Engels, F. (1968). *On Colonialism*, Moscow.

————(1970). *Selected Works*, 1 vol., London.

————(1974). *Collected Works*, vol. 6, London.

Malinvaud, E. (1977). *The Theory of Unemployment Reconsidered*, Oxford.

Mingay, G. E. and Chambers, B. D. (1966). *The Agricultural Revolution*, London.

Mitra, A. (1977). *Terms of Trade and Class Relations*, London.

——(1988). *China: Issues in Development*, New Delhi.

Moore, B. (1989). *Verticalists and Horizontalists*.

Mukherji, A. (1990). *Walrasian and Non-Walrasian Equilibria*, Oxford.

Nakamura, T. (1981). *The Post-war Japanese Economy*, Tokyo.

Naoroji, D. (1871). *Poverty and Un-British Rule in India*

Nayyar, D. (1978). 'Transnational Corporations and Manufactured Exports from Poor Countries', *Economic Journal*, March.

Norman, E. H. (1946). *Japan's Emergence as a Modern State*, New York.

Nurkse, R. (1954). 'International Investment Today in the Light of Nineteenth Century Experience', *Economic Journal*.

——(1958). *The Problems of Capital Formation in Underdeveloped Countries*, Oxford.

——(1959). *Patterns of Trade and Development*, Stockholm.

O'Connor, J. (1973). *The Fiscal Crisis of the State*.

O'Driscoll, G. P., Jr. (1977). 'The Ricardian Non-equivalence Theorem', *Journal of Political Economy*, February.

Okita, S., Jayawardena, L., and Sengupta, A. (1986). *The Potential of the Japanese Surplus for World Development*, WIDER, Helsinki.

Patel, S. J. (1952). *Agricultural Labourers in Modern India and Pakistan*, Bombay.

Patnaik, P. (1972a). 'A Note on External Markets and Capitalist Development', *Economic Journal*, December.

——(1972b). 'Imperialism and the Growth of Indian Capitalism', in R. Sutcliff and R. Owen (eds.) *Studies in the Theory of Imperialism*, London, New York.

——(ed.) (1986). *Lenin and Imperialism*, Delhi.

——(1986a). 'On the Economic Crisis of the Capitalist World', in Patnaik 1986.

——(1988). *Time, Inflation and Growth*, Calcutta.

——(1989). 'Some Aspects of the World Capitalist Economy in the 1980s', *Economic and Political Weekly*.

——(1991). *Economics and Egalitarianism*, New Delhi.

——and Ghosh, J. (1991). 'Deindustrialisation Without an Import Surplus: A Theoretical Note in the Context of a Stylised Colonial Economy', *Economic and Political Weekly*, annual number.

Patnaik, U. (1975). 'The Process of Commercialisation under Colonial Conditions', mimeo.

—— (1986). 'Neo-Marxian Theories of Capitalism and Underdevelopment: Towards A Critique', in Patnaik 1986.

—— (1987). *The Agrarian Question and the Development of Capitalism in India*, New Delhi.

—— (1991*a*). 'Introduction', in *Agrarian Relations and Accumulation*, Bombay.

—— (1991*b*). 'Food Availability and Famine: A Longer View', *Journal of Peasant Studies*, October.

—— (1991*c*). 'The Peasantry and Industrialisation', mimeo., Lectures at the Department of Sociology, University of Wisconsin, Madison.

Pollin R. (1990). 'Two Theories of Money Supply Endogeneity: Some Empirical Evidence', *Journal of Post-Keynesian Economic*, 13(13).

Prebisch R. (1950). *The Economic Development of Latin America and Its Principal Problems*, UN ECLA.

Radice H. (1985). *International Firms and Modern Imperialism*, Penguin.

Raj Committee (1982). *Capital Formation and Savings in India*, Reserve Bank of India, Bombay.

Raychaudhury, T. (1990). 'Colonialism and Mass Poverty', *Economic and Political Weekly*, Review of Political Economy.

Ricardo, D. (1951*a*). *On the Principles of Political Economy and Taxation*, in P. Sraffa (ed.) *Works and Correspondence of David Ricardo*, vol. 1, Cambridge.

—— (1951*b*). *Funding Systems*, in P. Sraffa (ed.) *Works and Correspondence of David Ricardo*, vol. 4, Cambridge.

Robinson, J. (1956). *The Accumulation of Capital*, London.

—— (1963). 'Introduction', in Luxemburg 1963.

—— (1966). *Economic Philosophy*, Penguin.

—— (1973). 'Beggar-My-Neighbour Remedies for Unemployment', in *Collected Economic Papers*, vol. 4, Oxford.

Robinson, J. and Eatwell, J. (1974). *An Introduction to Modern Economics*, New Delhi.

Rowthorn, R. E. (1971). 'Imperialism in the Seventies: Unity or Rivalry?', *New Left Review*, reprinted in Radice 1985.

—— (1977). 'Conflict, Inflation and Money', *Cambridge Journal of Economics*.

Saul, S. B. (1970). *Studies in British Overseas Trade*, Liverpool.

Schumpeter, J. A. (1939). *Business Cycles*, vol. 1, McGraw Hill

—— (1961). *Capitalism, Socialism and Democracy*, London.

—— (1966). 'John Maynard Keynes', in *Ten Great Economists*, London.

Seers, D. (1962). 'A Model of Comparative Growth of the World Economy', *Economic Journal*.

Sen, A. K. (1965). 'The Money Rate of Interest in a Pure Theory of Growth', in F. H. Hahn and F. P. R. Brechling (eds.) *The Theory of Interest Rates*, London.

——(ed.) (1970). *Growth Economics*, Penguin.

——(1970*a*). 'Interest, Investment, and Growth', in A. Sen 1970.

Sen, S. (1992). *Colonies and the Empire*, Calcutta.

Singer, H. (1950). 'The Distribution of Gains Between Investing and Borrowing Countries', *American Economic Review*, May.

Sinha, J. C. (1927). *Economic Annals of Bengal*, London.

Sivasubramonian, S. (1975). 'National Income of India 1900–01 to 1946–47', mimeo., Delhi School of Economics.

Solow, R. M. (1956). 'A Contribution to the Theory of Economic Growth', *The Quarterly Journal of Economics*, February.

Spaventa, L. (1959). 'Dualism in Economic Growth', *Banca Nazionale del Lavoro Quarterly*.

Spraos, J. (1980). 'The Statistical Debate on the Net Barter Terms of Trade Between Primary Products and Manufactures', *Economic Journal*, 90.

——(1983). *Inequalising Trade?*, Oxford.

Steindl, J. (1952). *Maturity and Stagnation in American Capitalism*, Oxford.

——and Bhaduri, A. (1983). 'The Rise of Monetarism as a Social Doctrine', *Thames Papers on Economic Activity*, Autumn.

Swan, T. W. (1956). 'Economic Growth and Capital Accumulation', *The Economic Record*, November.

Sweezy, P. M. (1942). *The Theory of Capitalist Development*, New York.

Sweezy, P. M. and Magdoff, H. (1987). *Stagnation and the Financial Explosion*, New York.

Tan Chung (1973). 'The Triangular Trade Between China and India 1771–1840: A Case of Commercial Imperialism', *Proceedings of the Indian History Congress*, Chandigarh.

Tarbuck, K. (ed.) (1972). *Imperialism and the Accumulation of Capital*, London.

Taylor, L. (1983). *Structuralist Macroeconomics*, New York.

Thomas, B. (1973). *Migration and Economic Growth*, Cambridge.

Todaro, M. P. (1969). 'A Model of Labour Migration and Urban Unemployment in Less Developed Countries', *American Economic Review*, 59.

Turner, H. A., Jackson, D., and Wilkinson, F. (1970). *Do Trade Unions Cause Inflation?*, Cambridge.

United Nations (1951). *Measures for the Economic Development of Underdeveloped Countries*.

Vaidyanathan, A. (1985). 'Trends in Poverty and Employment', in R. E. B. Lucas and G. F. Papanek (eds.) *Indian Economy: Recent Development and Future Prospects*, New Delhi.

Vernon, R. (1966). 'International Trade and Investment in the Product Cycle', *Quarterly Journal of Economics*.

Warren, B. (1973). 'Imperialism and Capitalist Industrialisation', *New Left Review*.

INDEX OF NAMES

INDEX OF SUBJECTS